"A VALUABLE CONTRIBUTION TO OUR UNDERSTANDING OF OUR ROOTS IN AMERICA.
. . . Thoughtful, balanced, and highly readable."
                    —KANSAS CITY JEWISH CHRONICLE

"It is rare to find a book that so vitally describes the religious, historical, economic, political, and social life of the common woman—or man for that matter . . . imaginative and sensitive."
                    —ST. LOUIS POST-DISPATCH

"Excellent and well-documented."
                    —LIBRARY JOURNAL

"Fascinating and instructive . . . a book we've needed for a long time!"
                    —CHICAGO TRIBUNE

"Absorbing, earnest . . . skillful, sensitive . . . and always readable."
                    —PUBLISHERS WEEKLY

CHARLOTTE BAUM is a New York City writer; PAULA HYMAN is Professor of Modern Jewish History at Columbia University; and SONYA MICHEL, who formerly taught Jewish-American literature at San Francisco State College, is on a Fellowship in American Studies at the University of Indiana. All three women grew up Jewish in America.

THE JEWISH WOMAN IN AMERICA

THE JEWISH WOMAN IN AMERICA

by
Charlotte Baum
Paula Hyman
Sonya Michel

A PLUME BOOK

NEW AMERICAN LIBRARY

NEW YORK AND SCARBOROUGH, ONTARIO

PLUME TRADEMARK REG. U.S. PAT. OFF. AND FOREIGN COUNTRIES
REGISTERED TRADEMARK—MARCA REGISTRADA
HECHO EN WESTFORD, MASS., U.S.A.

Signet, Signet Classic, Mentor, Plume, Meridian and NAL Books
are published *in the United States by*
New American Library,
1633 Broadway, New York, New York 10019,
in Canada by The New American Library of Canada Limited,
81 Mack Avenue, Scarborough, Ontario M1L 1M8

First Plume Printing, October, 1977

5 6 7 8 9 10 11 12 13

PRINTED IN THE UNITED STATES OF AMERICA

ACKNOWLEDGMENTS

Letter to the Editor by Diana Bletter: © 1973 by The New York Times Company. Reprinted by permission. Used with the permission of the author.

Excerpts from THE RISE OF DAVID LEVINSKY by Abrahan Cahan: Copyright 1917 by Harper & Row, Publishers, Inc; renewed 1945 by Abrahan Cahan. Reprinted by permission of the publishers.

"The Mother" by Kadie Molodowsky: Reprinted from ONIONS AND CUCUMBERS AND PLUMS, edited by Sarah Sweig Betsky, by permission of Wayne State University Press. Copyright © 1958, Wayne State University Press. Used with the permission of the author.

Lines from "From an Old House in America" by Adrienne Rich: Reprinted from POEMS Selected and New, 1950–1954 by Adrienne Rich. Copyright © 1975, 1973, 1971, 1969, 1966 by W. W. Norton & Company, Inc. Copyright © 1967, 1963, 1962, 1961, 1960, 1959, 1958, 1957, 1956, 1955, 1954, 1953, 1952, 1951 by Adrienne Rich. By permission of W. W. Norton & Company, Inc.

Grateful acknowledgment is made for permission to use the following photographs:

1. Courtesy Ida Hyman
3. Courtesy Paula Hyman
4. American Jewish Archives on the Cincinnati Campus of the Hebrew Union College—Jewish Institute of Religion
5. Jewish Daily Forward
6. International Museum of Photography at George Eastman House, Rochester, N. Y.
7. © Underwood & Underwood
8. Reproduced from the Collection of the Library of Congress
9. Reproduced from the Collection of the Library of Congress
10. New York Public Library Picture Collection
11–15. Courtesy of the Western Jewish History Center of the Judah L. Magnes Memorial Museum, Berkeley, California
16. Courtesy Garfunkel-Fialkoff Family

Our special thanks

to Berenice Hoffman and to
Professor Myra Jehlen for their
help; and to Professor Moses
Rischin, Dr. Ralda Sullivan, and
Harry Levine for their
thoughtful readings of sections of
the manuscript

CONTENTS

PREFACE

We grew up as Jewish women in America, but our backgrounds have not been uniform. Charlotte Baum was born in Philadelphia in 1934, Sonya Michel in New Haven in 1942, and Paula Hyman in Boston in 1946. Our families, environments, values, and aspirations were, at least during our childhoods, quite dissimilar. And yet, the experiences we shared as women and as Jews have brought us together to write about ourselves and the generations of women who preceded us in the American Jewish community.

Paula was brought up by parents who took pride in their Jewish heritage and saw to it that she received a far from ordinary Jewish education. Hebrew school was invested with as much importance as public school, and her Jewish education continued through her college years. Judaism has remained an important part of her life. She teaches Jewish history on the college level and is a member of the New York Havurah, a group of like-minded young Jews who have formed a community to celebrate and study Judaism in a warm and intimate atmosphere. She helped found Ezrat Nashim, the first feminist organization actively pressing for improvement of the status of women within the Jewish community. Although Paula experienced for the first time that sense of "otherness" while at Radcliffe College, for her it was a special quality she never wished to deny.

Sonya came from a family which, although it did not go so far as to deny its Jewishness, rarely celebrated it. Her parents left the close-knit community in New Haven shortly after she was born, and moved from one small New England town to another, often finding themselves the only Jews among established gentile populations. Sonya received little formal Jewish education, but enjoyed the holidays she spent with the New Haven branch of the family, and the noisy meetings of the "Cousins Club" formed by her mother's relatives. As an adolescent, she was urged to have her nose "fixed" and her hair straightened in order to improve her marriage prospects and, incidentally, to look more gentile. But, paradoxically, she was forbidden to date non-Jewish boys. Her identity was formed at the intersection of contradictory Jewish and assimilationist values.

Charlotte is something else again. Although both her parents were Jewish immigrants from Eastern Europe, theirs was a stormy intermarriage of ideologies. Her mother was a capitalist and her father a socialist; they sought salvation through opposite means. Their grocery store was the battleground and a truce was called every Sunday evening for a family visit to the Yiddish theater. To Charlotte, capitalism and socialism were two Jewish sects screaming at each other. Only the Holocaust silenced them both, and drew them together to fight a common enemy—anti-Semitism.

How we three distinct types found each other and decided to collaborate on a book about Jewish women deserves telling because it demonstrates the underlying commonality of our experience, and the problems and questions to which our status gives rise. We all became concerned with feminism when the women's movement began in the late sixties. Our focus on Jewish women followed a bit later.

Shortly after the publication of Philip Roth's *Portnoy's Complaint,* Charlotte attended a meeting of a Jewish women's "reading club." She had been asked to participate in a discussion of this latest attack on Jewish motherhood. Although Charlotte's experience in no way paralleled Alexander Portnoy's, she intended to defend Roth's point of view, and to support his right to demythicize the legendary Jewish family.

Most of the women in the group were in their sixties. They were the daughters of Eastern European Jews, either born here, or having immigrated as children. They were now upper-middle-class women whose husbands, none of whom had attended college, were manufacturers or owners of medium-sized businesses. Their sons were university-educated professionals, or associated with the family businesses. Their daughters were wives and mothers, married to successful men. The women themselves were all active in Jewish philanthropic organizations like Hadassah, ORT, B'nai B'rith, and synagogue sisterhoods.

The women began to defend themselves against Roth's highly critical view of Jewish women, as embodied in his character, Sophie Portnoy. They described their sacrifices, struggles, and hardships, and Charlotte knew she was hearing the truth. She remembered stories from her own past, about her aunts' involvement in the labor movement, her mother's friends who had taken in boarders to supplement the family's income, and her own mother who worked in the grocery store eighteen hours a day. She found herself agreeing with these Jewish women that if anyone had complaints to make, it was they!

Charlotte left that afternoon feeling wounded. Hadn't these women been severely maligned—and hadn't she been, too? Why were there no Jewish women novelists recording their experiences and hers? Had the daughters of these women been so psychologically damaged that they were incapable of generating a voice of their own? Charlotte's conflict, anger, and bewilderment grew.

Charlotte ran into Sonya, an old colleague from the antiwar and women's movements, at a seminar on "The Images of Women in American Literature." *Portnoy's Complaint* was on the reading list, and Charlotte and Sonya discovered that they shared the same angry reaction to Roth's attack. They decided to examine the portrayal of women by other Jewish American writers, and to report their findings to the seminar.

Early in their research, they realized that over a seventy-year period, the image of Jewish women reflected in popular fiction had undergone a radical transformation. In the stories of the old country and in the fiction of the immigrant period (up until the 1930s), there was a rich assortment of active women who fulfilled many roles both inside and outside the home. These fictional women were intelligent even if uneducated, energetic, protective toward their children, self-sacrificing, and very important to their families' economic security. They were shown grappling with political and ideological conflicts as well as with financial hardships. From the thirties on, however, they become frozen in one of two stereotypes: the stupid, domineering, over-protective "Jewish Mother" who pushes her children unmercifully to succeed; or the manipulative, self-centered, materialistic "Jewish American Princess," whose chief occupation is spending money.

What happened? Why was the Jewish woman once revered and now reviled? What accounted for her transition from veneration to vituperation? Charlotte and Sonya began to understand that the Jewish woman's literary image reflected a transformation in her real social role. They wanted to investigate this phenomenon more closely.

Soon thereafter they met Paula through Columbia University Women's Liberation. They knew she was a Jewish historian, and they discussed these problems with her. As a feminist, Paula had begun to study the position of women within the Jewish tradition and to explore the sources of her own anger at being deprived of the opportunity to express herself fully as a Jew. She had begun to ask questions, too. What, in fact, was the status of women within Judaism and the Jewish community? How had modern social conditions transformed the traditional roles of the Jewish woman? Had the economic opportunities available in the New World and the impact of American culture played some part in this process? Why was the history of the Jewish woman yet to be written? Why had we been deprived of our heroines?

The three of us decided to work together and this book is the result of our cooperative efforts. We want to make it clear that we've organized our book around our concerns and have not tried to write an exhaustive, definitive history of all Jewish women in America. It is instead a schematic approach to certain problems as we've defined them. We are offering no solutions and many of the problems we treat remain unresolved. We are asking questions that haven't been asked before and are describing the experience of some women during the course of Jewish settlement in America from the 1840s to today in order to understand the cultural and economic forces that have shaped their lives. Our research was not easy, for Jewish women have fared no better than their gentile sisters in history. We could, for example, find little statistical material on Jewish women in the labor force, the labor movement, or even in the most recent Zionist movement. Their absence in statistics did not, however, signify their absence in fact. When we were treating the role Jewish women played in the labor movement and in the Russian revolutionary movements before they came to America, for example, we were able to locate and interview many who had participated and who are still alive today.

We do not intend this book as an attack on Judaism or on Jewish men. Nor is it an apologetic defense of Jewish women. We have tried to destroy some of the myths about Jewish women that have severely affected their self-images, and to replace the myths with the truth about an admirable heritage that conventional histories have ignored. We are hereby reclaiming our past.

Charlotte Baum
Paula Hyman
Sonya Michel

New York 1975

THE
JEWISH
WOMAN
IN
AMERICA

1

"Woe to the Father Whose Children Are Girls"
Women in the Jewish Tradition

The Jewish woman in America is heir to a 3,500-year-old religious and historical tradition. Even if not religiously observant, she, as well as the Jewish man, has been influenced by practices they may no longer follow and attitudes of whose origins they are ignorant. Moreover, these traditional Jewish attitudes, then as now, shaped woman's self-image and the way in which men perceived her and related to her. For that reason, it will be useful for the reader to survey the position of women within the Jewish community from Talmudic times in the early centuries of the Common Era.

For the rabbinic Judaism under which all Jews lived in Western Europe until the early nineteenth century, and which held sway in Eastern Europe virtually until the twentieth century, has its roots in Talmudic law and custom. Of course, as we will show, rabbinic Judaism adjusted itself to the new conditions of medieval and, later, modern times. Since the Jewish community in America is composed primarily of immigrants from Eastern and Western Europe, it is also important to review some of the attitudes and laws that most affected women in those communities in order to locate many of the problems we will be confronting in this book. While Jewish law does not reflect all the

3

changes in the status of the Jewish woman—indeed her actual treatment was often superior to her legal status—it is a relevant indicator of her position within Jewish society at different points in time.

Women are temperamentally light-headed.

—*Ta' anith 7a*

Let a man be careful to honor his wife, for he owes to her alone all the blessings of his house.

—*Baba Mezia 59*

These very different sayings from the Talmud, the source of post-Biblical Jewish law and custom, sum up the position of women in the Jewish tradition. They are merely two sides of the same coin. As long as the woman followed her prescribed course as devoted helpmeet to her husband and responsible household manager and mother, she was accorded great respect. Should she seek to stray from what was defined as the female role, however, into the male's domain of study and prayer so central to Jewish civilization, she was demeaned and often ridiculed. This was a convenient and unquestioned division of roles thought to be ordained by God and dictated by nature. And even today, Jewish women still live with the consequences of this patriarchal world view whether they have contact with traditional Jewish law and customs, or identify themselves only as cultural Jews. For the conventional attitudes toward Jewish women rooted in these laws and practices are still transmitted from generation to generation through myth, behavior, and unconscious responses.

As far back as we can go in our history, it was the woman's primary responsibility to attend to family needs as they arose. Therefore, Jewish law exempted women from all positive religious obligations, like communal prayer, which had to be performed at a specific time (when they were to be engaged in other tasks). That Jewish women have fewer commandments to fulfill, by the way, is the theoretical basis for the oft-quoted blessing recited daily by Orthodox Jewish men thanking God for not having made them women. In a religious civilization like Judaism, ritual obligations were prized and one derived communal honor from their fulfillment. Women, having fewer religious responsibilities, were consequently assigned a religious and communal status inferior to that of men. Because women were not obliged to pray, they could not, according to traditional Judaism, be counted in a *minyan,* the quorum of ten necessary for public prayer; hence neither could they lead religious services. Women could, of course, visit the synagogue and pray in the small, curtained-off balcony reserved for them. But they couldn't participate as equals and they knew that they didn't really belong. Not the way the men did. The synagogue was a men's club, perhaps the most ancient in history. Only in modern times did Reform Judaism begin to treat women as equals in the religious service—though they could be neither rabbis nor cantors. And it was only very recently that Reform Judaism has ordained its first female rabbi; and the Conservative Jewish movement has decided, at the urging of a Jewish feminist group, Ezrat Nashim, to allow its congregations to count women in the *minyan.*

But this is a contemporary development. Throughout history, the Jewish ideal was the scholar, and the scholar was a man. It was the rare Jewish sage, in fact, who did not view women as frivolous, ignorant beings, performing vital tasks in the home and endowed with a simple spirituality, but otherwise regarded as diverting their husbands from their obligations to study sacred texts. Rabbi Eliezer's statement in the Talmud, "Whoever teaches his daughter Torah, teaches her obscenity," was merely an extreme formulation of the prevalent Jewish attitude toward education for women. Moreover, whatever equivocation is reflected in the sources, it is only whether or not women should be left illiterate. The *dominant* theme in Talmudic and later rabbinic literature was not to educate women to the same level as men no matter what their intellectual capacities. Again, only within the past generation or two, as a result of the influence of modern Western ideas and changed circumstances, have women been given the opportunity to acquire an equal Jewish education.

Not only were women deemed intellectually inferior to men, they were also not treated as independent, responsible adults in Jewish law. Like the minor, the deaf-mute, and the idiot, they could not—and as a rule still cannot—serve as witnesses in a religious court, for they were considered emotionally unreliable. Insulting, but hardly a major disability, you might say, for the modern Jewish woman—except in Israel, where matters of personal status are adjudicated according to traditional Jewish law in religious courts. More importantly, the Jewish laws of marriage and divorce, which originated in the polygamous culture of the ancient Near East, treated women as second-class citizens. The Jewish woman was the ideal passive bride, at least in the marriage ceremony. She said nothing at all while she was "consecrated unto her husband," that is, forbidden sexually to other men. (Needless to say, in a polygamous society, her husband was not forbidden sexually to other women unless they belonged to another man.) Long after polygamy had disappeared from the Jewish scene, it was the groom who enacted the one-sided Jewish marriage ceremony, while his bride still was a silent participant. In a traditional Jewish ceremony, this remains the case.

Dissolving a marriage was also a male prerogative and still is; even today only the husband can initiate Jewish divorce proceedings. According to the Talmud, a husband could divorce his wife if she burned his soup—though frivolous divorce was not encouraged—while an unhappy wife who came to the prominent Rabbi Judah, a second-century sage, to complain of her situation and petition that her husband be compelled to divorce her, was told, "Why are you different from a fish? You have no more right to complain against your husband's treatment than the fish has the right to object to the manner in which it has been cooked."

Not until the Middle Ages, when the woman's status rose along with her economic power, was it declared that a husband could not divorce his wife against her will. Then, as now, a husband refusing to grant a divorce, or disappearing or dying without witness, left his wife a grass widow, forever forbidden in Jewish law to remarry. A traditional Yiddish folk song expresses the plight of these women: "Brooks of tears flow out of my eyes; I am left like a piece of wood swimming on the water. The whole world has fallen on me since I am left alone; I sit day and night and weep bitterly. Rivers of tears pour forth from my eyes."

While a Jewish court could pressure a recalcitrant or vindictive husband through various means—mostly social ostracism —to give his wife a divorce, these safeguards did not always work and were virtually useless in America, where the community no longer exerted such a strong influence on individuals. After all, the individual Jew in America was not dependent upon the Jewish community for his personal status or economic survival, and belonging to a Jewish community had become a voluntary rather than compulsory matter. In Israel, where *halacha* (Jewish law) governs the personal status of Jews, the tragedy of the *aguna* (the grass widow) still obtains.

According to Jewish law a man is duty bound to marry in order to fulfill his obligation to propagate. Propagation, however, was and is not obligatory for a woman, although the *Shulhan Arukh*—the authoritative sixteenth-century Code of Jewish Law—warns that "nevertheless a woman should not remain single lest she be liable to suspicion." One need not comment that the same attitude prevails today. Moreover, for women, marriage was considered a protective institution, for every woman needed male protection, be it her father's or her husband's. Hence, the Talmudic saying, "Better a noodle of a husband than a life of widowhood."

The marriage contract, too, was considered a protective device for women. It provided for the wife's financial security both within marriage and in case of divorce or widowhood. It ordered her husband to support her and held him responsible, too, for her sexual satisfaction. In fact, the *Shulhan Arukh* stipulated the number of times per week that a husband had to have intercourse with his wife. And the weekly number varied with the husband's occupation! Interestingly, while a laborer was expected to perform twice a week, and a wealthy man of leisure every night, the pampered scholar had to satisfy his wife's sexual desires only once a week.

In return for her economic security and sexual satisfaction, a wife was legally bound to perform all domestic work, though servants could take over the grinding and baking and washing. But regardless of her social rank or the number of servants in the household, each wife was traditionally obliged to perform certain services for her husband—washing his face and hands, filling his cup, and making his bed—that symbolized her wifely submission. For the Jewish woman was expected to treat her husband deferentially and accept his "natural" dominion over her. To ensure that "natural" dominion, the husband was advised by the rabbis to "marry a woman who is inferior to you in social rank."

Because woman's sexual nature was always recognized, the "madonna syndrome" prevalent in the Western world did not develop in Judaism. The madonna syndrome denied that a good woman was endowed with sexual drives and needs. It thus divided womankind into two mutually exclusive categories: the sexually chaste (and sexually deprived) good woman—in its extreme formulation, the virgin mother—and the sexually promiscuous bad woman, the whore. Judaism, however, assumed that every woman's sexual drive was at least equal to man's. But marriage *was* considered a social necessity in order to regulate sexual desire and fulfillment, needs considered an evil impulse because they interfered with the male's scholarly-pursuits and distracted him from his obligations of worship. Within marriage sex was sanctified, both for procreation and pleasure, and celibacy was always condemned by Judaism. But sexuality was difficult to contain and it was woman who was considered the temptress who could entrap even the most pious man and lead him away from God. Hence the curtained-off women's balconies in the synagogues. One Eastern European rabbi, Reb Moishe by name, felt that "all the world's females seemed to be waylaying [him], trying to deflect him from the narrow path of righteousness and lead him to Gehenna." Male lust then was, as usual, blamed on woman.

While her sexuality was recognized, woman's biological functions were regarded with fear and repugnance by rabbinical Judaism. The attitude toward the menstruating woman reflected a blood taboo widespread in primitive cultures. For many cultures blood is regarded as a potent force with magical powers. In Judaism the power of blood lay in its role as the source of life. Because of its quasi-magical power, which could be dangerous, blood was to be shunned. According to *halachic* (legal) prescriptions observed by our female antecedents and by Orthodox women today, the menstruating woman was to have no physical contact whatsoever with a man. Like the person suffering from a gonorrheal discharge, she was impure, and to be shunned physically by all males, including her husband. Therefore, she could not have sexual relations with her husband nor touch him or hand him anything directly. A man whose work had kept him away from home for many months might be disappointed to return to a wife who was menstruating. When one husband brought this matter before a rabbi in Eastern Europe, he received only the reply: "A Jew must be a Jew."

Contact with a woman could be resumed only after she had been free of her discharge for seven days and had undergone ritual purification in a *mikvah,* or ritual bath. After leaving the *mikvah,* the woman was publicly and unabashedly wished good health and fertility. But she would not speak openly to her husband of the fact that she was once more sexually available, for that would be immodest. Rather, she would hand some object directly to him. She could not do this while still menstruating, for during her period of impurity, anything she touched became impure. While this state of impurity was a legal rather than a hygienic concept, it charged woman's primary biological functions with a negative animus hardly calculated to enhance a woman's self-esteem and attitude to her own body.

Moreover, woman's sexuality was so threatening that it had to be shackled not only by rigidly separating men and women socially, but by imposing strict standards of modesty as well. It was considered immoral, for example, for a man to listen to a woman sing, to look at her hair, or to walk behind her on the street. Thus, the most pious men shunned all contact with

9

women other than their wives, would not look directly at women, and avoided hearing their voices by refusing to address them by name or ask them questions ("for the voice of woman leads to lewdness"). In the marketplace, a man might grab a boy to go through the crowds with him, "for, according to the Law, 'two men together may walk through a group of women since one can guard the other.' " Married women were expected to keep their hair covered or even shave their hair off, and modesty also dictated long sleeves and long skirts. Moreover, it was considered most prudent to prevent women from infringing upon the domains of male activity. While it was the responsibility of men to avoid women, some men saw it as the other way around. In some houses, women had to eat in the kitchen when there were male guests, and might be forbidden to sing. Such isolation therefore closed off a significant portion of worldly experience from most women's reach, at least until modern times.

It was no wonder, therefore, that the birth of a male was a time for rejoicing, the birth of a female for stoic acceptance. A female child was destined to be merely a good wife, and she was a financial burden as well since she would need a dowry. But a male child would not only ultimately assume all the religious responsibilities of Judaism—including reciting the memorial prayer for his parents—he might even bring renown to his family as a scholar. And, of course, only a male could be the Messiah! As a pithy saying in the Talmud phrased it, "Woe to the father whose children are girls." Such attitudes persisted among Jews in Eastern Europe into the nineteenth and twentieth centuries. I. J. Singer, the novelist, describes in his memoir, *Of a World that Is No More,* the events surrounding his sister's birth.

The Hasidim snickered in the house of worship as my father named the new child Sarah. Siring a female child was a shameful act for which they occasionally flogged a young father with their belts. Naturally, the birth wasn't celebrated at our house except for serving egg cookies and whiskey to the few men who bothered to drop in. For a girl this was considered sufficient.

A *shtetl* saying summed up this attitude: "Many daughters, many troubles; many sons, many honors."

From the first days of life a religious distinction was made. Pomp and ritual surround the birth festivities of a male. Through the circumcision ceremony, joyously celebrated among friends and relatives, the male infant is inducted into the covenant of Judaism. In Biblical times, firstborn males were considered the property of God and were expected to be consecrated to God's service in the temple or redeemed through a monetary contribution. The redemption of the firstborn son (but not daughter—she was not worthy to serve God) became ritualized in the Jewish tradition. Even today, if the firstborn is a male, he is redeemed, amid great festivity, from symbolic service to God through a donation to a *kohen,* one of priestly descent. These *pidyon ha-ben* and *brith* ceremonies have no parallel for a female. Within a week of a girl's birth, with neither fanfare nor partying, and in the absence of the mother, the father merely declares her name during a regular service in the synagogue.

The next major religious ritual in a boy's life is the *bar mitzvah,* which marks his assumption of the religious responsibilities of an adult. In America the *bar mitzvah* ceremony itself has been overshadowed as never before in Jewish tradition by the *bar mitzvah* party, often a splendid catered affair. Although Reform and Conservative Judaism within the past century have introduced the *bat mitzvah* for girls, such a ceremony has been essentially meaningless as long as women have enjoyed only limited rights and responsibilities within the synagogue. For many girls, particularly in Conservative synagogues, the *bat mitzvah* is not a beginning. It marks the only time she will be able to chant the *Haftarah,* a reading from the prophets, before the congregation. Besides, unlike the boy, who is called to the Torah on Saturday morning, the girl performs her ritual on Friday evening, in a brief service during which the Torah is not even read. The *bat mitzvah* party, too, is a pale imitation of the male's. Moreover, the *bat mitzvah* is generally not celebrated in Israel, where traditional Judaism holds sway. The *bat mitzvah* has been merely a halfhearted attempt to adapt to the American reality of equal religious education for girls.

Within Judaism these attitudes toward women did not preclude treating them with a full measure of humanity in familial relations as long as they fulfilled their expected role. But these attitudes gave rise to the most rigid beliefs regarding the nature and duties of women. The Jewish woman, we are told, was responsible for the moral, but not strictly religious, development of the family, since she was endowed with an exceptional capacity for moral persuasion. At the same time, and somewhat contradictorily, the female in Judaism was regarded as inherently close to the physical, material world, while the Jewish male was immersed in religious matters. Therefore, conveniently, the male-female role division was perceived in the Jewish tradition as a most natural one, based as it was on the fundamental polarity of male and female characters. Consequently, the Jewish woman, in the eyes of the male, was not spiritually deprived by her virtual exclusion from synagogue and study, for her spiritual capacity was simply inferior to his. Better for her to supply his and his children's material needs, while he supplied her spiritual wants. A most efficient division of sexual characteristics and labor! And one that relegated women to the historical anonymity which was their lot in most cultures.

There were some women who achieved positions of prominence within Jewish history, but those who are known to us are few indeed. Deborah, Esther, and Beruriah—the heroines of countless Sunday School texts—leap instantly to mind. The advanced student of Jewish history can add a few more exceptional women: Mibtahiah of the fifth-century B.C.E. Elephantine colony in Egypt, or the scholarly daughter of the twelfth-century scholar Samuel ben Ali, or a number of educated and powerful women in Renaissance Italy, Pomonada Modina, Bathsheba Modena, Benvenida Abrabanel, and Gracia Mendes, or the colorful seventeenth-century merchant, Glückel of Hameln, one of the many who helped run the family business. Just a handful of Jewish women throughout a period of some 3,500 years of Jewish history!

In historical terms, then, these few were truly the most exceptional of women, products of unique historical circumstances. Because Deborah was active in the period of early Israelite religion, before strict monotheism eliminated the last vestiges of the female figure from religious life, she was able to serve as her people's judge and leader. Mibtahiah lived in a marginal community cut off from normative Judaism, from the mainstream of Jewish development. In her community women could engage in independent business activities in their own right and divorce their husbands. Samuel ben Ali, with no sons to educate, raised his daughter to follow in his footsteps as a rabbinic authority. In a later period, upper-class Jewish women in Renaissance Italy profited from the general rise in status of all wealthy women in this period to become well-educated patrons of learning, and active as well in business and politics. And finally, Glückel was a member of a wealthy merchant family in Germany and her husband's partner in a flourishing business. Bourgeois and literate (as well as pious), she was fortunate enough to have her diary—a literary and historical work—saved for posterity.

Of the oft-cited women in Jewish history, Esther and Beruriah attained immortality by excelling in traditional feminine roles. Esther traded on her beauty and charm to gain the king's favor and thus was in a position to follow Mordecai's advice, save her people, and earn a place in Jewish history, while Beruriah's reputation rests as much upon her piety and devotion to her scholar husband as upon her unusual scholarship. When Beruriah's two sons died on the same day, the Talmud tells us, she tried to find the gentlest way to break the news to her husband, Rabbi Meir. After some thought she asked his advice about the case of a man who had lent two jewels and was now demanding their return. "Why, the jewels must be returned to him," Rabbi Meir replied. Leading him to their sons' room, Beruriah softly stated, "These are our jewels. God has given, and God has taken. May His name be blessed." Yet, of the same

Beruriah, who had been able to control her maternal emotions at the time of her sons' death in order to spare her husband, it was told that she was tempted into adultery by her husband, who was jealous of her achievements as a scholar. According to the famous medieval commentator Rashi, he deliberately left her alone with one of his students, who was instructed to try to seduce her. When Beruriah was discovered responding to his overtures, she committed suicide. Clearly, Rashi was trying to point out, learning was not a proper feminine attribute, for it resulted, even for the best of women, in a sorry end.

There were undoubtedly other Jewish women we ought to know about and celebrate, but their lives have gone unrecorded. Certainly the social and economic roles women have played at different moments of Jewish history merit serious scholarly investigation as well as retelling for popular audiences. Until that scholarship becomes available and known, however, we are left with mere token women. For the anonymous Jewish woman has been portrayed in a form that only obscures her real history.

In spite of the secondary status of women within Jewish religious life, there was much in the Jewish historical experience that enabled the woman to develop her human capabilities. Perhaps the most important phenomenon she was spared—as women from other Western cultures were not—was the impact of the "macho" mystique, which was shunned within Jewish culture. Deprived of political independence and, in most places, of the right to bear arms, Jewish men denigrated physical prowess as a cultural ideal. Instead, they cultivated intellectual and spiritual pursuits. They expressed their masculinity in the synagogue and in the house of study, not on the battlefield and not through the physical oppression of their women. The absence of the macho mystique also freed Jewish men and women—until they assimilated into modern Western societies—from the sharpest differentiation of gender characteristics: the strong, emotionally controlled, yet potentially violent male versus the weak, emotional, and tender female. Jewish culture "permitted" men to be gentle and emotionally expressive, and women to be strong, capable, and shrewd. These qualities were suitable for women who were responsible for sustaining their families in environments that were often hostile.

Not only did women perform all domestic chores; as early as medieval times, and especially in modern Eastern Europe, from which most American Jews originate, they assumed heavy economic responsibilities. Like Glückel of Hameln they were often partners in their husband's business, although considered to be "just helping out." Often they relieved their husbands entirely of economic responsibilities so they could devote themselves to the ideal masculine pursuit of study. Frequently they made a significant economic contribution to the family by selling their home-produced wares in the marketplace, and they worked in shops, as well as factories. The role of household manager and supplementary breadwinner was respected, and the *baleboste* (housewife) who could make a meal from a potato became a legendary figure. It was she who met on a regular basis the practical needs of her family by bargaining in the marketplace and dealing with government officials. When economic conditions and persecution brought the Jewish woman from Eastern Europe to the United States, she carried her abilities and self-confidence as well as her pots and pans with her. It was in keeping with her developed strengths that she became active in political and labor movements, both there and here; and as educational opportunities became available to her, she proved that she shared the Jewish passion for education and availed herself of the learning denied her within the traditional Jewish milieu.

Jewish culture's division of roles by sex scarcely reflected the reality of most modern Jewish communities, and particularly not the American one. As the immigrant Jews and their sons abandoned Jewish study as their ideal and focused their ambitions on the economic and professional success valued in America, the newly American Jewish woman, like her non-Jewish counterpart, was encouraged to restrict her activities increasingly to the home and mothering. Her energy, which had found a variety of outlets both in the old country and in the immigrant ghetto, became focused almost exclusively on her family. She found, too, that the qualities of strength and competence with which her mother and grandmother had served their families so well outside the home in Eastern Europe and in the immigrant ghettos of America were no longer respected. The self-sacrificing *Yiddishe mamma,* celebrated in song and story well into the 1930s, had been transformed in literature by the 1950s into a domineering and guilt-producing monster. It was not the Jewish woman who had changed so much as the way in which she was perceived. The characteristics Eastern European Jewish culture had fostered and admired because they served to maintain a stable family life in the midst of poverty and persecution were found unacceptable in mid-twentieth-century America.

The Jewish religious tradition has been abandoned, wholly or in part, by most American Jews. Yet, in secularized form, many of its attitudes toward women prevail within the Jewish community. Others have given way to attitudes more recognizably "American" or simply "Western." The history of the American Jewish women which we are about to recount is the product of that encounter between the forces of Americanization and the traditions of the Jewish historical experience.

2

Assimilation Was Their Goal
The German Jewish Woman in America

The first Jewish women to escape from the traditional Jewish definition of what a woman should be and do were the Jewish women of Western Europe in general and Germany in particular. And it was these women who began to arrive in the United States in large numbers beginning in the 1840s. Besides helping to build the American Jewish community, they became, in some ways, models of the successful American Jewish woman for the Eastern European immigrants who followed them to the American shores in even larger numbers in the last quarter of the nineteenth century.

Not that German Jewish women were the first to become Americans. German Jews had been preceded to the New World, after all, by a small group of Sephardi Jews. Originally from Spain (called *Sepharad* in Hebrew), where a highly cultured and affluent Jewish community flourished during the Middle Ages, Sephardi Jews had dispersed throughout the Mediterranean world after the expulsion of Spanish Jewry by Ferdinand and Isabella in 1492. Other Sephardim had become Marranos (crypto-Jews), outwardly converts to Christianity, but secretly preserving their Jewish identity and whatever Jewish practices they could. To escape the hated Spanish Inquisition many Marranos established themselves as supposed Christian merchants in France, England, Holland, Latin America, and the West Indies. When it became politically feasible, they cast off their Christian guise and emerged as Jews. It was Marranos like these who became the original Jewish settlers of the American colonies in the mid-seventeenth century. As wealthy traders they often moved in the best circles of colonial society. But the Sephardi Jews in colonial times never numbered more than a very few thousand, and their impact on the cultural patterns of later American Jewry was small indeed. Though they contributed their share of illustrious and notorious figures to the gallery of American Jewry, we are starting our story of the American Jewish woman with the formation of the German Jewish community in America, which in 1825 already outnumbered the Sephardi Jews, and which left a permanent mark on American Jewry.

The German Jewish women who emigrated to the United States in the mid-nineteenth century belonged to a Jewish community that had already begun to take giant steps along the path of modernization. By the end of the eighteenth century German Jews, particularly those of the middle and wealthy classes, had heard the call of the Enlightenment, the liberal eighteenth-century ideological movement that introduced the concepts of equality, natural law, and democracy into modern political thought. To the Jews Enlightenment writers promised equality if only they would shed their traditional ways, which the men of the Enlightenment found uncultured and superstitious. Though the promised equality dangled before their eyes was not to be granted fully to German Jews until the unification of Germany in 1870, they made every attempt to purge themselves of the ghetto mentality and to prove themselves worthy of German citizenship. Many took the route of baptism, noting, along with the German Jewish poet Heinrich Heine, that baptism was the admission ticket to European society and culture. While most refused to take that final step, they still accepted as their own the values and standards of modern German culture and began to evaluate their Jewish tradition by these new criteria of Western culture.

In several ways the German Jewish woman may have become modern even more rapidly than her male counterpart. As early as the seventeenth century, she was often the first member of the family—if the family was part of the rising mercantile bourgeoisie—to learn foreign languages, for the successful Jewish merchant, emulating his gentile competitor, considered the social graces of his daughter, her ability to speak and read French and Italian and play charming tunes on the piano, as a sign of his success. One of the most colorful female figures in Jewish history, Glückel of Hameln—merchant's wife and later merchant in her own right—records this practice in her memoirs. Eighteenth-century rabbis preached sermons and wrote moralizing tracts against those fathers, derelict in their duty, who hired gentiles to teach their daughters foreign languages instead of the Bible, Hebrew, and prayers more appropriate to the pious Jewish woman. Not surprisingly, the rabbis also complained that the women who came into contact with the culture of the gentiles were less observant than was expected of them and spent their Sabbath afternoons reading French novels. Jewish males continued to be educated in traditional Jewish studies and enjoyed positions of high status within the Jewish community, but the women received no comparable Jewish education. As the Israeli social historian Jacob Katz has pointed out,

> When enlightenment and secular education penetrated into Jewish society, it had to compete with the study of the Torah that had come traditionally to occupy the whole of a man's free time. This was not so in the case of women. Thus, the daughters of the well-to-do families in the ghetto were the first to benefit from the new opportunities. . . . They were also the ones to acquire the social graces that enabled them to move easily in a society not limited to Jews.

Thus, Western society offered the bourgeois Jewish woman a social and intellectual status denied her within the confines of the traditional Jewish community.

The social world outside the ghetto beckoned the educated

and upper-middle-class Jewish woman even more strongly than it did her brother. Not only did he feel the pull of traditional Jewish studies, he also could win fame and fortune in the economic sphere, where the bourgeois woman's role was progressively limited with the development of capitalism and the separation of home and workplace. The majority of Jewish men did, in fact, seek to prove their equality in the business world. The most educated and sensitive of Jewish women in Germany, however, chose another path. They abandoned their Jewish tradition and their community because the society and culture of the Enlightenment seemed to offer them freedom and opportunities to excel intellectually and win admirers from the worlds of literature and politics, experiences they might dream of but never have if they remained within their native community.

Most famous of the German Jewish women who left the Jewish world for the heady atmosphere of gentile society were the "salon Jewesses" of the early nineteenth century. Though hardly typical of their sister Jews in Germany, they show at their most extreme the effects of being educated within the Western culture that despised both Jews and Judaism. They also reveal the effects of their alienation and isolation from the Jewish community, which kept them ignorant of Jewish culture and made no effort to facilitate the development of their talents.

The most notable salon Jewesses were Dorothea Mendelssohn, daughter of the renowned philosopher Moses Mendelssohn; Rahel Levin Varnhagen, daughter of a wealthy merchant; and Henriette de Lemos Herz, whose father was a physician. Raised under comfortable circumstances and with only the most superficial of Jewish educations, they took advantage of their wit, their familiarity with European culture, and their social position as Jews, who were therefore not bound by social conventions, to open literary salons where the elite of the nobility, the bourgeoisie, and the Bohemian world of the artist could freely mingle. Their salons were frequented by such figures as Goethe, Count Mirabeau, the Humboldts, the philosopher Fichte, and the theologians Schlegel and Schleermacher—all drawn to the company of these salon Jewesses by the lure of the exotic and the opportunity to overlook class divisions.

The salon Jewesses fulfilled the romantic ideal of womanhood according to which a woman was to serve as muse to the talents of men. Spiritually and intellectually independent of their husbands, they cultivated their personalities and sensibilities to provide inspiration to creative men. They found their deep need for faith and spirituality unmet by a Judaism which they saw only in its worst guise. As Henriette Herz, who was married off at the age of fifteen by her father, wrote in her memoirs, "The Jewish children, particularly the girls, were not . . . really instructed in the faith of their parents but were constrained to observe its *forms*. . . . Girls had to pray in the Hebrew language without understanding what they were praying." Dorothea Mendelssohn, too, came to loathe what she saw as the stale rationalism and empty ritual of her father's and husband's Judaism as well as her husband's unexciting stolidity. Neither her husband nor his religion could compete with the new Christian theology she learned from Friedrich Schlegel. No wonder, then, that she abandoned both when she eloped with Schlegel in 1802, becoming baptized as a Protestant in 1804 and later turning to Catholicism, drawn by its aesthetic appeal.

Henriette Herz and Rahel Levin also forsook Judaism, Herz at the age of fifty-three in 1817 after the death of her mother, whom she had not wished to wound, and Levin in 1814, on the day of her wedding to the Prussian noble and diplomat, Karl Varnhagen von Ense. Christianity was seen as the religion of Western culture, Judaism only its despised stepmother. Because Judaism and the Jewish community offered them so little, these women were doubly sensitive to the social stigma and cultural inferiority they bore as Jews. Rahel Levin wrote with pain of her status as a Jew: "I imagine that just as I was being thrust into this world a supernatural being plunged a dagger into my heart, with these words: Now have feeling, see the world as only a few see it, be great and noble; nor can I deprive you of restless incessant thought, but with one reservation, be a Jewess! And now my whole life is one long bleeding."

Courted by members of gentile society who proclaimed, "Among the Jews . . . the women . . . are 100 percent better than the men," the salon Jewesses served as the agents of social assimilation at the topmost rungs of society. Free from the conventions and prejudices of the social elite, they brought the fresh creative insight of outsiders to the ranks of German intellectuals. While Jewish men of their generation devoted their time and passion to their business activities, the educated Jewish woman played out the drama of leaving the ghetto, both physically and spiritually, in their own salons.

Besides fascinating their gentile admirers, the salon women taught a lesson as well to the men of the Jewish Enlightenment, the *maskilim,* who sought civic rights for Jews and preached the necessity of self-improvement to their own community. It became clear to them that more and more educated Jewish women would rebel against their status in traditional Judaism unless that status were improved. So the *maskilim* in Germany made room for female students in the modern schools which they established. However, they instituted a separate curriculum for boys and girls. While boys studied Bible translation, Hebrew grammar, and rabbinics, girls were taught the less demanding and supposedly more feminine subjects of Bible history, ethics, and customs and ceremonies. In their German-language periodical *Sulamith,* the *maskilim* also attempted to appeal to female readers. They did so with a special feature designed for the delicate and sensitive female nature—a column entitled "Letters to a Respectable Young Lady of the Jewish Religion" —which consisted of moral homilies and Bible stories. Although they realized that in this period of transition the Jewish community could not ignore its female members, the *maskilim* were bound by the mores and ideas of their time and class in their approach to women. The traditional restrictions on women were to be relaxed, but the new role found acceptable for them was to be that of the German bourgeois woman. No longer denied an education, the modern Jewish woman still was not to be given an education equal to a man's. Like her gentile sister, she was considered the weaker and less intellectual sex. It should be remembered, after all, that so noted a *philosophe* as Jean-Jacques Rousseau was a misogynist who saw the destiny of women to be the ignorant servants of men.

As German Jews assimilated Western ideals and culture, they

also adopted Western attitudes toward women. The pioneers of Reform Judaism in Germany in the mid-nineteenth century placed the status of women in Judaism on the agenda of their 1846 synod not merely because of an abstract commitment to the notion of equality but also because of their embarrassment at the non-Western customs evident in the treatment of Jewish women. The segregation of women in balconies during worship, the absence of confirmation for girls, the male blessing thanking God for not having been born a woman, and the ban on women in choirs were seen as atavistic Oriental customs that had to be uprooted from Jewish behavior. As a Hungarian Reform rabbi declared proudly, Judaism had surpassed "the barbaric ages when . . . it was thought sinful to put woman on the same level with men." One thing German reformers wished to prove was their progressiveness and successful adaptation to Western culture and to deny their non-European origin. They worried as well about keeping the loyalty of the modern Jewish woman who was repelled by her inferior status within the synagogue. Abraham Geiger, one of the most prominent Reform rabbis of his generation, went so far as to declare that only by granting her equal rights "will the Jewish girl and . . . woman [become] conscious of the significance of our faith and . . . fervently attached to it." Though the 1846 synod did not publicly discuss the status of women, it accepted the need for the ratification of the proposals brought to it. Moreover, the congregation of Reformers in Berlin on their own had already taken the lead in introducing the changes proposed at the 1846 synod, and those changes, which essentially introduced religious equality for female laity, soon became widespread among Reform congregations in Germany.

Some German Jewish women themselves pressed for improvement of their religious status, particularly insofar as it appeared to lag behind that of the Christian women of their own class. Thus, they resented the custom of the bride bringing a dowry to her husband and sought a double-ring ceremony, which was alien to Jewish tradition. One German Reform rabbi commented, "These young brides of the most cultured families . . . stated that they did not wish to be completely passive at the marriage altar, as if they were objects and as though the marriage ceremony could be performed without their equal participation." Thus, a combination of women's demands to be equal and the desire of men to be modern led to significant improvement in the religious status of Jewish women.

In the New World

The German Jews who immigrated to the United States in the nineteenth century brought their Reform Judaism with them and provided the mass base for the success of a Reform movement that had been initiated independently in the United States in 1824 by a group of Jews in Charleston, South Carolina. Like the early reformers in Germany, the members of Congregation Beth Elohim in Charleston who split with the traditionalist majority in their synagogue sought a dignified service, largely in the vernacular, which would uplift and edify their spirits in accordance with the esthetic standards of the American Protestant middle classes. Many of the immigrants from Germany rapidly assumed the same standards and found Reform Judaism congenial to their tastes.

Between 1840 and 1880 some 250,000 German Jews settled in the United States. Like other immigrants, they sought greater economic opportunity than had been available to them in Germany, where many states, particularly in southern Germany, limited the number of Jewish families permitted to settle permanently and establish businesses. Second and third sons who did not receive permanent residence rights often took off for America. There were also a large number of single women among the Jewish immigrants from Germany. They emigrated because they were not allowed to marry and establish homes in their native state of Bavaria. Ineligible for full citizenship, German Jews also immigrated to the United States in search of political rights. However, they were not coming straight from the ghetto to a vibrantly modern America; they had taken the first steps toward modernization in Germany.

Unlike many other immigrants to the United States, the Jews from Germany were not peasants but primarily city and town dwellers. Even though many of the Jewish immigrants from southern Germany came from small rural village communities, for the most part they had not worked the land. Their fathers had been horse and cattle dealers, storekeepers, artisans, or traders in agricultural produce. While not all were middle class and many were unskilled, most were not prepared to become either farmers or industrial workers.

The German Jewish immigrants settled in the cities and towns of the American Midwest, along with their gentile fellow immigrants from Germany, who became their customers in commercial enterprises. And like the gentile German immigrants, they also spread throughout the Great Lakes region and into the big cities and farming towns of the Far West. From its pioneer days, San Francisco had a small Jewish community whose numbers grew as merchants who had prospered in mining towns moved into the city to settle. German Jews settled in a host of southern towns as well. Even today scores of towns and small cities throughout America boast local jewelry and department stores with Jewish names, heirs to the German Jewish immigrants of the nineteenth century.

Not that the immigrants arrived as prosperous merchants. Usually they had little money, and they started as basket peddlers, carrying their merchandise to customers in the countryside. When sufficient capital was acquired they purchased a horse and wagon to carry on their mobile enterprise. Only later were the successful ones able to obtain stores and become settled merchants, or "store princes," as they were popularly known. While some of these store princes actually founded important department store dynasties—such as the Strauses of Macy's, the Gimbels, Bloomingdales, Bergdorfs—most German Jewish businessmen remained of moderate means, respected members of the local business community but hardly barons of commerce.

German Jewish immigrant males tended not to marry until they had acquired some capital. But their wives, needless to say, generally helped in the family business until their husbands were sufficiently successful to afford the luxury of a housewife-wife. A typical case is that of Gustav Kussy and his wife, Bella Bloch.

Though they lived in Newark in the 1860s rather than in the Midwest, their pattern was a familiar one. As their daughter recounts, Gustav was a butcher who peddled his cuts of meat on foot throughout the Newark region in the early days of his marriage. His wife, a former milliner who had immigrated to the United States with her sister, "waited on customers in the butcher shop; cooked, washed, sewed for her family, while every drop of water had to be carried into the house from the pump that stood in the yard."

As a group the German Jewish community in America rapidly ascended into the middle classes and beyond. However, there were variations of life-style. An unmarried immigrant girl might live with relatives and provide unpaid domestic help or find gainful employment as a schoolteacher or a saleswoman in a refined shop. Such employment became more respectable, even for the daughters of the middle class, in the second half of the nineteenth century. Henrietta Szold, the unmarried daughter of a prominent Baltimore rabbi, taught private school and contributed her salary to her family.

The married woman, like Bella Bloch Kussy, helped her husband in his business only as long as was necessary. Then she retired to manage a household—a job that entailed frequent marketing, the preparation of meals, canning fruit and vegetables, sewing clothes for the family or having time-consuming fittings with the seamstress, and laundering the family's wash by hand. With domestic help relatively inexpensive—the "servant problem" is a twentieth-century phenomenon—the wives of middle-class businessmen, merchants, and rabbis took advantage of the situation to hire servants. A cook and a maid were most desirable (the Szold family employed both Lizzie and Maggie Muller, gentile Hungarian sisters, for some twenty years) but a family might make do with one servant whose chores began, and centered, in the kitchen and extended to the rest of the house as well. The Levys of San Francisco, described by Harriet Lane Levy in her memoir *920 O'Farrell Street,* kept their Maggie O'Doyle busy with thirteen-hour workdays. As soon as a servant woman was hired, the wife became the overseer of her domestic help, preparer of menus, and manager of accounts with the local tradesmen who kept the household stocked with goods. She made sure that the home, with its ornate parlor for guests, its sitting room, music room, sewing room, bedrooms, and kitchen, was always in order. With or without servants, that was no small task.

The majority of these German immigrants quickly became Reform Jews, if they had not already done so in Germany, for Reform Judaism, which accepted the aesthetic standards and cultural patterns of Protestantism, seemed appropriate for the American scene. Immigrant Jews reveled in the American climate of equality and sought to be as much like their neighbors as possible. With its proud trumpeting of its consonance with "the spirit of the times," Reform Judaism offered them that opportunity.

Immigrant women seeking equality found Reform leaders responsive to their demands. Isaac Mayer Wise, the most dynamic leader of American Reform Judaism, who was responsible for the creation both of Hebrew Union College in 1873 and of the Union of American Hebrew Congregations in 1876, was particularly anxious to retain the loyalty to Judaism of those young women repelled by orthodox Judaism. He favored female suffrage, the establishment of a special academy to provide religious instruction for girls, the inclusion of women as trustees and members of temple school boards, and the ordination of women as rabbis (something that was not to occur until the 1970s). Under his leadership, the Philadelphia Rabbinical Conference of 1869 replaced the traditional marriage ceremony, in which the bride is a silent partner, with a reciprocal declaration and a double-ring ceremony. Furthermore, the religious divorce, the *get*, which can be granted only by the husband, was abolished in favor of reliance solely upon civil divorce. And it was left to civil courts to decide as well whether a missing husband could be declared dead, thus enabling his widow to remarry.

As in Germany, this attempt by the Reform movement to equalize the legal position of women reflected the desire of Reform leaders to be as Western, and in this case as American, as possible. But it was also at least partly a response to the demands of two decades' duration on the part of immigrant German Jewish women. In Isaac Mayer Wise's first congregation in Albany, his female congregants demanded to sit on the main floor along with the men. Temple Emmanuel of New York City abolished the women's gallery in 1854, and in Reform temples in the Midwest it had disappeared generally by 1860. Around the time of the Civil War family pews had become widespread, and confirmation for girls and mixed choirs were coming extensively into use.

The elevation of woman's status did not always proceed smoothly. Occasionally, conflicts over the proper role for women erupted, as in Congregation B'nai Jeshurun of New York City, where traditionalist members brought a suit against the congregation for permitting mixed seating. Moreover, under the leadership of Isaac Leeser, educator and editor of the *Occident,* traditionalists within the American Jewish community marshaled their arguments against the changes introduced by the Reform movement in religious law and custom regarding women. According to the *Occident,* because of their vanity, women "join in the shout of progress, not knowing, poor things, that with its advance . . . they are the actual losers in the estimation that they were formerly held at home, as wives, mothers, daughters . . . the true characters in which women should excel." (Or, shut up and stay on that pedestal!) The solution proposed by the *Occident* was accommodation to woman's traditional role in Judaism: "Our rabbis . . . should call attention to the wives and mothers of Israel to that portion of the holy law . . . specifically addressed to them . . . and it should be the duty of our women to attend to it, instead of forcing themselves into positions which our religion wisely did not open to them."

Despite their quarrel over the legal position of Jewish women and their participation in religious activities, both reformers and traditionalists alike adopted the attitudes toward women currently in fashion in mid-nineteenth-century middle-class America. Whatever new roles were made available to Jewish women in America followed the patterns of gentile society, which at the time embraced what we have come to know as the Victorian ideal of womanhood—the woman of delicate sensibility, source of morality and the noblest feelings, pillar of the family (and its prisoner as well). Conveniently, this concept of womanhood meshed with that aspect of the Jewish tradition that had stressed the importance of family life for Jewish strength and survival. Although the Victorian model attributed to women a fragility absent from the Jewish ideal (which was based on the reality of the role division within the Jewish family), it was accepted by the American Jewish community as a sign of its own progress and modernity.

Typical of this stance are the following effusive comments addressed to women from the *Israelite* of April 5, 1861—comments that would appear equally at home in many a non-Jewish journal of the same period:

> . . . you are a wife and mother, and therewith your position is nobler and grander than that of the master mechanic, the merchant prince, the man of letters, the soldier and the statesmen of the land; your position gives you the power to sway over all; but do you use the power which civilization and nature have bestowed upon you, rightly? If you are true to your husband, if you take a lively interest in his occupations, if you are economical and do your best to live below his income; if you strive to be worthy of his entire confidence; if you advise him to what is good and noble; if you speak kindly to your children, reason with them and impress upon their minds that 'Honesty is the best policy,' if you bring them up domestically; if you set them a good example with a sweet temper and good manners . . .—then you are worthy of your exalted position; then peace and harmony prevail in your house; your husband gathers strength in your loveliness, in your noble counsel and your manners . . . he earns abundantly because he is a happy man, and a happy man is a host within himself.

This paragon of feminine virtue and humility described above seems to have existed solely to serve as a source of inspiration for those around her. She was the adult version of the "nice girl," whose modesty and proper place were described by the *American Israelite:* "In public she is not in front showing her shoulders; she sits quiet and unobtrusive, at the back of the crowd most likely. In fact, it is not often we discover her. Home is her place."

Home may have been her place, but the synagogue was considered much more within her sphere than it had been in premodern Judaism. Whereas Jewish men had always been the "pillars of the synagogue," now one of the organs of the traditionalist Jewish press in America, the *Jewish Messenger,* applied that term to women in its comments on their piety and devotion. Isaac Mayer Wise, too, wrote that "American [Jewish] women, we find, are more religious, and in many instances more intelligent than their 'lords of creation.' They are the religious teachers of their children, the priestesses of the house, and we are morally obligated to attach them closer to the synagogue."

Just as women's natures were expected to be predisposed to piety, they were also expected to be endowed with an extra measure of charity and mercy. Philanthropic concern, particularly on a personal level, was considered one of the few activities that might legitimately draw a middle-class woman—a lady— from her home. Charity was considered an extension of the home and family obligations that women bore, and it became another example of her religiosity and purity. While there had always existed special "women's societies" within the traditional Jewish community, especially for providing the necessary care for the female sick and dead, charity had always been a communal activity, controlled and executed by men. Now many synagogues and most cities and towns boasted a Ladies' Hebrew Benevolent Society. It was Rebecca Gratz of Philadelphia who established the first Female Hebrew Benevolent Society in that city in 1819 and, along with other women, the Philadelphia Jewish Foster Home in 1855. During the Civil War, American Jewish women, like their non-Jewish counterparts, extended their charitable work. As participants in Red Cross activities, they rolled bandages, sewed uniforms, made blankets, raised funds, and tended the wounded. Though small in scale the philanthropic societies established by women throughout the nineteenth century became the forerunners of the great American Jewish women's organizations of the twentieth century.

To attain her perch on the Victorian pedestal, the American Jewish woman in the mid-nineteenth century was expected to have an education long on the social graces and short on serious content. The traditionalist Isaac Leeser commented in the *Occident* that "it would be regarded as mean in a wealthy father not to give his daughters an ample opportunity, at least, to acquire the science of music, and to learn French, say for a space of ten years at the smallest calculation. . . ." Fathers hired private tutors for their daughters and the wealthiest sent them to Jewish finishing schools with such names as Mrs. H. Simon's Select School for Young Ladies of the Hebrew Faith, Dr. Joseph Ridskopf's Select Male and Female Academy, or the Boarding and Day School for Young Ladies of the Jewish Faith. It was understood that education for women should equip them for their family responsibilities. As the *Israelite* intoned, "Young wives acquire useful knowledge of household affairs first; other education can follow afterwards."

While finishing and polishing in the genteel arts was not lacking, most nineteenth-century American Jewish women had the most meager Jewish education. Although women attended, and later taught in, Jewish Sunday Schools, the orthodox *Jewish Messenger* lamented that they "learn little or no Hebrew and Jewish religion." And a European Jew writing of his three-year visit to America found little to recommend in women's frivolous behavior and lack of Jewish education. Should a parent decide to add a Hebrew teacher as a crowning touch to the music, singing, drawing, and French teachers already engaged, the foreign observer noted, ". . . she will find this last teacher . . . a bore. She will find Hebrew too dull and also too difficult; she will weep over her lessons so that her yielding parents will give the teacher notice. . . ." If the American Jewish girl was to keep up with her gentile playmates, then religious education would have to be sacrificed. It had not, after all, ever been a priority for females. Jewish education for girls had become of importance to American Jewish leaders only because they realized that in a society with no ghetto walls a girl ignorant of her

Jewish heritage could easily be drawn away from the Jewish community by the glittering attractions of the world around her. And traditionalists realized that education could be used to teach Jewish girls their proper place (within the home) and to guard against the lure of Reform.

In mid-nineteenth-century America, then, Jewish women were scarcely distinguishable from their non-Jewish middle-class counterparts. They were found on both sides during the Civil War, and they were fierce partisans of the particular cause to which they owed their allegiance. Confederate Jewish women lamented the ravishing of the South while their northern sisters cheered on the boys in blue. Along with other middle-class women in the second half of the nineteenth century, they formed numerous literary societies which became a badge of their culture and afforded them an opportunity on occasion to leave their homes and meet together. Though there were teachers and nurses, shopkeepers, and operators of boarding houses among them, the cultural ideal held aloft for the Jewish woman still remained the perfect and submissive helpmeet whom the *Occident* described as "ever seeking equality with man, but in vain." The Jewish woman in America had become essentially a housewife and consumer. In the 1890s a periodical directed specifically to Jewish women, and entitled appropriately enough the *American Jewess,* could point out as an inducement to advertisers that women buy soap, china, glassware, flour, baking powder, carpets, and all other household articles—and "Jewish women buy the best." Elevated for her supposed spiritual qualities, the Jewish woman was still deemed intellectually inferior. She was caught in a double bind. Though she was more or less confined to domestic routine, and deprived of educational opportunities, she was mercilessly criticized for her frivolity and lack of seriousness when she sought diversion in fashion and fancy dress balls. Dr. Marcus Jastrow, a Philadelphia rabbi and scholar, who brought up his daughters according to the axiom that too much education makes a girl an unfit wife, later found their chatter about dresses and household furnishings unstimulating. For his own companionship he preferred the likes of Henrietta Szold, daughter of an old friend and fellow rabbi, who had not been reared solely for social pleasantries. (But she remained a spinster—so the common wisdom seemed realized in her state of unmarried intelligence.)

Not all Jewish women, even then, accepted with equanimity the role reserved for them and the advice tendered them by solicitous males on how best to perform that role. One woman subscriber in 1864 angrily protested the *Israelite*'s advice to women, finding it "obnoxious." A decade later another woman expressed her outrage at a male correspondent's disparagement of the education of Jewish women with the comment: "I am one of those familiarly known as the weaker sex—who are very often mentally the stronger." If Jewish women resented the uncharitable assessments of their abilities and their sensibilities, they had few means of protest available other than letters to the editor, and few alternative models other than that of wife, mother, and homemaker, a role that was certainly more desirable than holding the jobs reserved for women in mills and factories. The home reigned supreme in middle-class America. In fact, by the end of the nineteenth century most middle-class Jewish women, like their gentile counterparts, had internalized the view that theirs was the duty to reign as the spiritual element within the home. It was the *American Jewess,* published by a woman, Rosa Sonneschein, that printed a poem that sums up the prevailing image of the Jewish woman:

The girls that are wanted are good girls—
Good from the hearts to the lips;
Pure, as the lily is white and pure
From its heart to its sweet leaf tips.
The girls that are wanted are home girls—
Girls that are mother's right hand;
That fathers and brothers can trust to,
And the little ones understand.

. . .

The girls that are wanted are girls with hearts;
They are wanted for mothers and wives;
Wanted to cradle in loving arms
The strongest and frailest lives.

The clever, the witty, the brilliant girl
There are few who can understand;
But Oh! for the wise, loving home girls
There's constant and steady demand.

The Spinster

Virtually the only nineteenth-century Jewish women in America who left their mark upon history were spinsters or, occasionally, childless wives. Though most spinsters undoubtedly became maiden aunts who served as unpaid domestic help in return for their home and board, spinsterhood offered an opportunity for the talented and energetic woman to do what she wanted with her time, given the limitations of her socioeconomic class. She, after all, was not kept at home by the responsibilities that fell so heavily upon the wife and mother and by the accompanying social sanctions. She may have needed as well to earn her own livelihood. And she may have sought a way to feel socially useful and to win in public the recognition other women were expected to attain in private within the family.

The obstacles that social climate and internalized constraints placed in the way of purposeful activity outside the home for married women—particularly if they were mothers—is reflected in the life and memoirs of Rebekah Bettelheim Kohut. Growing up as a rabbi's daughter in post-Gold Rush San Francisco, she was encouraged by her father to attend college, despite the disapproval of his congregation. As a woman of many talents, she entertained hopes of "a career of service . . . rather than a life limited to housewifely duties [for she was moved] by the desire to do some useful, significant work." Like so many others, she sacrificed her dreams and ambitions upon the altar of marriage. In fact, her marriage to Alexander Kohut, a prominent rabbi of Hungarian origin, became her career. Kohut was a widower, some twenty years Rebekah's senior, and the father of eight children, so Rebekah's responsibilities were immediate and heavy. She accepted them with grace and with the kind of rationalization women have traditionally adopted whenever compelled to abandon their cherished dreams. As she wrote to her sister, "I go to New York to be the wife of a great man and to become a mother to the motherless." Her ambition to be of service was merely transmuted into wifely duties, for she felt "that possibly my life's work was to serve him and his children."

Serve him she did. Besides assuming all the tasks associated with running a household of ten persons, she tried to "lessen his burden" and took over the chore of his correspondence as well as translating his Sabbath sermons for publication. When he became ill in 1893, she nursed him for fourteen months, never leaving his side.

In spite of her devotion and her feeling that she had "little time and little call" for the social and communal work which would occupy much of her later life, she managed to establish and preside over the sisterhood of her husband's synagogue. Her charitable activities attracted attention, and she was asked to deliver a speech for the Women's Health Protective Association. Her communal work did not receive unquestioning approval, however, from her husband, who in Rebekah's words,

> was dubious of the wisdom of a public career for me. He felt that I had much to do at home and was more or less jealous of any time I gave to others. However, I continued with the Association for a number of years until pressure of household and other duties became so great that I had to give them my undivided attention.

Even for a woman as capable and strong as Rebekah, it must have been difficult to face her husband's guilt-provoking disapproval as the price for the worthwhile activity to which she was drawn. While she is consistent in her admiration for her husband, her covert resentment surfaces from time to time in her memoirs. So powerful was the inner conflict that Rebekah decided at the last minute not to travel to Chicago to read a paper which she had been invited to present at the First Congress of Jewish Women, held in 1893 as part of the Chicago World's Fair. She had been "thrilled" by the prospect of traveling to the exposition and by the honor of being invited to speak. She had prepared her paper. But Alexander was feeling sick and Rebekah's concept of wifely duty did not allow her to leave him for two or three days. As she wrote in her autobiography *My Portion,*

> My heart gripped me at his absolute dependence and his sadness. "I didn't really intend to go," I cried impulsively. "Isn't it nonsense to travel twenty-four hours in order to read a fifteen-minute paper?" "Why then," he said happily, but in a quiet tone, "did you allow me to be unhappy all day?" . . . The disappointment was keen. . . . But in later years I felt it was one of the finest sacrifices I had ever made for Alexander Kohut.

Ironically, it was Kohut's death and the prospect of a life of impecunious widowhood that both impelled and allowed Rebekah to pursue a career. At first, she delivered literary talks to a circle of wealthy German Jewish ladies convened under the patronage of Therese Loeb Schiff, the wife of Jacob Schiff, the New York banker and philanthropist. Seeking financial independence, she turned to education. After teaching the confirmation class at the fashionable Temple Emmanuel, she founded the Kohut School for Girls, which she served devotedly as headmistress for five years. When she sold the school, she was able to invest her returns to yield a living income.

Besides her purely professional work, Rebekah was active in public service, and she was criticized by friends for "neglecting" her household duties. As she recalled, "It was a period in American history when women's careers were looked upon askance. . . . I had always felt that while a woman's interest ought to begin at home and ought to end there, they need not necessarily confine themselves to it alone."

Only the spinster escaped some of the conflict and criticism (though spinsterhood naturally entailed its own economic and psychological problems). Spinsters also found their social roles limited since they were still expected to fulfill typically female functions. The earliest of the spinsters who achieved fame among American Jewry was Rebecca Gratz. She hardly challenged the accepted norms of her society. Born in 1789 to a successful merchant family in Philadelphia, she remained single partly because of her Jewish loyalties. As a pious Jew, she refused to marry out of her faith, though she was reputed to have been deeply, and mutually, in love with the scion of a wealthy and socially prominent Christian family. Since there were few eligible Jewish bachelors of her own class, she opted for spinsterhood instead of intermarriage. In this respect Rebecca Gratz typifies the lot of many American Jewish women in the nineteenth century and later, particularly those who lived in small southern and western communities with few Jewish families. These women had limited marital possibilities. As Leah Morton wrote in *I Am a Woman—and a Jew* of her own experience in such a community at the turn of the century,

> The Jewish girls whose fathers were the first to settle in the American small towns faced a double misery as women. They were received, very often, into the social group of the community, went to parties and dances. They had not the seclusion of the Jewish girls living even in a small city, such as I had known. As soon as they became women, however, they found themselves left alone, isolated. Their girl friends married the young men they met in churches and church societies. The Jewish girls met few, if any, of their faith.

Rebecca Gratz was the model spinster, raising her sister's children after her sister's death and ministering to the needs of her unmarried brothers. Graceful, modest, and charming—and devoted to "good works"—she is supposed to have served as the model for the gentle Jewess Rebecca in Sir Walter Scott's *Ivanhoe.* Thus, in spite of the fact that she never married, she followed the traditional woman's role throughout her long life. And when she turned to community service, it was as an extension of female caretaking and nurturing roles. Philanthropy, both nonsectarian and Jewish, became her major activity. From the age of twenty-one she was secretary of the Female Association for Relief of Women and Children in Reduced Circumstances, and in 1815 she helped to organize the Philadelphia Orphan Society. Her most important contribution to the Jewish community was the establishment of the Hebrew Sunday School Society in 1838. Since moral education and the inculcation of religious piety, and not serious study of the Jewish classics, were the purpose of Jewish Sunday Schools, they fell within woman's realm. It was appropriate, then, that the first Jewish Sunday School in the United States was founded by a woman. Rebecca Gratz was held up as a paragon of feminine virtue, and she served as a role model for the upwardly mobile German Jewish immigrant women of the second half of the nineteenth century.

Another nineteenth-century American Jewish spinster, Emma Lazarus, was too exceptional to be a role model. But she was publicly esteemed, and the moving lines of her poem, "The Colossus" are inscribed on the pedestal of the Statue of Liberty. Though of Sephardic rather than German origin—her family dated back to the colonial period—she lived in New York City from 1849 to 1887, when American Jewry was dominated by Jews of German origin. The daughter of a wealthy and assimilated family, she was privately tutored and well-educated. From her earliest childhood she wrote poetry. Her first book, entitled *Poems and Translations,* was published in 1868 when she was only nineteen years old. As a literary figure she entertained a friendship, primarily through letters, with Ralph Waldo Emerson and corresponded as well with Ivan Turgenev, Henry George, and John Burroughs. She was probably the most prominent American Jewish writer of her generation.

Though it has often been claimed that Emma Lazarus's Jewish consciousness dates from her contact with Russian Jewish immigrants who arrived in the United States in 1881 fleeing from pogroms, in fact her literary interest in Jewish subjects goes back to her girlhood. Her poem "In the Jewish Synagogue at Newport" was written when she was eighteen, and in 1876 she published *Songs of a Semite,* which included "The Dance to Death," a poem recounting the persecution of Jews in fourteenth-century Germany. In 1881 she published as well a translation, along with a biographical introduction, of the works of the German poet Heinrich Heine, whose concern with his Jewish identity was lifelong. Nevertheless, her Jewish interests were sharpened by the anguish and empathy aroused within her by the persecution of the Jews of Russia. It was her feeling for the immigrant Jews, noted Henrietta Szold (the founder of the women's Zionist organization, Hadassah) who experienced a similar empathy, that made her "a poet of the people." Rebekah Kohut, another of her acquaintances, similarly claimed that the persecutions of Russian Jewry "made her the supreme poetess of Jewish suffering."

Inspired to action in behalf of her fellow Jews of Eastern Europe, Emma attempted to rouse the acculturated and comfortable Jews of America to respond to their needs. In "An Epistle to the Hebrews" she called on American Jews to acknowledge their heritage instead of denying it in the name of universalism: "Not by disclaiming our 'full heritage,' but by lifting up our own race to the standard of morality and instruction shall we at the same time promote the advancement and elevation of the Gentiles." One way American Jews could both express their heritage and improve their people's lot was by aiding the victims of the pogroms: "By virtue of our racial and religious connection with these hapless victims of anti-Jewish cruelty, we feel that it devolves upon us to exert our utmost strength toward securing for them permanent protection. . . . Until we are all free," she wrote, "we are none of us free." To aid immigrant Jews in their adaptation to American society she was the first to propose the creation of a Hebrew Technical Institute. Her concern also led her to believe in a more far-reaching solution—the establishment of a Jewish state in Palestine as a homeland for the oppressed Russian Jewish masses.

Emma's Jewish identity also informed her general social ideals. She found support for her proclaimed socialism in the Mosaic code and even in the Jewish descent of Karl Marx. The Sabbath, according to Lazarus, was not merely a day of spiritual meaning but also of social significance, for it bestowed the right to rest equally upon employer and employee. "However degrading or servile might be their avocation during the secular week," she declared, "The first star of the Sabbath eve restored to them their human dignity. . . . The only limit to these [Sabbath celebrations] was the equal right of every individual to undisturbed rest from labor."

While Emma Lazarus's poetic voice and her social concerns were strong and vital, her position as "lady poet" relegated her to the margins of the literary world. In one poem she gave expression to her sense of exclusion from the world of male poets:

> Late-born and woman-souled I dare not hope,
> The freshness of the elder lays, the might
> Of manly, modern passion shall alight
> Upon my Muse's lips, nor may I cope
> (Who veiled and screened by womanhood must grope)
> With the world's strong-armed warriors and recite
> The dangers, wounds, and triumphs of the fight. . . .

She perceived a real problem facing the woman poet. It was possible to accept her poetry and her social concerns as expressions of her femininity and equally possible to dismiss them for the same reason, as the outpourings of an emotional woman. While feminine charity and spirituality were admired, they were honored more in the breach than in the observance. At best Emma Lazarus was regarded as the exceptional woman whose talent earned her the attention of the Jewish community and of the literary lights of her day.

Equally prominent and equally atypical was the militant feminist Ernestine Rose. Like Emma Lazarus, she was not of German Jewish origin, but she came to America during the period of German, rather than Eastern European, immigration. She was born in Poland, the daughter of a rabbi, in 1809. When her father attempted to marry her off against her will at the age of sixteen to a man many years her senior, she rebelled against his authority (and likewise against the Jewish tradition he represented). Even as a teen-ager Ernestine was an independent spirit whose religious faith had been eroded by a questioning and skeptical turn of mind. Determined to break the engagement contract her father had signed as her guardian, she took the matter on her own to a Polish court—and won her case! Shortly thereafter she left the Jewish community and Poland behind her.

Ernestine's travels took her through Central and Western Europe to England, where she became a disciple of the Utopian socialist Robert Owen and married a fellow Owenite socialist. In the 1840s she and her husband arrived in the United States. As a convinced atheist, she had severed her connection with the Jewish community after leaving Poland. With a husband who saw her as a companion in political action and not as his servant, and with no children to care for, she devoted herself to the causes of feminism and abolitionism, two of the most controversial issues of the time. Along with Susan B. Anthony she was a stellar attraction on the feminist lecture circuit. Her political activity would hardly have won her the sympathetic attention of the German Jewish community. In general, it was a conservative community, still establishing its social and economic security, and while some northern rabbis preached against slavery, few Jews appear to have been partisans of either the nascent feminist movement or the abolitionist cause. The pressure for equal religious rights for women within the Reform movement was dominated not by militant feminism but by the desire to make the status of women within American Judaism conform to their social situation in nineteenth-century America.

Ernestine Rose did earn favorable recognition from some members of the American Jewish community, however, for her vigorous defense in 1863–1864 of Jews and their religion. Enraged by an anti-Semitic article written by her former friend Horace Seaver, the editor of the liberal Boston paper, the *Investigator*, to which she had often contributed, she engaged in a debate with Seaver (who had, by the way, been ignorant of her Jewish origins). She refuted his charges that Judaism was inferior to Christianity and that Jews were by nature corrupt and exploitative. While no admirer of any religion, Rose was quick to point out that Judaism was no worse than any other. Likewise, she asserted that Jews merely shared in the failings common to all groups and, given the opportunity, made praiseworthy citizens.

Ernestine Rose's involvement with the Jewish question and with the Jewish community was transitory, and her influence on American Jewish history consequently was negligible. Far different was the case of Henrietta Szold, the most notable of Jewish spinsters, who devoted her entire life and her considerable talents to Jewish communal and intellectual activity both in the United States and in Palestine. As a woman she did not easily gain the recognition and power which she deserved. Not until her old age, long after she had founded Hadassah and had spent more than thirty years guiding its medical activities in the poverty-stricken Palestine of the early decades of the twentieth century, was she accorded the honor and status which many of her inferiors—who were males—had more easily earned.

One of eight daughters of a Baltimore rabbi, Henrietta was given an exceptionally fine Jewish education along with her secular studies. College, however, was out of the question in her time—she was born in 1860—and after her graduation from high school, she became herself a high school teacher. She also continued to contribute articles to American Jewish publications. Though her erudition was considerable, her sex, rather than the content of her articles, became the focus of criticism. Her attack on the assimilationist tendencies of Reform Judaism, which she as a traditional Jew opposed, were not accorded a serious reply by the *American Israelite,* the Reform newspaper. Instead, they were dismissed as unworthy of serious attention because they came from the pen of a "pot and pan scourer." Sharing the prejudices of their age, American Jewish leaders seemed incapable of treating an intelligent woman as a worthy opponent.

The Jewish community did see fit, though, to utilize Henrietta Szold's talents, but always in subordinate positions. She began her literary career in the typically feminine way, as a volunteer on the editorial board of the Jewish Publication Society of America, for whom she edited the five-volume English version of Heinrich Graetz's *History of the Jews.* From 1893 she served for twenty-three years as the paid "literary secretary" to the Society, devotedly contributing her talents as editor of the *American Jewish Yearbook,* proofreader, and translator of many of the publishing ventures of the fledgling group. When she became a special student at the Jewish Theological Seminary in

New York—the first woman granted the privilege of attending its classes, on condition that she not presume to apply for rabbinical ordination—she assumed similar tasks for Louis Ginzberg, a young rabbinical scholar and teacher at the seminary. Louis Ginzberg and Henrietta Szold shared a close friendship and working relationship for several years. Ginzberg respected her intelligence and put it to good use in his own scholarly endeavors. For him, their relationship was primarily intellectual; for her, the personal aspects of their relationship were as important as their mutual scholarly interests. When Ginzberg, seven years Henrietta's junior, became engaged to a young woman whom he met while on a visit to Europe, the remarkable friendship between Henrietta Szold and Louis Ginzberg came to an abrupt end.

Along with the end of the friendship came Henrietta's realization that her talents had been exploited, albeit with her consent. That realization finds expression in Szold's personal papers. There we find a letter from Louis Ginzberg, dated February 21, 1909 (after the termination of their friendship):

Dear Miss Szold:
I have finished my preface to "the Geonica" and I would like to ask you whether you have any objection to my reference to your kind assistance without which this book would never have been published in English. I do not think I have any right not to mention it, on the other hand I have no right to mention your name in connection with this book without asking your permission.

Henrietta's firm response reveals her resentment, which is more than that of a woman scorned:

I appreciate the motive that prompted your letter of Feb. 21, but all things considered—the change in our personal relations, the fact that I was not afforded an opportunity of seeing the last proofs, etc., and the other fact, that *you always regarded most of the work as being of subordinate importance*—it seems advisable to me not to make mention in the preface to "The Geonic Responsa" of my share in your volume.

To this reply Henrietta appended a private comment: "To be noted: He did not have the courtesy to let me know what form the reference to me in the preface would have and he did not offer to put my name on the title page as translator."

Henrietta had always accepted woman's traditional place within the family. But the roles of wife and mother were denied her, and her experiences as a working spinster in the world outside the home led her to recognize the absurdity of the ways in which women were denigrated.

At a time when most people have settled into the routine of their lives, in middle age, she undertook a new career—as a Zionist leader. After visiting Palestine in 1909, she was determined to bring modern medical care and standards of hygiene to that land. A member of a literary Zionist women's society, called Hadassah Circle, she steered the group in a new direction. On February 24, 1912, it was reconstituted as an organization dedicated to meeting the health needs of the peoples of Palestine. She herself directed much of the new organization's work in Palestine, and in 1919 she accepted an invitation from the International Zionist Commission to assume leadership of its medical unit in Palestine. However, she was not granted a seat on the Commission. As she wrote to a friend, on November 30, 1919, "The Commission will not consider seating a woman, particularly not in view of the women's suffrage question among the orthodox leaders in Jerusalem." (Needless to say, they opposed women's suffrage.)

It was with a mixture of bemusement and anger that Henrietta Szold responded to the way she was treated as a prominent woman in a country where women were expected to follow orders, not give them. She noted in 1922 in one of her evocative letters that "the fiat ha[d] gone forth that [she was] to be boycotted" by the Christians with whom she served on numerous boards and committees in Palestine, because she was "too intelligent." In anger rather than tolerant amusement, she herself boycotted the 1921 Zionist Congress at Carlsbad when it became clear that the Zionist leadership wanted to incorporate the medical unit into another body and thereby merge her position out of existence.

She retained her post and kept her sense of self-worth intact, despite her isolated position as a woman whose intelligence and indomitable spirit were intimidating to many men. While she certainly recognized the ways in which Jewish tradition and the Jewish establishment of her day denied equality to women, she never lost sight of what she regarded as the true spirit of Judaism which had reigned within her childhood home. When a male friend volunteered to recite *Kaddish,* the memorial prayer, for Szold's mother because women were customarily exempted from doing so, Henrietta rejected his offer. Her thoughtful reply reveals her personal understanding of the higher ethical concerns of Judaism and of her obligations as a Jewish woman:

The *Kaddish* means to me that the survivor publicly . . . manifests his wish and intention to assume the relation to the Jewish community which his parent had, and that so the chain of tradition remains unbroken from generation to generation, each adding its own link. You can do that for the generations of your family, I must do that for the generations of my family. I believe that the elimination of women from such duties was never intended by our law and custom—women were freed from positive duties when they could not perform them, but not when they could. It was never intended that . . . their performance of them should not be considered as valuable and valid as when one of the male sex performed them. And of the *Kaddish* I feel sure this is particularly true.

My mother had eight daughters and no son; and yet never did I hear a word of regret pass the lips of either my mother or my father that one of us was not a son. When my father died, my mother would not permit others to take her daughters' place in saying the *Kaddish,* and so I am sure I am acting in her spirit when I am moved to decline your offer. . . .

Henrietta Szold's opinion was not legally correct, but it enabled her to make her own peace with Judaism.

The Organization Women

Henrietta Szold's most lasting contribution to American Jewish history is Hadassah, the women's Zionist organization she founded in 1912 and which today boasts a membership of more than 300,000 women. As Henrietta mused in 1920 in a letter to her friend and co-worker Alice Seligsberg, "Isn't it curious how the Hadassah idea has taken hold of women? Here at home the sections absolutely refuse to go out of existence. . . ." Yet as a Zionist organization, Hadassah reached only a tiny minority of Jewish women in the early twentieth century, a period when American Jewry of German origin was noticeably cool to Zionism. If Hadassah succeeded in its organizational efforts, it was because the time had come for women's organizations, particularly when they embraced noble causes.

It was middle- and upper-middle-class Jewish women who became most actively involved in organizational work. The ladies of the Jewish financial aristocracy of New York, the distaff side of "Our Crowd," for the most part remained aloof from the daily activity of the new women's organizations. Following the social leadership of Betty (Mrs. Solomon) Loeb and Henriette (Mrs. Jesse) Seligman, they continued to meet together for their regular social afternoons, working all the while on fashionable beadwork and embroidery. Entertaining each other at lavish dinners served by their English butlers seems to have been one of their major preoccupations. But they represented only a very small segment of the Jewish bourgeoisie.

With the rise of a prosperous middle class in the last third of the nineteenth century, there also arose a class of women who had the leisure time (thanks to affluent husbands and the availability of household help) to meet together socially. To give their get-togethers a purpose other than the social, they organized literary societies for the cultivation of their minds and garden clubs for the cultivation of flowers. In the last two decades of the nineteenth century the literary societies and garden clubs were supplemented by civic organizations—deliberately called women's clubs rather than ladies' societies to indicate their serious commitment to the eradication of the urban social problems to which American society was becoming increasingly sensitive. For this was the progressive era, when Americans fervently and optimistically believed that social problems could be solved by a combination of serious attention, good intentions, and scientific knowledge.

The women's organizations that busied themselves with social work enabled women to engage in worthwhile and socially approved activity. As ladies, they could not, of course, seek paid employment, but they were expected—*noblesse oblige*—to be concerned with the welfare of the community. Individual women of talent had already taken an interest in major issues of the day. Annie Nathan Meyer, daughter of a distinguished Sephardi family and cousin of Emma Lazarus, devoted herself to the cause of education for women and became in 1889, at the age of twenty-two, one of the founders of Barnard College. Her concern with women's education was perhaps, in part, a reaction to her father's objection to higher education for women—an objection summed up in his comment, "Men hate intelligent wives." Despite her father's foreboding, Annie Nathan married (a doctor!) at age twenty and pursued nonetheless a career as a writer, playwright, lecturer, and philanthropist.

Women's organizations set out to attract those women who were less exceptional than Annie Nathan Meyer. To be sure, they attracted their share of "ladies bountiful" who enjoyed patronizing their "inferiors." However, they also drew scores of thoughtful women who devoted the better part of their free time not to personal amusement but to civic undertakings which in some measure improved the lot of the urban poor. Orphanages, training schools, settlement houses, and facilities for juvenile delinquents were all the beneficiaries of their largesse.

The Jewish women's organizations founded at the end of the nineteenth century and the beginning of the twentieth were thus part of a larger American movement. They were part of an effort by middle-class women to expand the options available to them. Though most of their members were not feminists in the current sense of the word, some of them saw in their social and charitable work an opportunity to reach out for equality for women. If they did not seriously challenge the accepted notion that woman's proper place was in the home, they tried to extend the concept of home to embrace the larger society as well.

All these trends were reflected in the National Council of Jewish Women, the most important organization of American Jewish women of German origin. It was a child of the First Congress of Jewish Women, organized in 1893 through the heroic efforts of Hannah Greenebaum Solomon as part of the Parliament of Religions held at the Chicago World's Fair. As Hannah Solomon recounts in her autobiography, *Fabric of My Life,* the decision to go ahead with a separate Jewish women's congress rather than join the Jewish men in their sessions was the result of typical male attitudes of the time. Though male Jewish leaders in Chicago invited the women to "cooperate," the women agreed to do so only if allowed to participate actively in the program. When the program committee finished its deliberations, however, not a single woman had been placed on the program. Accordingly, Solomon withdrew her offer of collaboration. Instead, the First Congress of Jewish Women was convened with great pomp and much publicity. Its speakers included such notable women as Henrietta Szold, Josephine Lazarus (Emma's sister), and Rebekah Kohut. The Congress voted to establish an ongoing organization of Jewish women, to be called the National Council of Jewish Women, which had grown by 1896 to include sections in fifty United States cities and two in Canada. (In 1975, the National Council was composed of 100,000 women.)

The National Council of Jewish Women combined in its goals the religious, philanthropic, and educational activities considered to be within women's domain. It established Jewish study groups for its own members and Sabbath Schools for children. It concerned itself with social problems and social legislation. And as we shall see, it established a network of immigrant aid facilities for women and children that won recognition from the United States government. Though it hoped to unite Jewish women of diverse religious and social backgrounds, in fact most of its members were Reform Jews and virtually all were middle-class women of German origin.

The activists of the Council were clearly aware of the challenge they posed to the accepted stereotype of the lady. As Rebekah Kohut, then president of the New York section of the Council, declared at the organization's 1896 convention, "The idea existed that women had inherent incapacity for convictions and cooperation. Women could never work together, so it was said. It cannot be said now. . . . Jewish women can work together, and working, can achieve definite results."

Sadie American, the national corresponding secretary, added that the Council's activities were, in fact, appropriate for women: "We do claim that for a woman to give in words and publicly of her enthusiasm or of the wisdom of her experience to make life fuller and better for others, is quite as womanly as to sing operatic arias in a parlor voice, to execute sonatas . . . or to imitate poor actresses—all of which meet with general approval."

While not denying the importance of the home, Council leaders suggested that limiting oneself to one's family was in some way a dereliction of duty, for other responsibilities beckoned. In the words of another speaker at the 1896 convention, "It seems to me the pressing need here is, that those of the leisure class of our Jewish women who have no conflicting home duties should be aroused to personal and active interest in philanthropic and religious educational work."

Likewise, Flora Schwab of Cleveland attacked those women who used their household responsibilities as an excuse for inactivity: "We might mildly insinuate to those mistaken women that to spend an hour or two in the society of intellectual women . . . may not be more derogatory to their love and devotion for home than a two hours' gossip or shopping or dressmaking."

The new association's success greatly enhanced the self-image of its active members. Recalling the 1893 Congress, Sadie American noted that to woman "it accorded for the first time the recognition of her individuality, her independence of thought, and of her right to represent these herself and not by proxy."

Women were called upon to rely on themselves—even in spheres traditionally closed to them, such as Jewish studies. The new assertiveness of the Council women and their recognition of the need for greater respect for their abilities led them in 1896 —though radical feminists they were not—to appoint two delegates to the Elizabeth Cady Stanton celebration.

Because they saw themselves as modern and progressive women, Council leaders stressed the importance of scientific social work. Sympathy and tact, they exclaimed, were not enough. With this new approach they consciously transcended the type of charity that had long been the avocation of wealthy women. By calling upon their members to be dedicated and reliable volunteer workers and to seek guidance for their social work endeavors, they were, in effect, asking them to view themselves, even if unpaid, as professionals who regarded social work as a scientific discipline.

The Council continued in the early decades of the twentieth century to combine progressive attitudes with respect for the traditional values of home, family life, and devotion to religion and community. In 1911 the Council stressed the importance of sex education so that children would not associate sex with filth. As Dr. Rosalie Morton stated in an address to the Council's 1911 convention, "I think it is a crime to allow any girl to reach the menstrual period without having her understand before the time is at hand what it means. . . . The old idea that a woman must suffer . . . has happily been exploded." Surely a break with the Victorian past (though Dr. Morton did advocate that girls take it easy during their periods as a means of protecting their health).

Council women recognized that delinquency stemmed more frequently from being underpaid than from inherent character defects and urged their members to lobby for adequate salaries for women workers. Moreover, one speaker noted with insight, "As long as we are willing to buy bargains . . . regardless of the return which the worker gets from them, we will never find a solution of the terrible social problem, we will never be able to improve the condition of the industrial class in the world."

The Council also continued its flirtation with feminism. In

1914 it invited Desha Breckenridge of Kentucky to speak to its convention on "the feminist movement," which at the time was focusing primarily on women's suffrage. Fears for the disruption of the home were women granted the vote were groundless, Breckenridge declared. Furthermore, she turned on its head the argument that women belonged in the home. What was the state if not the home writ large? Therefore, women's salutary influence should be exercised on the state as well as her own family. That could be accomplished only through the institution of female suffrage. Besides, female suffrage was the best way, she argued, to secure protective legislation for working women, for women in the states that had already enfranchised females had the best legal protection. In addition to inviting Breckenridge to speak, the Council that year had also sent Sadie American— personally a feminist—as its representative to the International Council of Women in Rome. There she participated in an outdoor suffrage meeting which attracted a crowd of 5,000 people.

The war and the accompanying mobilizations of women's talents confirmed for Council women their self-worth. By 1917 the Council had increased in size to eighty-nine sections with 19,715 members. It had expended more than $231,000 for its endeavors and had participated in both national defense work and overseas relief. The war had legitimized the participation of women in sectors previously closed to them, and the Council's 1917 convention reflected this new climate. The national president, Mrs. Nathaniel Harris, noted with pride, "Through the war, men have learned, and are learning every day, to respect women . . . and that is great and glorious; but there is something infinitely greater than this which has happened: women have learned to respect women." Like many American women of their generation, Council women liked the new freedom and sought recognition of their contributions. As Mrs. Hugo Rosenberg passionately declared: "The Jewish woman, once having felt the stimulating influence of larger work cannot and should not withdraw from it. . . . Let the watchword of this convention be equality, equality in all things for . . . both sexes." Her sentiments were echoed by Rebekah Kohut in her report on philanthropy: "We refuse as women to be used merely to raise money and to act as figureheads in the management of sewing societies and ladies' auxiliaries. We have earned the title to larger responsibilities than this. It is now that woman can show for all time that she is able to meet the greater demands, not only in the social spheres, but in the productive fields of work as well."

Council leaders also heralded the greater participation of women in politics and the expansion of professional and industrial fields now open to women. One speaker, Mrs. Carl Wolf, noted that ". . . the scope of [the Jewish woman's] activities had broadened to include every phase of that worldwide movement of revolt against artificial barriers which we call feminism." Yet, despite that assessment, a resolution that the Council endorse the proposed suffrage amendment was *not passed* by the same convention which had heard ringing declarations about the need for women to influence circumstances outside the home and stem the tide of the "mad militarism [that] has plunged a world in war." While many Council women had assumed new responsibilities and hailed the growing recognition of women's abilities and right to decision-making power, the larger Council membership was unwilling to take a stand on a political issue, which was, moreover, still the subject of controversy.

The National Council of Jewish Women was only one of the organizations to which the middle-class Jewish women of the early twentieth century might dedicate her leisure time. The Reform and Conservative movements in the United States had established national women's auxiliaries in 1913 and 1918 respectively to unite the local sisterhoods to which their female adherents belonged. Nonreligious Jewish organizations like B'nai B'rith and the American Jewish Congress similarly set up women's auxiliaries.

Middle-class Jewish women in America, most of German origin, thus had no lack of institutions vying for their time and volunteer energy. Yet the real positions of power and authority within the American Jewish community belonged to men. The Federations of Jewish Philanthropy, sprouting in virtually every significant Jewish community in the first three decades of the twentieth century and determining the priorities of the local community and allocating its funds, were controlled by men. Organizations devoted to matters of both national and international Jewish concern were likewise dominated by men. While women's auxiliaries were useful for fund raising and for keeping Jewish women attached to the Jewish community, they were generally excluded from any real share in the decision-making process. Only by actively lobbying—as the Reform National Federation of Temple Sisterhoods did in 1921 to secure the acceptance by the Reform movement of women rabbis, at least in principle—could the women's associations influence the decisions of the male leadership of American Jewry.

From 1840 to 1920 the German Jewish woman in America was affected by all the social and economic currents that determined the status of the gentile American woman, for the German Jewish community in America, while retaining its Judaism, with seeming ease assimilated the mores, attitudes, and ideological patterns of the rising American middle class of which it was a part. Even its Judaism was Americanized through the Reform movement. Moreover, it regarded Judaism as a purely religious phenomenon, and not as one aspect of an entire ethnic culture. In this—as in its origins and its socioeconomic status—it differed from the new wave of Jewish immigrants who would make American Jewry the largest Jewish community in the world. These new immigrants, this new source of strength for American Jewry, were the persecuted and impoverished Jews of Eastern Europe.

3

Fit for Survival
Jewish Women in Eastern Europe

The scholastic education resulted in producing men entirely unfit for the battle of life, so that in many families
energetic women took charge of the business and became
the wage earners, while their husbands were losing themselves in the mazes of speculation, somewhere in the re-
cesses of the rabbinic Bet ha-Midrash or the Hasidic Klaus.

—S.M. DUBNOW, *History of the Jews
in Russia and Poland*

The largest influx of Jews—those from Eastern Europe—
began to arrive in the United States around 1880. By this time,
the German Jewish community was already functioning
smoothly within the mainstream of American society. Its men,
by virtue of their mercantile skills, had taken advantage of
expanding commercial opportunities to become solid members
of the middle class; their wives, as we have seen, readily assumed
roles appropriate to their position, leaving financial matters to
their husbands, and devoting themselves to their families, their
homes, and a variety of cultural and charitable activities.

East European Jewish women—energetic, pragmatic, and

often financially astute—created quite a different impression from their German Jewish counterparts. Their robust image was to become the dominant one associated with Jewish women, as Jews from Eastern Europe came to outnumber those of German origin in the American Jewish community. By Western bourgeois standards, East European women seemed "masculine," for they were forthright and aggressive. Their husbands, on the other hand, sometimes appeared "feminine," for some were gentle, dreamy, and soft-spoken.

These personality traits become understandable within the context of the history of East European Jews in the decades preceding their emigration to America, for Jewish men and women had evolved their gender ideals in response to the difficult conditions under which they were living. Women, in addition to their domestic duties, were accustomed to functioning as part of a family economic unit, a pattern typical in preindustrial societies where husbands rarely earned enough to support an entire family. Customarily, Jewish women also participated in making decisions for the family, even though, according to the religious tradition which held sway until late in the nineteenth century, women's status was inferior to men's. When, contrary to their expectations, Jewish immigrants encountered in America many of the same difficulties they thought they had left behind, they were prepared to cope with them. Because of their particular experience, women, in many cases, found the initial adjustment to the new land somewhat easier than men.

During the nineteenth century, about half of the world's Jewish population lived in the Russian empire, most of it confined to the Pale of Jewish Settlement, an area consisting of twenty-five northern and western provinces out of the total of eighty-nine provinces making up the empire. Throughout the century the areas open to Jewish settlement were progressively restricted as the government drove Jewish residents from smaller to larger towns and banned them from certain occupations that had supported many Jewish families. After the pogroms of 1881–1882, the reactionary regime of Czar Alexander II issued further Draconian measures against the Jews. They were allowed neither to buy nor rent land in rural areas, and were on e more expelled from villages where they had lived for years. Even the small elite of the Jewish population that had enjoyed special residency rights outside the Pale—professionals, bankers, rich merchants, university students, master craftsmen—lost their special status in 1891. Dislocated Jews poured into already overcrowded urban Jewish settlements where nearly all the inhabitants suffered severe economic hardships.

Although prior to 1882 many Jews lived in small villages in semirural areas, these *shtetls,* as they were called, were not the all-Jewish towns with but a single road pictured by American Jews when they think of their East European forebears. Even the smallest *shtetl* had several hundred people, not all of them Jewish. Many East European Jews also lived in cities, where they usually settled in certain quarters, but, except for a handful of middle-class families who became integrated into cosmopolitan gentile society, most Jews had little desire or opportunity to socialize with their Russian or Polish counterparts. *Shtetl* and city Jews had commercial ties with the "others," but the focus of their social and cultural life was almost entirely Jewish.

Don't Ask, Do

Until secular influences made their inroads during the last half of the nineteenth century, religious tradition informed nearly every aspect of the life of these Jews. For women, religious obligations were home centered. To be good Jewish wives, they had to observe daily numerous laws concerning personal and domestic cleanliness. They had to see to it that their families ate only kosher food, keeping milk and meat strictly separate in cooking and serving.

It was also women's task to prepare their homes for the Sabbath and for each holiday. In order to finish all their work by sundown on Friday, they would do their Sabbath marketing on Thursday, and begin to bake and cook that night. On Friday the house would be swept and tidied, the silver (if there was any) polished, and the table laid with a white Sabbath cloth. In most families the mother, even if she worked outside the home, made the preparations herself, sometimes aided by a daughter or her mother or mother-in-law.

At sundown, their work finished, the women of the house would share a few quiet moments lighting the Sabbath candles while the men were at *shul*. When the family sat down to dinner, the housewife, who had been poised on the edge of her chair all week so that she could leap up to satisfy her family's needs in an instant, could sit back and relax for the first time, taking pride in her work. A memoir of Eastern Europe describes how one woman behaved during the Sabbath blessings:

> Grandmother always went through a kind of pantomime. Gazing at the twisted loaves, she nodded at the other women gathered around the table. Every inch of her beamed with satisfaction when the hallahs turned out well and drooped with despair when they did not. . . . Fortunately, the hallah was usually excellent.

Although women had fewer religious obligations than men and were excluded from Talmudic study, it was expected that they, too, would be pious in their own way and most of them fulfilled that expectation. Some women voluntarily attended services as often as men were required to. Few women were well-instructed in Hebrew, but in each *shul* there was usually one woman who could lead the prayers behind the *mehitza* (the curtain), reading aloud from Yiddish translations of prayerbooks while the other women followed. They had several texts: *Lev Tov* (*Good Heart*), *Ts'eno Ur'eno* (*Go Out and See*), and the *Tehinot,* devotional prayers written by women for women.

Religious education was, of course, formally the province of men, but by their own piety, women set an example for their children. In many cases, a mother's lessons were more vivid than those of the children's teacher, the *melamed.*

Bella Chagall, painter Marc Chagall's wife, remembers that in *shul* on *Yom Kippur* and *Tisha B'av,* "the women's section is filled with stifled weeping. In every corner a woman sighs and laments." On the Sabbath of Vision, a special Sabbath, groups of women would gather in one house to read a Yiddish translation of the Pentateuch and grieve over each story. Sometimes at Purim a special reader would come to recite to the women of a family the whole *Megillah*—the story of Esther's brave defiance of the wicked Haman.

The Zionist Schmarya Levin remembered his mother's moral lessons. She made him observe *Yom Kippur* by resolving quarrels with his playmates. She never missed her own prayers, and taught her children to have faith in the coming of the Messiah. After the pogroms began, she became even more pious. Convinced that the tribulations of the Jews signified the arrival of the Messianic age, she spent increasing amounts of time in synagogue, and added her own fast days to the ones already decreed by the rabbis after each tragedy struck the Jews. Her devotion evoked criticism from Levin's father:

> "Elke, is it your business to provide the entire world with piety?" And my mother used to reply: "Let me fast, Samuel Chaim; let me get some sort of pleasure out of life."

Abraham Cahan, the Socialist editor of the *Jewish Daily Forward,* the leading Yiddish newspaper in New York, wrote of his mother, "Her piety was a source of deep serenity." If she could not attend *shul,* she read her prayerbook at home. Isaac Bashevis Singer reports that his great-grandmother wore a ritual fringed undergarment *(tsitsit)* "just like a man," and his own mother took him to task for his enlightened antireligious views.

These men are not, of course, describing all East European women, only those whom they knew intimately. Yet piety appears to have been widespread among women, though it was not a piety based on learning. A daughter might bring baskets of food to her father or brothers in the house of study, but she was never taught the meanings of the words she heard the men murmur as they swayed over the scrolls. Her role, as ordained by God, was different from the male's, and, daughter of her traditional culture, she accepted her place, at least overtly. Only as modern trends invaded the *shtetl* did women begin to see the injustice of their situation. If there was covert rebellion before, it was not reflected in literature by and about the East European Jews of that time, most of which was, coincidentally, written by men.

Bella Chagall, a child at the turn of the century, was led to ask why she could not participate in important rituals like her father and brothers did. On *Succoth,* the males in her family would take their meals in the courtyard in a *sukkah* built of pine branches and palm leaves.

> Neither mother nor I nor the cook goes there. The three of us have only been allowed to go up to the door of the sukkah to hear father's benediction over the kiddush cup.
>
> And the meals are served to those in the sukkah through a little window; as through a hole, one plate after another. My brothers can make believe that the plates with the food came to them straight from heaven.
>
> Do they give a thought to us who have been left in the house?
>
> In the apartment it is cold. It seems empty, and it feels as if there were no doors or windows. I sit with my mother and eat without zest.
>
> "Mother, why have we been left here with the servants, as though we too were servants? What kind of holiday is that?" I keep tormenting her. "Why do they eat apart from us?"
>
> "Ah, my little child, they're men," says mother, sadly, as she eats her piece of cold meat.

When rain interrupts the men's meal and they rush in from the *sukkah,* little Bashke (as Bella was called) can't help feeling glad.

The religious distinction between the sexes began at birth. Boys and girls were educated separately for the different roles they would take up as adults. While most Jewish boys attended *cheder* until the age of thirteen, girls received only a year or two of tutoring. A woman, often the *melamed*'s wife, would teach them to read and write Yiddish, and to recite, although not translate, prayers in Hebrew. Girls might also learn arithmetic and letter writing, and sometimes studied the local language—Polish, Russian, or German—to enable them to deal with peasants in the marketplace.

After their few years of schooling were completed, many girls went on to learn on their own, in their spare moments, even though *shtetl* custom did not encourage them in this direction. Advanced education, whether in religious or secular subjects, was seen as an impediment to a girl's performance of her proper domestic duties. Too much learning might reduce her eligibility as a bride, for she would not be content to leave matters of learning to her husband. Nevertheless, some girls taught themselves to translate Hebrew and read the Talmud.

Girls were also forbidden to read novels that fostered romantic notions about love and conflicted with the *shtetl* custom of arranged marriages. Despite this prohibition, they bought Yiddish novels from traveling peddlers, and some even learned Russian so they could read the great works in that language. One young woman, Sarah Yetta Reznikoff (whose son Charles became a noted Jewish American poet and novelist), complained to her mother that she was being stifled:

"Do you remember when Grandfather Fivel gave me the *Tree of Life* to read and memorize? In that it said, 'He who does not know how to read is blind.' "

"A man is meant," Mother answered.

"I don't believe intelligent people think a woman is not as good as a man." And I made up my mind not to listen to Mother or Grandmother and learn as much as I could.

Unlike their sisters, boys were encouraged to study, and no sacrifice was too great for their families to make for their education. Even as toddlers, boys began to identify with their fathers, "studying" with them in preparation for the day they would be old enough to have real lessons. As young as three or four, a boy, wrapped in a prayer shawl, would ride on the shoulders of his proud father through the streets to *cheder,* where his first utterances in Hebrew would win him a shower of nuts and raisins, "God's reward" for learning. There was, of course, no parallel custom for girls who went off to their lessons.

No matter how poor they were, families struggled to keep their sons in school. Women would pawn their Sabbath candlesticks or beg for money to pay the *melamed*'s fees. While the rest of the family ate only dry bread, a mother would somehow produce hot soup for the *cheder* boy. Mary Antin writes of winters when her grandmother, her own shoes in tatters, would carry her grandson on her back through the snow to *cheder*, because the family could not afford to buy him shoes.

Mothers pampered their sons, but expected their daughters to share in the housework and watch younger children. While boys spent long hours in *cheder*, girls followed their mothers around, learning the housewife's duties by example. "A girl's real schoolroom," wrote Mary Antin, "was her mother's kitchen."

> There she learned how to bake and cook and manage, to knit, sew, and embroider; also to spin and weave, in country places. And while her hands were busy, her mother instructed her in the laws regulating a pious Jewish household and in the conduct proper for a Jewish wife; for, of course, every girl hoped to be a wife. A girl was born for no other purpose.

Indeed, there was no place in the Jewish community for unmarried women. To be left an old maid was "the greatest misfortune that could threaten a girl, and to ward off that calamity the girl and her family, to the most distant relative, would strain every nerve, whether by contributing to her dowry, or hiding her defects from the marriage broker, or praying and fasting that God might send her a husband."

Courtship was officially forbidden in the *shtetl;* men and women married young, often as early as fourteen, their matches arranged by their parents through the efforts of *shadchens,* or marriage brokers. The bride and groom might arrange to catch glimpses of one another at the signing of the marriage contract or in some public place; otherwise, they had no contact before the wedding.

On both sides, parents looked for evidence of piety and

wealth. If the groom was a poor but promising scholar, the bride's parents might offer *kest,* several years of support including room and board, for the young couple while the groom advanced his studies. The most eligible brides came from long lines of scholars themselves or had ample dowries. In poor families, girls would save dowries out of their own earnings but they did not really expect to marry scholars. Many young women were pleased to be matched to someone who had a trade or craft.

According to custom, Orthodox Jews did not consider love to be an important factor in marriage, at least not before the fact. As Abraham Cahan noted, "If a Jewish bridegroom loved his bride, one said, 'He wants her,' or 'She pleases him,' or 'He faints for her.' But love—love was for gentiles, primarily the wealthy gentry." Inasmuch as husbands and wives did not choose each other, it is remarkable how well some of these marriages worked, although some couples did become embattled for years. In a number of cases, husbands deserted their wives, leaving them grass widows unable to obtain a divorce or remarry unless their husband's death or desertion could be proven. When a woman died in childbirth, her husband sought to remarry as quickly as possible, favoring a strong young woman who could keep house for him and care for his children. It was not uncommon for men to be many years older than their wives.

Despite the customs keeping them apart, young people sometimes did form romantic attachments to one another outside of marriage, although their feelings could be expressed only surreptitiously. A recent study of Yiddish folk songs reveals that most love songs concern themselves with transitory relationships which would be unacceptable to their parents and the community.

Many songs, this study points out, reflect the pain felt by lovers who cannot marry. One singer laments:

. . . God help me, I'm so unhappy.
We have loved each other for three years,
and we cannot resolve our love.

And another lover complains,

> Love has shackled me
> Like a prisoner in chains. . . .

Despite the unrest created by this romantic undercurrent, lovers, at least as far as this body of folk song reveals, rarely confronted Orthodox custom openly. Except among middle-class Jews living in cities where the ideas of the *Haskalah*—the Jewish Enlightenment—had taken firm hold, these young people did not insist on having the right to choose their own mates. The study concludes that

> the revolt of youth against parental control was emotional rather than stemming from any deep-rooted conviction. While ridiculing the traditional attitudes of their parents, the young people accepted the customs of their elders, and perhaps secretly even admitted the wisdom of this accept-ance. . . . In a sense, the song was an escape valve for the frustrations and repressions which, had they been directed against their actual source, would have resulted in the os-tracizing of the individual from the community. No song suggests that the singer is willing to relinquish identifica-tion with the Jewish community and the traditions of his Jewish heritage.

In any case, the new bride had little opportunity to dwell on lost love, for pregnancy usually followed close upon marriage. Women nursed their babies on demand, for they felt sure that infants shouldn't cry, and they also found nursing pleasurable. They talked to their infants and identified closely with them. Sayings like, "You shall grow strong and healthy for me," "My crown, my jewel, my heart," and "It should hurt me for you" were common. Women acted protectively toward their children almost instinctively, for the rate of infant mortality was high. Malaria, typhoid fever, and tuberculosis were rampant. In *Life Is with People,* their study of the *shtetl,* Mark Zborowski and Elizabeth Herzog found that "worry is viewed not as an indulgence but as an expression of affection and almost a duty."

Yet childhood was not prolonged, for women had too much work and too many children to allow for such luxury. Boys, believed to be stronger than girls, were weaned earlier, and toddlers were given over to the care of an older sister or grandmother. Because the Jewish community was tight-knit and no child was a stranger to neighboring families, women who worked in shops or peddled in the marketplace could leave older children on their own, trusting that they could find a friend or relative to help them if they needed it.

Housekeeping was laborious and time-consuming in the *shtetl;* food preparation in itself took many hours of a woman's day. The traditional Jewish emphasis on food has become the target of a great deal of humor and even derision and criticism in America. The Jewish mother who offers food to her children or guests is accused of forcing her goodwill on them, smothering them with her desire to nurture. But in the Pale, such gestures had quite another meaning. "Food is always good for people, always a token of good feeling. There is no malicious food sorcery in the *shtetl.* To give food symbolizes not only maternal love but also the friendliness of the household to its visitors," Zborowski and Herzog found. It was a blessing, a *mitzvah,* to feed another Jew for the Sabbath or a holiday; it was a *mitzvah* to cook for the rabbi, to make an extra dish for someone who was ill, or provide an "eating day"—dinner once a week—for a penniless *yeshiva* student.

The only limitation on hospitality was poverty. A housewife never knew when her husband might come home from *shul* with a guest—perhaps a distinguished visiting scholar, perhaps a ragged beggar—for dinner, and while her husband enjoyed his own generosity, it would be up to the wife to produce the food. The novelist Shalom Asch described *shtetl* cookery in mystical terms:

They were wonderful, those cooking-pots of mother's! They looked exactly like ordinary pots. . . . But still they were different; if one regarded them casually, it might seem as though nothing were clinging to the inner surface of their sides; and still mother could get a supper out of them.

Sarah Rifke could "milk" her pots as though they were cows. They never denied her anything. She gave them cold water—and the pots yielded yesterday's carrot soup anew; she gave them boiling water—and the pots returned a royal dish to mother. Just *one* formula of extortion did mother possess for use on her pots—a sigh. When the pots heard mother sigh it was as though she had repeated a secret incantation over them with which she adjured them to supply the pitifully meager bit of nourishment which was all she demanded for her large brood.

Asch's portrayal, charming though it is, is somewhat misleading. Women had no magical powers; what they did use were their labor to earn some money to buy ingredients, and their skills in preserving food and stretching small amounts to feed many mouths.

Another writer from Eastern Europe, Yuri Suhl, remembers how his Tanta Malke, "an artist at potatoes," varied their meals.

The potatoes never failed us. . . . For each meal, they looked different and tasted different. Once in a great while she'd even manage a spoonful of chicken fat to flavor them with. For days afterward the smell of chicken fat would linger with me. And I'd even dream about it in my sleep. But the main stand-by for flavoring and trimming was the onion. There was no limit to its use and versatility and there was no meal without it. Sliced, browned, or cooked, it was there. But onion or no onion, there was always the appetite. It was like a curse.

Bathsheba Singer (mother of writers Isaac Bashevis and Israel Joshua) was sometimes too poor even to buy onions, so she would brown flour to flavor the soup, and often when she served her family, there was "nothing under the broth."

When the family could afford it, they presented homemade preserves, accompanied by a glass of tea, to an honored guest. Berries were more common than other fruit because few Jews had access to orchard land, even in rural areas. Carrots, beets, and onions became known as the "Jewish fruits." *Shtetl* Jews rarely tasted any others; oranges were imported, but given only to those who were ill. Women supplemented the monotonous diet of grains and beans by filling barrels with pickled beets and cucumbers, putting up cranberries, and chopping enormous quantities of cabbage for sauerkraut. In addition, most women baked their own bread. So it was not by magic but by hard work and resourcefulness in making the most of what was available that these Jewish women fed their families. Every housewife tried to manage a chicken or goose for the Sabbath, but the occasional eggs, herring, and other fish were considered luxuries in many homes.

Similarly, women made the most of their family's clothing, patching and reworking garments to make them last as long as possible, and cutting down large-size garments to fit children. When they sewed for infants, they made garments many sizes too large and put in tucks to be released as the children grew. Until the Singer sewing machine appeared in Eastern Europe, late in the nineteenth century, all sewing was, of course, done by hand. Little girls were taught to sew early, and they helped their mothers.

Love Is Sweet, But More Sweet with Bread

The varied domestic skills of Jewish women were no different from those of all women living in preindustrial economies where families bought few items manufactured outside the home. In these societies, women also customarily shared with their husbands the burden of supporting the family in addition to their other responsibilities. What distinguished Jewish women was that sometimes they provided the *sole* support of their families, while their husbands studied Torah.

No dishonor was attached to these economic arrangements. In fact, quite the opposite was true. Throughout Jewish history the man as scholar was the cultural ideal, and it was considered a *mitzvah* for a woman, whether she was a wife, sister, mother, or daughter, to support a learned man while he studied. In I.B.

Singer's memoir, *Of a World that Is No More,* he describes his grandmother's role:

> She was a saintly woman who never assumed that it was her husband's duty to support her. She left him to his beloved Torah and [Kabala] and herself traveled to Warsaw to buy goods and earn a living for her family, since her husband's wages [as a rabbi] could not keep a bird alive. . . . It never occurred to her that one day her precious son would be expected to earn a living. She always considered this a wife's responsibility.

Most men were not rabbis or Talmudic scholars, though; they were workers. Even so, in families that could not boast of males preoccupied by religious pursuits, Singer's grandmother's attitude and behavior were not extraordinary. In *Life Is with People,* the authors found:

> The earning of a livelihood is sexless, and the large majority of women . . . participate in some gainful occupation if they do not carry the chief burden of support. The wife of a "perennial student" is very apt to be the sole support of the family. The problem of managing both a business and a home is so common that no one recognized it as special. The economic area is more nearly an extension of the woman's domain than that of the man's. To bustle about in search of a livelihood is merely another form of bustling about managing a home.

Jewish women found various ways to earn "the living." The most successful owned shops where they sold food, staples, linens, piece goods, crockery, china, glassware, and fancy goods. But frequently, women were peddlers who stood in the marketplace or went from house to house, baskets over their arms, selling rolls and bagels they had baked, or tea, beans, and other foodstuffs. Others bought small lots of manufactured articles in the cities to barter with peasants who brought their produce to market. In the marketplace, women were in their element, each

one hawking her wares with a unique patter. I.B. Singer gives
us a goose dealer's soliloquy:

> "You think this is a goose? God in heaven, it's a calf! Look
> how the fat pours off—our enemies should only melt from
> envy. If this goose doesn't feed you for a week, may I get
> a fire in my belly, a heart attack; I shouldn't live to marry
> off my youngest daughter—dear God, she should stand
> beneath a black canopy! You think I'm making money
> from you? For every groschen profit you give me, I should
> get a plague. . . . Someone offered me a ruble more, we
> should both live so long, but it's Thursday and I don't want
> to be stuck with the bird over the Sabbath. I don't keep
> meat on ice—may our enemies lie on the ground with
> boils and blisters on their heads, and poison in their
> blood. . . ."

As this sales pitch reveals, Jewish women were not only hyper-
bolic, but outspoken and aggressive as well. The barren
economy of the *shtetl* demanded these traits; women who would
be considered "feminine" by Western standards could not have
survived in this environment.

Not only women, but girls at an early age were expected to
supplement the family's income. In Asch's novel *The Mother,*
the daughter Deborah is only ten or eleven when her father
complains, "In other families girls of her age have already begun
to contribute money at home, but she runs around all day
without doing a thing." Shortly afterward, she becomes a seamstress's apprentice.

When Sarah Reznikoff was a girl, she kneaded dough for the
rolls her mother peddled, and, by trampling a mixture of chalk
and oil with her bare feet, made putty for her father to sell to
a shopkeeper. In Warsaw I.B. Singer found young girls stringing
coral for necklaces and winding thread from spindles onto
smaller bobbins.

Both girls and women sewed clothing to sell, either independently or through small contractors. They made blouses and
skirts for neighbors, jackets for the peasants, and underwear,

pillowcases, and other linen articles. These seamstresses earned less than those who tailored and embroidered gowns, coats, and linens for trousseaux, or worked on clothing for wealthy land-owners.

The Jewish community itself also provided seasonal and sporadic employment for women. The rabbi's wife usually had the concession of selling ritually approved yeast to the other Jewish housewives. One woman might have the paid task of securing donations and "eating days" for *yeshiva* boys, while another might earn a few coins delivering baskets of Purim gifts from one family to another. At Passover, many women rolled and baked *matzohs,* and there was steady work for attendants at the *mikvah.*

In rural areas, women took in washing, worked in gardens, and gathered berries. They searched for down in the meadows where geese were fattened, and plucked feathers from slaughtered fowl to stuff in pillows, cushions, and the famous feather-beds they carried across the ocean to the dank basements and unheated flats of America's ghetto tenements.

Ironically, men often received at least nominal credit for their wife's work. Schmarya Levin described how the wife of one "Mottye the *melamed* and baker" actually did the baking, while "he merely helped her and delivered the loaves. . . . But the townlet was not much interested in the division of labor between man and wife, so that Mottye the *melamed* and Mottye the baker were one and the same person." I.B. Singer mentions a similar case: "Reb Joseph Goosedealer" earned his surname by virtue of his wife's occupation.

Given the amount of time women spent out of their homes earning money, it is not surprising that many households did not run smoothly, that meals were haphazard, and children were often left in each other's care at an early age. Mary Antin writes:

My mother had less to do than anyone with our early training, because she was confined to the store. When she came home at night, with her pockets full of goodies for us, she was too hungry for our love to listen to tales against us,

70

too tired from work to discipline us. It was only on Sabbaths and holidays that she had a chance to get acquainted with us, and we all looked forward to these days of enjoined rest.

Memoir literature and fictionalized accounts of Jewish life in Eastern Europe have provided this picture of the role of women in the *shtetl* communities which were relatively stable up to the last quarter of the nineteenth century. Thereafter, social, political, and economic changes, in conjunction with the *Haskalah* movement, profoundly affected the Jewish way of life in these localities. Religious orthodoxy, which had regulated most people's lives, was being seriously undermined by the ideas of *Haskalah* at the same time as outside forces in the form of governmental decrees and prohibitions against the Jews were causing an upheaval and severe dislocations within the various Jewish communities.

The *Haskalah* movement had begun in Western and Central Europe at the end of the eighteenth century. As early as the 1850s, the movement had gained a foothold among middle-class Jews living in the metropolitan areas of Eastern Europe. Twenty years later, the ideas of the movement had begun to penetrate the *shtetl* communities and to alter Jewish outlook and behavior.

Looking to the West, where Jews were experiencing social and economic mobility and acquiring political equality, *maskilim* in Eastern Europe called for the self-improvement of their fellow Jews in order to make themselves worthy of emancipation. Abandon superstitious practices, they advised; learn the language of the land and a productive trade, for there was hope for the betterment of the status of the Jews in Russia.

The *Haskalah* had the greatest influence on poor young men studying in traditional *yeshivot*, who greeted its literature as a breath of fresh air and secretly read *Haskalah* tracts behind their Talmuds, and on the upwardly mobile sons of the Jewish bourgeoisie studying in gymnasia. It had an effect as well upon Jewish women, particularly those who were privileged to acquire an education and saw possibilities for change. For one thing, the *maskilim* were sensitive to the degraded status of impoverished Jewish women in the *shtetls*. Early marriage—brides and grooms as young as fourteen and fifteen were not uncommon—saddled teen-agers, who had little hope of ever earning an adequate livelihood, with responsibilities for which they were not prepared, and *maskilim* railed against the custom. Moreover, *maskilim* wrote, women in particular should be freed from the religious restrictions that made them second-class citizens within the Jewish community. One of the most moving poems of the Russian *Haskalah,* Yehuda Leib Gordon's *"Kotso shel Yod,"* describes the plight of a virtuous Jewish woman, Bas-Shuah by name, who is left a grass widow when a fanatic rabbi, the incarnation of insensitive piety, refuses to recognize the validity of a divorce issued by her husband. Since the husband has, conveniently for the plot, drowned without witnesses, there is no way that Bas-Shuah can marry the modern young *maskil* who is anxious to rescue her from her life of poverty.

By calling for the reconstruction of Jewish life in Eastern Europe, the *maskilim* thus called as well for an improvement in the status of women. For the first time, bourgeois parents influenced by the *Haskalah* saw the importance of educating their daughters as well as their sons, at least in secular subjects. Schmarya Levin decried the fact that while these parents continued to see to it that their sons received some religious instruction, they completely ignored this aspect of their daughters' education. As an ardent Zionist, Levin was concerned with preserving the Jewish community and fostering a strong and positive Jewish identity. Assigned to teach religion to Jewish girls at a government school in Ekaterinoslav (to which only the most assimilated Jews sent their children), Levin found them almost totally ignorant of Jewish history and literature. "The Jewish girl, the future Jewish mother, grew up like an exotic plant in her parents' house," he complained, "and often enough her entire Jewishness consisted of a fear of pogroms."

And Levin was right to worry. Like some of their German counterparts, these secularly educated, middle-class East European Jewish women did turn their backs on the religious tradition. Some became part of the cosmopolitan Russian intelligentsia and they, too, turned their homes into artists' and literary salons much like those which flourished in Berlin in the mid-1800s. Others were eventually drawn into revolutionary political movements which promised equality and made use of their enlightened outlook and developed skills.

Despite the transformation of values in middle-class urban Jewish society, in general women did not assume a position of real equality outside of certain professional and political circles. Abraham Cahan has described the relations between young men and women in Vilna, the cultural center of enlightened Lithuania, around 1870. Men who were studying at the Vilna Institute would keep company with young women of the town attending the gymnasia. These "cavaliers would deal with a young woman in a spirit of equality. . . . She, in turn, must speak Russian fluently, have a modern approach and a command of the social graces." But Cahan comments that even if a couple agreed on the issue of equal rights for women, "she would proceed to make the most of her feminine helplessness." Although Cahan implies that these women acted out of coyness, it is more likely that a double standard was operative in this situation. These women weren't *really* expected to be equal, independent beings, but rather to serve as ornaments, displaying their cultivated tastes to enhance the status of their mates.

Nevertheless, some women did take full advantage of their new educational opportunities, going on to universities after the gymnasia. Russian universities had a quota on the number of Jews they admitted, so daughters of the wealthy who could not get in under the quota sometimes went to Switzerland, Paris, and Berlin. Jewish women who lived within the Pale had another problem; since they were forbidden residency in the Russian cities where the universities were located, some had to pose as members of the one class of female Jews who were welcome —prostitutes. S.M. Dubnow, the noted Russian Jewish historian recounts that

[a]ll Russia was stirred . . . by the sensational story of a young Jewess, who had come to St. Petersburg or Moscow to enter the college courses for women, and in order to

obtain the right of residence, found herself compelled to register fictitiously as a prostitute and take out a "yellow ticket." When the police discovered that the young woman was engaged in studying, instead of plying her official "trade," she was banished from the capital.

Before 1891 university women trained as physicians, dentists, and midwives had the choice of remaining outside the Pale or returning home to establish their practices. They were well respected, and usually well paid. These women could not have obtained their training without the encouragement and financial support of their families. Besides the influence of the *Haskalah,* several other factors might have stimulated parents to provide educations for their daughters as well as their sons. Ambitious parents saw the professions as an avenue of upward mobility. Too, Jews were aware of the increasing precariousness of their position in the Pale and realized that professional skills were more portable than mercantile businesses. Daughters of *shtetl* merchants had often entered the family business and become successful, but shifting political and economic conditions made that occupation less reliable.

Civilization and Its Malcontents

The May Laws of 1881 forced Jews out of rural villages into the more urbanized towns and cities of the Pale, affecting the lives of young women from poor families as well as those of the middle class. Many of the localities to which Jews were forced to migrate were rapidly becoming industrialized. While the Jews suffered severe economic hardships, there were also new job opportunities for some. Young women who might have followed their mother's occupational patterns in the *shtetl* now began finding work in the rapidly growing clothing trades and the tobacco industry. They worked in small factories or artisans' sweatshops. Some turned their own homes into shops. They bought sewing or knitting machinery on time and produced goods for small-scale distributors. Some families were supplied machinery and raw material by entrepreneurs who would pay piece-work rates for the finished products. They either kept the business within the family or hired outsiders to help.

Working conditions in this embryonic period of industrialization were miserable, and many women believed that only a miracle would save them from the fate of endless toil. The folklorist Ruth Rubin found that "these working girls poured out their hearts in plaintive songs which described their hard, colorless, often celibate lives. . . . Only a Prince Charming in a dream could take them out of their misery." In the lyrics of one folk song from the period, the working girl pleads for rescue:

Day and night and night and day

And stitching, stitching, stitching!
Help me, dear God, may my handsome one come
    along,
And take me away from this toil.

But if her "handsome one" were a fellow worker, he would probably be unable to support her, so she would still have to work. Their despair yielded to hope as they became members of the emergent Jewish proletariat whose self-consciousness was stimulated by the efforts of the clandestine Jewish labor movement. Instead of dreaming of escaping oppressive working conditions through marriage, young women sought to improve them by joining the ranks of the labor movement, and at the same time they began to seek equality for their sex. Their participation in the movement drew them, unavoidably, away from the influence of their families and the Orthodox tradition.

The first leaders of this workers' movement were not, however, workers themselves, but the children of middle-class families who had been influenced by the *Haskalah,* and who were financially able to provide their children with the secular education that often led to revolutionary activism. As these young people became increasingly dissatisfied with conditions in Czarist Russia in the last quarter of the nineteenth century, they developed the impetus for change. Some of this energy found an outlet in the growing Zionist movement, many of whose members eventually emigrated to Palestine and built the first Jewish settlements there. But others felt that the situation of the Jews would be ameliorated only if barriers between them and the rest of the population were broken down—that the problems of the Jews were rooted in the evils affecting all of Russia.

Looking for the possibility of real economic, social, and political change as early as the 1870s, a small number of educated Jewish men and women were propelled into anti-Czarist groups dominated by Russians.

Narodnaia Volia (The People's Will), an offspring of the unsuccessful Populist movement, had attracted some of these enlightened Jewish youths. Eager for immediate change, the Narodniks theorized that direct political action would best serve this purpose, but direct political action became transmuted into terrorist tactics as a means to an end—the overthrow of the government. This aim eventually destroyed the movement but not the government. Even though the Narodniks succeeded in assassinating Czar Alexander II in 1881, this act did not result in the popular revolution they hoped for. At the time, the assassins were living in the home of Hessia Helfman, a Jewish woman who was also a member of *Narodnaia Volia,* and who was, along with the others, sentenced to death for her involvement.

Using Helfman's association with the movement, the government blamed the Jews for the Czar's assassination. They insinuated, moreover, that the Jews were responsible for the economic woes of the populace. Fearful of a revolution, the government attempted to redirect the anger of the already demoralized and frustrated Russian peasantry by inciting them to wage pogroms against the Jews. *Narodnaia Volia,* hoping that the pogroms would culminate in a general revolution, took up the government's cry that the Jews were exploiting the peasantry, who were the real producers. The Jews, therefore, became the scapegoat for both sides, and *Narodnaia Volia*'s tactic lost it many of its Jewish members.

Now aware that the Jewish masses might be sacrificed in the general revolutionary struggle, Jews of various political persuasions began secretly meeting in some of the towns and cities of the Pale in the 1880s. They were responding in part to the new anti-Jewish measures and were searching again for some way to resolve the hardships of the general population as well as the particular problems of the Jews. By this time, many of those who formed these study circles had come under the influence of Marxist ideologues. They came to believe that the Jewish worker could also be indoctrinated and Jewish labor organized into a revolutionary force to help create a new order of society. For the Jewish economy in the Pale had changed considerably, developing from largely self-employed individuals into a class of wage laborers. By 1888 a Russian government commission investigating the Jewish question reported that "about 90 percent of the whole Jewish population . . . come near being a proletariat." Many of the "enlightened" political Jews were probably attracted to Marx because his logical, indeed scientific, approach to history meshed with their rationalist-oriented search for possible avenues of change. Moreover, most of them became convinced that only socialism could bring equality to the oppressed Jewish masses of Eastern Europe and solve, for once and for all, the Jewish problem.

The study circles were abandoned as an organizing device in the early 1890s because they neither fostered the proper revolutionary activism nor responded to the immediate economic needs of the impoverished Jewish workers. They were replaced by local workers' *kases*—embryonic labor unions which dealt not with theory but with action. It was these local unions, led by young middle-class Jews emancipated from the religious tradition, that became the source for the Jewish Socialist Labor Bund. In 1897 seven of the leaders of the movement, centered in Vilna, established the Bund. Of these seven pioneers, two were women.

Educated Jewish women were probably drawn to the Bund and to other revolutionary movements at least partly because these movements promised women equality and offered them opportunities for leadership denied them by the traditional Jewish community. Their actions have resonated through the generations, for they served as models worth emulating for the young women who later emerged as a significant force in the Jewish labor movement in America. In Russia, some of the women did not choose to remain identified as Jews, but instead, like Rosa Luxemburg, subscribed to the notion that their Jewish identity was irrelevant. The realization of a socialist society would destroy ethnic and national distinctions, they thought, and they joined revolutionary groups dedicated to breaking down and eradicating separate identities. The Bund, on the other hand, tried to reach the workers on their own terms, addressing them in Yiddish first as an organizing tactic and later as an affirmation of Yiddish culture. Within the ranks of the Bund, then, women were encouraged to retain their Jewish identity.

One woman who joined the Bund in Vilna in the late 1890s and stayed with the movement until 1941 remembers that it was well known in the late nineteenth century that "Jewish girls were making all kinds of troubles for the Czar." Indeed, over 64 percent of the women imprisoned for political activity from March 1903 to November 1904, for example, were Jews, although Jews constituted only 4 percent of the Russian population at that time.

Within the Bund women served in various roles and were well represented among the leadership of the local cells. Although many early women leaders came from the upper middle class and were well educated, their political activism, their commitment, did not differ widely from that of Bundist women who came from far less privileged backgrounds.

Pati Srednitsky (Kremer) was born in Vilna in 1867 and attended the gymnasium there, which was not a rare occurrence for the daughters of the Jewish bourgeoisie in the 1880s. Pati became politicized through her acquaintance with Liuba, a Jewish woman who went from door to door selling her homemade sauerkraut. Liuba always brought letters written in Yiddish from her sons in America for Pati to read to her and help her answer. Although Pati, coming from the assimilated bourgeoisie, spoke Russian at home, she had been taught to read and write Yiddish by a tutor. One day, when Pati was about fourteen, she asked Liuba why her own daughters did not read and write for her. Liuba explained that her daughters could neither read nor write. They had never been to school because they worked at home making socks on machinery placed in the house by a distributor who supplied them with the raw materials and paid them piece-work wages for the finished goods. (This was a fairly common family occupation in Vilna at this time.)

The next day Pati asked her schoolteacher why some girls did not go to school. The teacher replied that schooling was unnecessary for them because they had their work to keep them busy. Pati, who loved reading, decided that these girls must be unhappy and that she could do something about it. She bought several notebooks and pencils. Wrapping a shawl around herself to look like a poor person, and taking some books and pencils and notebooks, she walked to Liuba's home in the poor section of Vilna. She told Liuba's daughters, in Yiddish, that she had come to teach them to read and write. One of the daughters asked if they would have to pay. Pati said no. Another daughter then asked Pati if she were going to pay them. Pati replied, "Why should I pay you?" The girl answered that, since they could not work during the time that they were learning, they would lose money. Pati, therefore, decided she would come each day and just read to them while they worked. The daughters loved the stories she read aloud to them, and looked forward to her visits. Finally, they asked Pati to teach them to read for themselves. After they had all learned to read, Pati went on to teach the daughters of other Jews in the area.

After Pati finished the gymnasium, she was sent to the university in St. Petersburg. There she met other Jewish students, became familiar with socialist ideas, and joined the workers' movement. Sent back to Vilna by the police, in 1890 she became one of the seven members of the first central committee of the Vilna workers' organization which later became the Bund. Because of her fluency in Yiddish, Pati organized cells, and spoke and taught at the workers' circles. (Many of the male intellectual leaders of the Bund were so assimilated that they spoke Yiddish only poorly.)

Pati was arrested in 1897, but was released soon after. She remained a central figure in the Bund until 1908, when her husband, Arkedy Kremer, known as the "father of the Bund" was released from prison, and they both decided to retire from their leadership positions. Arkedy felt that the revolutionary movement needed skills that neither he nor Pati possessed, skills in writing and making speeches. They remained involved in Bundist activities, however, until Arkedy died in 1935.

Pati remained loyal to the Bund until her death. In 1943, the Jews of Vilna, Pati among them, were rounded up by the Nazis and taken to Ponar, a village on the outskirts of Vilna, to be shot. One of the Jews who escaped the execution said that Pati gathered a group of women Bundists around her and said to them: "We will join hands and together sing the Bundist hymn, 'The Oath' [*Shevuah*], then death won't be so terrible." And so she died at the age of seventy-seven.

She was one of the few Jewish revolutionary women who lived a long life. Many of them were killed while still in their twenties or thirties. As one woman Bundist who knew Pati from that period and who is still alive today, and living in America, said: "Thirty years is a lifetime for a revolutionary. None of us expected to live longer than that."

Another Bund pioneer, a contemporary of Pati Kremer's, followed a different route into the movement. Lyuba Levinson was born in Vilna in 1866. After finishing the gymnasium at seventeen, she was sent to Switzerland to study biological sciences. There she met members of the recently formed workers' liberation group. Lyuba had been very much influenced by the Narodniks, and was familiar with their ideology. In Switzerland she joined a youth group led by Plekhanov, the noted Marxist ideologue. While previously she had espoused the Narodnik view that the revolution could be carried out by the peasantry, she now supported the Marxist view that the industrial workers were the group to be organized to lead the revolution. Lyuba decided to forego her studies and return to Vilna to organize among the masses. At the border she was arrested for carrying illegal literature and conspiratorial letters. She was imprisoned for three years where conditions were so bad that she twice tried to commit suicide.

After her release she returned to Vilna and contacted the pioneering circle of the Bund which had also become Marxist oriented. This was the first central body of the yet-to-be-organized Bund. These members prepared and distributed propaganda, and began laying the foundation for the Bund's official birth.

Lyuba was responsible for creating cadres of class-conscious socialist activists for the future mass movement. She became one of the heartiest supporters of the tactic of mass agitation in Yiddish. In 1896 Lyuba, by then married to Isai Eisenstadt, another founding member of the Bund, was assigned to work in Bialystok, while her husband was sent to Odessa to organize. That same year they were both arrested, imprisoned for a year, and exiled to eastern Siberia. Lyuba bore a child during her exile. When she and her husband were released in 1902, Lyuba was determined to continue her life as a revolutionary, and felt it would be impossible to give the child proper care, so she arranged for her son to live with her sister in New York. She brought the child to America, and on the eve of her return to Russia, she died accidentally, by drowning in a bathtub.

Another Bundist, Zhenia Gurvich, ought to be known as the first translator of Marx's *Capital* from German into Russian. She was born in Vilna in 1861, and upon her graduation from the gymnasium was sent to St. Petersburg to study medicine. She became involved in the propaganda group of *Narodnaia Volia,* and was arrested in 1879 and again in 1881. After her release, she went to Minsk, convinced that the urban worker rather than the peasant would be "easier to organize and would yield more readily to agitation and propaganda."

In 1903 Zhenia Gurvich came to America, but she soon became disillusioned by the American political scene and returned to Russia in 1906 to continue her revolutionary activity there. She belonged to both the Bund and the Russian Social Democratic Workers' Party in Minsk. In 1917 she was elected to the Minsk City Council, but was ousted in 1920 when she refused to join the Communist Party. The Bolsheviks arrested her in 1922 because she was a member of the Bund, which, after the Revolution, was again considered a subversive organization.

Infuriated by her situation, Zhenia wrote a letter from prison to D.B. Riazanov, head of the Marx-Lenin-Engels Institute. How ironic, she noted, that she, the first translator of Marx into Russian—whose translation, in fact, had just been reissued and was being used in the schools throughout the Soviet Union—was rotting in their stinking prison. She was released shortly thereafter when Riazanov interceded on her behalf. He then hired her to work at the Institute even though she still refused to join the Communist Party. When Riazanov was dismissed in 1931, accused of being a Menshevik, Zhenia probably lost her job as well. It is claimed that she died, anonymous, in Moscow in 1940.

An early Jewish feminist who remains uncelebrated and unknown, except in Bundist circles, was Anna Heller Rosenthal. She was born in 1872 in the Grodno district. As a young girl, she joined the Vilna social democratic group which later grew into the Bund. Along with her husband, Pavel Rosenthal, one of the founding members of the Bund, she worked from 1899 organizing in Bialystok. Like so many other revolutionaries, both she and her husband were arrested in 1902 and exiled to Siberia, where they once again began organizing among the political prisoners. They both participated in the 1904 Siberian revolt known as the "Romanovke Uprising" because the meetings were held at the home of Yakut Romanov.

Anna Heller was in the center of this activity. She helped build defenses around the walls of the governmental building in which the fifty-seven participants of the uprising barricaded themselves. She stood night guard, procured food, medical supplies, and the weapons for the rebels. She even managed to find a bit of material and some red dye to make a flag. The revolutionaries then hoisted the first red flag to fly from the roof of a governmental building in Czarist Russia. So Anna Heller was our Russian Jewish Betsy Ross, but there the parallel ends.

Anna Heller Rosenthal deserves a place in the annals of feminist history for laying her life on the line by demanding that the women rebels be treated as the men. The fifty-seven rebels —six of whom were women, nine of whom were Bundists— managed to hold out for seventeen days, engaged in battle with the soldiers surrounding them. After their surrender the judges separated the women from the men for the purposes of the trial. On the day of the trial the defense lawyers notified the women that they were to be tried separately so that they would receive lighter sentences; it was rumored that the men would be shot. Anna and the other five women held a caucus in the courtroom and then Anna stood in the court and asked to be heard.

> I speak in the name of all the women. The women fighters want no favors from the Czarist power. There was no division among the Romanovkes between men and women. We were treated equally. Together with the men, we stood up in a just struggle and we feel that for the realization of the ideals towards which we strive, a human life is not too dear a price to pay. We take upon ourselves complete moral responsibility for all that has happened.

All were sentenced together to twelve years of hard labor. After the 1905 Revolution, they received amnesty and were released.

Returning to Vilna, the Rosenthals resumed their activities with the Bund. Anna was a member of the Vilna committee and active during the years of reaction. While she dropped out of political work during the First World War, she became involved again after the 1917 revolution, when she became secretary of the central committee of the Bund. In 1921 she returned to Vilna, disillusioned, as most Bundists were, with the Bolshevik Revolution, and remained active in evening educational programs. She wrote memoirs and pieces about the Bund and worked for the Vilna committee and the children's and women's organizations after her husband's death in 1924. After the Nazi-Soviet pact she was arrested by the NKVD and ironically died in a Soviet prison in 1941.

It was probably these revolutionary women whom Dovid Edelstadt had in mind when he wrote the words for the Bund song, "To the Women Workers." He held them up as models for the women he wished to recruit for the movement:

> Working women, suffering women,
> Women who toil and languish at home and factory,
> Why do you stand at a distance, why don't you help
> Build the temple of freedom, of human happiness?

Help us carry the red banner
Forward, through storm and dark nights,
Help us spread truth and light
Among unknowing lonely slaves.

Help us lift the world from its filth,
Be ready, as we are, to give up what you treasure.
We'll struggle together as mighty lions
For freedom, equality, and our ideal.

More than once have noble women
Made the throne and his bloody hangman tremble.
They have proven that we can entrust them
The holy flag—through the bittermost storm.

Among working-class women there were also outstanding
Bundists. While the middle-class women pioneers may have
disappointed their families when they gave up their studies to
join the Bund, a recently published history of the Bund suggests
that the working-class women who entered the movement might
have had a really hard time of it. Given the cultural attitudes
of the lower-class Orthodox Jewish family, it is probable that a
woman would have had to endure arguments and beatings if her
affiliation with the movement was discovered. Traditionally,
unmarried girls were expected to obey their fathers, who were
politically cautious. Revolutionary activity was considered dangerous and likely to bring down the wrath of officials upon the
entire Jewish community. Joining the Bund rightly was seen as
rebellion; moreover, it signified a radical break with religious
tradition. It was this turning away from the religious and social
traditions of the past that exacerbated the rift between parents
and daughters, for the Bund, like other Marxist groups, considered the religious establishment to be the pillar of an oppressive
and reactionary system.

But sometimes the emotional bond between parents and children was stronger than their ideological differences. While
members of the older generation might not understand their
children's radical activities or be willing to become involved in

them, they could not turn away from their children entirely. In a poem about a mother's vigil outside Paviak, the prison that held those arrested on political charges in Warsaw, the Yiddish poet Kadie Molodowsky notes the link between the two generations:

The Mother

The green-sweatered mother walks and walks
    the street.
In Elul the wind swings,
In Tebet it snows,
at Passover sun floods the windows.

. . .

There a prison burns like a wound,
a prison rocks through days and nights;
a daughter sits shut behind those gray heights,
locked in,
mute,
with folded hands,
with sharpened ears,
and saws the gratings with her glance
and counts the stars.

. . .

The green sweater walks and walks the street.
Elul is not wet,
and Tebet is not cold,
and Passover no holiday.

Despite the traditional attitudes with which they had been raised, young working-class Jewish women moved easily into all the positions open to them in this exclusively Jewish movement, assuming leadership roles and carrying out some of the most dangerous missions. Perhaps the actual experience of assuming responsibility at home and entering the work force at an early age had given them confidence in their own abilities, so they did not internalize the patriarchal notion that women had limited intelligence and capabilities. They saw themselves as strong and independent, and they had the skills and courage to reinforce this belief.

One of the women of this class was Teibetscke Oshmianska. Although only semieducated, she gave lectures in grammar to workers at night. One Bundist book of biographical sketches memorializes Oshmianska, "Women like her in every city, who remembers them? They are the unknown souls whose names history has not even recorded." Esther Riskind is another. She was raised in an Orthodox Hasidic home, and on the eve of her arranged wedding, aged sixteen, she ran away to Kharkov where she learned a trade and joined a propaganda circle. In Bialystok she joined a workers' movement and then went to Warsaw and was associated with a group of young writers around I.L. Peretz. She was arrested several times for her political activities and was finally exiled to Siberia. Fleeing abroad, she returned when the 1905 Revolution broke out. When a military patrol fired upon workers in Bialystok on August 12, 1905, Esther Riskind was among the victims on the barricades, killed by a Czarist bullet at the age of twenty-five.

Sara Fuchs was a sock maker, self-educated, who worked in Switzerland and in Germany. As a Bundist, she was active in Lodz, Warsaw, and southern Russia. One person reports that she appeared at the Conference of Jews in Kiev in 1917, the only woman among hundreds of delegates. No one seems to know whether she was invited or not, but it has been reported that the rabbis roared their disapproval when they saw her on the platform. As a response to the Bolshevik Revolution, Sara Fuchs wrote that she "opposed social democracy without the democracy." Ironically, Sara, too, who had spent so many years in Czarist prisons, was arrested for "counterrevolutionary" activity after she made that statement. Popularly known as "the revolutionary from head to toe," Sara, despondent over the Bolshevik terror, drowned herself in the Dnieper River on July 25, 1919.

Another working-class Bundist, a talented orator, was Maria Dzalodski. On May Day, 1896, she stood up on a fallen tree in the woods near Vilna, where the Bund was having a secret celebration, "called out in her high, strong, energetic voice, 'Sisters and mothers,' " and began to talk. When she had finished, the entire audience of 185 workers rose to their feet and began to sing "The Oath." Then Maria presented the speaker.

From its beginning, young unmarried women seem to have made up about one third of the Bund's membership, a proportion that remained constant as the organization grew and spread. The fact that the Bund germinated in the growing industrial areas of the Pale, where women were a substantial part of the Jewish labor force, only partially accounts for their significant representation in this organization. They were probably attracted to the Bund because it offered them equality as women, and included them on every level of its structure.

Jewish women had never before played a political role in such large numbers. While Jewish men also became dissidents for the first time by joining the ranks of the Bund, they had had some prior political experience in *kehillot,* communal governing bodies, and in *hevrot,* self-governed mutual aid societies. Women usually participated, although often covertly, in decision-making processes within the home, but they had traditionally been excluded from public and political participation. By joining the Bund, they were able to escape assigned roles and the second-class status with which they were dissatisfied, and express their rebellion against a patriarchal religious system which had not adapted itself to the realities of most women's lives. The Bund offered the possibility of a society in which they could be fully enfranchised.

Equality was not perfect, however, even in Bundist circles; particularly among the rank and file, the old attitudes toward women died slowly. Economic competition between the sexes also caused organizing problems, as Arkedy Kremer, Pati's husband, noted:

There was also the problem of the women workers in the tailor shops where women's clothes were made—women were assistants to men in those shops, and relations between the two groups were bad.

While the Bund itself adopted advanced attitudes about sexual equality, they could not always enforce their views in work situations where they lacked control. Despite the time lag between behavior and attitudinal changes on the part of some men, women's political participation reflects their gradual social emancipation and a real change in the traditional structure of the Jewish community. The very independence of the modern Bundist women challenged the values of Jewish culture. Many women remained unmarried, unless they married other members, and of those who did marry, few had children. While women were not, according to Jewish law, obligated to marry and produce children as males were, motherhood was a cultural ideal, and the community pitied women who didn't bear children and saw the spinster as a familial tragedy.

The women who rebelled against these cultural values by becoming political activists, refusing to marry or become mothers, also made demands upon the revolutionary community. Not only did they seek equality; they meant to be treated seriously. In his recent history of the Bund, Henry Tobias, discussing women, notes:

> Many came to regard references to their physical appearance as out of place and frivolous, and security conditions as more important than personal emotional considerations.

These women were committed revolutionaries upon whom the movement depended. Many were imprisoned, exiled, or killed because of their involvements. They engaged in illegal activities such as carrying and distributing propaganda material; they were responsible for getting workers out to secret meetings, often leading the way; and they also wrote much of the material, ran the printing presses, smuggled arms and ammunition into Russia and distributed them from locality to locality, and participated in uprisings and fought alongside the men. The names of most of these women have gone unrecorded in conventional histories.

Though many Jewish women stayed behind in Europe to carry on the revolutionary struggle there, thousands of their sisters who may not have belonged to the Bund but were aware of its activities came to America and became active in the Jewish labor movement here. There is a strong connection between the two groups of women, for those involved in the Bund and various other revolutionary movements in Eastern Europe were models for those who emigrated to the United States. The "new Jewish woman" originated in Eastern Europe, not America. Jewish women's political and union activism had already been established in Eastern Europe and it was carried steerage class to America.

It is not surprising that the conditions under which Jews lived in Eastern Europe produced few women who fit the image of what Americans took to be "feminine." Many of those who undertook the journey to the new land, either alone or with their families, were prepared, both by skills and by personality, to survive and transcend the harshest conditions. Indeed, one historian has suggested that Jewish women were often more decisive than the men (particularly those isolated in Talmudic scholarship), and these wives, surveying the precarious position of Jews in the Pale, convinced their dubious husbands to take the difficult step of emigrating. While the scholars might feel displaced in the secular culture of America, the sociologist Philip Slater has pointed out that it would be men who were not primarily scholars and women ". . . who would have least to lose in terms of status, who would be best adapted to transact successfully the difficulties of the journey, and who would find themselves most at home in the new environment."

4

They Made a Life
East European Jewish Women in America

. . . the refugee couple with their cardboard luggage
standing on the ramshackle landing-stage

he with fingers frozen around his Law
she with her down quilt sewn through iron nights

—the weight of the old world, plucked
drags after them, a random feather-bed. . . .

—ADRIENNE RICH, "From an Old House
in America"

Philadelphia's outdoor market on Marshall Street was typical
of those found in every Jewish ghetto in America at the beginning of the twentieth century. Reminiscent of the *shtetl* marketplace of Eastern Europe, the street was crowded with pushcarts
by day, and at night empty but for the leavings on the cobbled
brick sidewalk and along the curb: banana peels, squeezed-out
orange halves, chicken feathers, fish scales, bits of ground
horseradish—the overflow from a grater—yellow blobs of
chicken fat here and there, an occasional squashed egg, thin
shreds of printed fabric, and loose pages of the *Jewish Daily*

Forward blown back and forth across the street by the wind. Even after everyone had left, the strongest smells lingered in the air—herring, pickles, sauerkraut, garlic, goose and chicken droppings.

Every Monday night, Molly Chernikovsky and her *landsleit* turned left on Girard Avenue and walked down Marshall Street to Rappoport's *schvitz,* known in America as the Turkish baths. Monday and Wednesday were women's nights; for many married women a night at the *schvitz* was "her" night. Monday nights were crowded; Wednesday nights were sparsely attended —who knows why? Sunday, Tuesday, and Thursday at the *schvitz* were for men only. On Friday and Saturday, Rappoport's was closed.

Molly Chernikovsky's night at the *schvitz* was for pleasure, not purpose. The *schvitz* was not the *mikvah;* it was a place of fun and games. Some rituals were observed, but they were not religious ones. Noise prevailed: loud voices, laughter, the sucking of ice wrapped in a terry washrag, thighs slapping moist wood as the girls and women dropped their work-weary bodies heavily onto the slatted benches lining the walls of the steam room. After sweating out the week's grime, the women took a cold shower, wrapped themselves in thick white towels, the kind they never had in their own homes, and sat down to eat.

Molly always ate a thick corned beef sandwich on seeded Jewish rye bread, spread with a particular yellowy mustard and filled with creamy dripping cole slaw that trickled from the palm of her hand onto her wrist and ran in a narrow rivulet down her forearm, collecting in a tiny pool in the bend of her arm. After taking a bite, Molly switched hands and sucked up the collected liquid, continuing this procedure until the sandwich was finished. Then, with licked fingers, she squirted cold seltzer out of a blue glass siphon bottle to "wash down" the remains of the sandwich, and belched. She got up and walked across the room to wash her hands in the sink. After drying her hands, she began brushing her long dark hair, braided it and pinned it up, and sat down to a poker game that usually lasted until midnight.

Sometimes she went home, but more often she spent the night on a cot in the bathhouse's dormitory. At six in the morning

Molly was up. She dressed and went straight from the bathhouse to her sewing machine, while other women left to set up their pushcarts. Those who had brought their children went home to prepare breakfast for them and for the husbands they had left behind.

During their menstrual periods, women had to forego the *schvitz*. They usually stayed away until they had been to the *mikvah*. Molly didn't have to give up the Monday night ritual in those days because she didn't start menstruating until she was eighteen, which, she said, was not rare for Jewish girls from Odessa. It was also one of the reasons she gave for having married late—at the age of twenty. She said she was a real beauty and could have had any man she wanted, had she wanted any. But she was looking for someone a little special, because *she* was not an ordinary girl, a common person. She describes herself:

Already at the age of fourteen, I was big and buxom and beautiful. With large, white, even teeth, and a long, big straight nose. A real Russian Jewish type. I had this thick, black shiny hair—you should only wash it once a month if you want to keep it. I made two fat braids, and I wound them around my head. I had these big red cheeks, just like you see now, and good skin, the same. I had wonderful eyes, you can see. And I was smart, very smart. Smarter than most men. And I was bigger, too. From leftover pieces of material I used to take home from the factory, I made all my own clothes. Shirtwaists, skirts, even underwear. I always wore a long-sleeved shirtwaist, high at the neck. Not because I was Orthodox, but because I liked my arms covered. Maybe it was a habit. But I think I liked the way it made me look. I wore sometimes a skirt of print, sometimes a solid. And I covered myself with a shawl, like in the old country. I liked it. I could have had a coat, but I liked to hold myself together. It was a nice look. I didn't wear a hat like other women, or even a kerchief, because I wanted to show my hair.

Most people like Molly do not write memoirs; indeed she is illiterate. Their lives have been described by their literate, educated children—usually their sons—whose own acculturation prevents them from fully understanding their mother's experience. The oral biographies of these women, when available, reveal feelings and attitudes which their children did not detect, and they also help to explain how women facilitated the successful adaptation of Jewish immigrants to American life.

By 1910 Jewish women outnumbered men, according to one history of New York City's East European Jews, indicating that from the very beginning they meant to stay—it was a permanent move. This was apparently not the primary motive of many other major ethnic groups emigrating during approximately the same time period. While it was true that young Jewish males made up the largest proportion of this group's émigrés in the early movement to America, they sent back money to enable other members of their families to join them. The men of other ethnic groups were derogatorily labeled "birds of passage" because many stayed here only long enough to accumulate money to enable them to return home and buy land. Of course, their motives and their aspirations differed because of a substantial difference in their status. Immigrants from other groups were nationals of countries to which they felt they belonged, whereas East European Jews were a disenfranchised, persecuted minority living in a host culture that found their ways distasteful, if not contemptible. They never felt they fit in and were grateful if they were left alone—merely tolerated.

Making a Life

In 1909 about 40,000 Russian Jews emigrated to America, Malka (Americanized to Molly) Chernikovsky among them. She was thirteen years old, the youngest of eight children, three of whom had died in childhood of unknown diseases. She had come alone, with just the words "New York" printed on a label pinned to her coat, to join the four others in her family who had already settled in, two boys, two girls.

Molly's sister Ida and Ida's husband, Sam, had come to

America in 1903. They arrived in New York and there they stayed. It was, by historical count, the twenty-second year of the mass emigration of Jews from Eastern Europe. While prior to 1881 a small number of Eastern European Jews had come to America to seek new opportunities, beginning in that year Jewish emigration from the cities, urbanized towns, and *shtetls* of Eastern Europe increased dramatically. Young women, married couples, and whole families, as well as the usual young unmarried men, made up the movement. Between 1881 and 1885, about 54,500 Jews from those areas entered the United States.

This increase in emigration is usually seen as the direct result of the deteriorating social, political, and economic conditions discussed in the previous chapter. Between 1885 and 1898 some 411,650 Jews followed their *landsmen* to America, and by 1914, about 1,382,500 more had joined them. Despite the efforts of various Jewish immigrant aid societies to disperse the newcomers throughout America, by some estimates as many as 70 percent of the Eastern European Jews who arrived in New York stayed there, although Philadelphia, Chicago, Cleveland, and Boston each attracted enough Jews to establish its own ghetto and more than enough to support traveling Yiddish theater companies by the end of the first decade of the twentieth century.

Molly and Ida were born in a *shtetl* near Odessa. They tended a garden and helped their mother keep store on a square of cloth spread on the ground in the town's open marketplace. Carrying the best of her parents' few possessions—a samovar, some cut-glass vases, the brass candle holders, two homemade feather comforters used as mattresses, pots, and a silver thimble, Molly arrived in America speaking only Yiddish and some Russian. She had been sent for, brought over by her "rich" brother Morris—an auctioneer on the boardwalk of Coney Island.

Once here, Molly went to work as a servant for a family of East European Jews who had already become successful, a job which she found humiliating because it was an occupation fit only for the very lowest-type Jewish girl, while she—she was the daughter of a merchant. While working for this family, Molly learned to operate a sewing machine, and then she moved to

Philadelphia where she got a job as a seamstress in the factory where her other sister, Sophie, was employed. Now a member of the outside world, Molly learned to speak English, and "made the acquaintance of many girls just like me. We had a life. We went on Sundays to Fairmount Park. We packed a big meal. We sang. We danced Russian dances. Believe me, it was better than it was in the old country. Then I met my husband and that's another story."

Molly married at twenty, became pregnant immediately and left her job at the factory. Her husband worked for a manufacturer of men's suits. He was a tailor and a union organizer.

He was Russian born, but an American type. He wasn't scared of nobody. We had a crowd of married and single people. We went to the Yiddish theater on Sunday and then to the Automat for coffee. We had picnics, we went to the zoo, to the amusement park, all over. I had first a boy, then two years later a girl. We didn't have much money, but it was enough to get along and we enjoyed. Sometimes in the summer we went to Atlantic City for a week. Always on Saturday night there were people in our house. We told stories about our lives in the old country and here. Some of the women in our crowd had been in the Bund, they were political types, and here they were active in the union. My sister Sophie was also a union person. My brother-in-law Meyer was a carpenter and a real dancer. A lively man. After having a few *schnapps* he would dance for us. We made a circle around him and some of the women would join him in the circle. Everybody brought their *kinder* and we put them to sleep on the floor or on chairs we pushed together. Everybody had a good time. I made boiled potatoes with sour cream and we had herring. This was our Saturday night.

When Molly's husband died, leaving her with two small children and no insurance, she opened a grocery store in the cellar of her house on Christian Street.

I sold whatever I could get. One day I stopped the milkman on the street and asked if he could deliver to me. He sent an egg man. Then a bread man came and also we have a friend, a baker, and he began bringing me bagels on Sunday morning and *challah* on Fridays. It didn't take any capital. I opened up and suddenly I had a store. The neighbors bought. The children stayed with me in the store or played in front. I managed. One day a man came and asked me if I wanted to sell fruits and vegetables he would deliver. He came twice a week. He fell in love with me, so I married him. I thought, enough struggling, now I would have somebody to take care of me and the family. But what he brought in, you could do without. So I kept the store open and I still ran it alone. And I had right away two more children—two girls.

Molly's house burned down in 1939, and she gave up religion. Why? Because the fire was started by the *Shabbos* candles. "What kind of God would take away the house and business of a poor person who observed? I'm not one who thanks God for bringing *tsores.*" The following day she took a bus to New York to borrow money from her rich brother Morris and her sister Ida, who was in real estate. When she returned she bought "a real store with a house over it, from my friend Sadie who wasn't doing so well there. Her husband, don't ask. It was cheap and *I* knew I could always make something out of nothing. Except for my husband. He was nothing when I met him and so he remained. I supported the family, and him, too."

During the Second World War, Molly became an operator in the black market. Molly said she didn't make a fortune, but she did "all right." She took numbers, bought real estate, and put up bail money for her neighbors on which she made "a small commission." She said she made quite a lot of money this way because somebody was always in jail where she lived, and eventually she was, too. She ran an illegal chicken and meat business that supplied most of the Jewish shopkeepers in North Philadelphia. Molly said her friend Sadie was very jealous. She said, "To hear Sadie tell it, I had my hands in starting the war so I could make a profit from it. But people have to eat, and I had some contacts in chicken and meat, so what should I do, tell them to give it to somebody else?"

Minding Their Own Business

Jewish men and women in the old country had been small merchants, traders, artisans, and craftsmen, and when they got to America most engaged in similar pursuits. As they had in the old country, women continued contributing to the family's income in significant numbers. One study of an immigrant community in Philadelphia found that one out of every three Jewish households had a female wage earner. In the community surveyed, over 73 percent of unmarried Jewish females were part of the labor force, but only about 7 percent of the married Jewish women worked outside their homes. Since the wages of one worker—either male or female—were usually too low to support an entire family, many married women with small children who could not leave the home found other ways to contribute to the family's income. Some took in laundry, did hand sewing, produced goods for various industries at home, looked after the children of other women who worked in stores and factories, and many took in boarders and lodgers.

Like Molly, many Jewish women were an integral part of the small retail shop system that supplied the needs of the neighborhood. In numerous "mom and pop" stores, women were full-fledged partners, taking their turn at opening and closing up, and running the shop alone while their partners ate or had a rest, for most of these stores were open from six in the morning until ten at night. Despite the fact that women spent as many hours in the store as they could, probably almost if not as much time as men did, women were often described as "minding" the store, while men were "working" there. This situation is the source of the refrain commonly heard even today among Jews who, when they meet a Jewish woman on the street without her husband, often ask her, "So, who's minding the store?" Although the words imply that women took a passive role, this does not necessarily reflect the nature of the partnership, nor the real relationship between the man and the woman, but rather the patriarchal assumption that the man is "boss" or head of the household. Indeed, some women had more experience as merchants in the old country than their husbands, and they often took the initiative in opening up a small business. They were known to do the ordering and keep track of the merchandise, as well as selling and keeping the store clean.

In addition to running the business with their husbands, these women of course still had full responsibility for the home and family. Women managed their dual roles with typical efficiency. Mary Antin reports that her mother ran back and forth between the shop counter and her kitchen behind the store, where she did the family's cooking and washing, and writes that "Arlington Street customers were used to waiting while the storekeeper salted the soup or rescued a loaf from the oven." But the double burden was not without its toll on some women. Michael Gold, in *Jews Without Money,* noticed the effect the multiple work had on one wife, Mrs. Ashkenazi, who was married to Reb Samuel:

She was a tiny, gray woman, weighing not more than ninety pounds, and sapped dry as a herring by work. Her eyelids were inflamed with loss of sleep. She slaved from dawn till midnight, cooking and cleaning at home, then working in the umbrella store. At forty she was wrinkled like a woman of seventy. She was always tired, but was a sweet, kindly, uncomplaining soul, who worshipped her family, and revered her impractical husband.

Butcher, tobacco, and shoe repair shops, bakeries, candy stores, groceries, and delicatessens run by couples became the daytime social centers for Jewish men, women, and youth. They were often the hub of a neighborhood; people came in just to chat, not to buy. Visitors or customers exchanged news and gossip, made dates and arrangements between families, passed on word of job openings, complained about their children and the difficulties of adjusting to American ways. These small stores often served, too, as communications centers for disseminating information about strike meetings.

In America, East European Jewish women took other occupations similar to those they had in the old country. Standing by their pushcarts, for example, some women peddlers found themselves back in their element, doing the familiar. Louis Wirth, writing about immigrant life in the Jewish ghetto of Chicago, comments that

> [i]n accordance with the tradition of the Pale, where the women conducted the stores . . . women are among the most successful merchants of Maxwell Street. They almost monopolize the fish, herring and poultry stalls.

The situation was similar in New York, where female peddlers had to accede to a somewhat perverted form of chivalry in order to pursue their trade:

> There are many women in the pushcart business . . . who rent their carts at eight or ten cents a day, just as the men do, but who get them by proxy, delegating to some men the task, it being a law, unwritten but acknowledged, that women should not undertake pushcart trundling. In addition to these women who have no husbands to take the initiative, or perhaps such incapables as cannot be trusted, there are a whole army of pushcart women trained and habituated to the business, who from long custom or love of excitement follow their consorts about the streets and help in the selling, even if they do not have a cart themselves.

The pushcart trade had its own class distinctions. The highest status was awarded those women who had their own carts and a regular place and clientele. Next in prestige were the women who rented carts by the week and occupied spaces on the street where and when they were available. Snobbery among the women in the business assigned the very lowest status to the pushcart trundlers, those who walked along the streets hawking their wares and whose daily stock varied with what was available. Sometimes these trundlers were fortunate enough to find a busy corner that hadn't already been taken. There they would set up shop for the entire day, if the police didn't interfere. Some women went into the business legally by taking out a license, but many just went about hoping they could talk themselves out of any trouble that might come their way. These illegal merchants often took a small child with them both to help out with the selling and to act as a front to arouse the sympathy of potential customers or bothersome police. Frequently these children did not even belong to the pushcart trundler, but were "borrowed" from neighbors, and paid a few cents a day.

Making Do

Jewish women from Eastern Europe brought with them social patterns and skills that served their families well. They had judged wisely when they chose the few possessions to carry with them across the ocean. In small, cold rooms they bedded down their children under warm down comforters, and on stoves fired with coal instead of the wood they were accustomed to, they put their treasured pots to simmer. Although the tenement flats seemed strange and the names of the streets sounded unfamiliar to them, they faced some of the same daily problems they had had before, and they lost no time in dealing with them.

No strangers to bargaining, these women held their own against the peddlers of New York's Hester Street or Chicago's Maxwell Street, and they stretched their few dollars as far as possible. A contemporary observer describes the scene at a New York pushcart around the turn of the century:

> Buying and selling were not, as elsewhere, a mere affair of looking at a price mark and making up one's mind. The price asked was only meant as a declaration of war, the act of purchase was a battle of insult, the sale was a compromise of mutual hatred.
>
> "*Weiberle* [ladies], *weiberle,*" cries the merchant, "come by me and get a good *metsiah* [bargain]."
>
> The woman stops with a sneer, pokes contemptuously at the merchandise, insults it and the salesman, underbids

him half. He tries to prove that he would die of starvation if he yielded to her disgusting bid. She implies that he takes her for a fool. In a moment he is telling her he hopes her children may strangle with cholera for trying to make a beggar of him. She answers that he is a thief, a liar, a dog of an apostate Jew. She makes as if to spit on his wares; he grabs them from her and throws them back on the heap. At length a sale is made and she moves on to the next bout.

Shopping was only half the skill; preparing small amounts of food to feed large families required another kind of expertise. From a herring, two onions, and a piece of day-old bread, a woman could make a four-course supper:

> First she chopped the milk roe with onion—this the appetizer. The herring brine was the base for a potato soup. The second onion was sliced and flavored with vinegar—the salad, to be sure. The herring itself was the roast, which she wrapped in a wet newspaper and then placed on the red coals in the range.

The total cost for one person: five pennies.

When it came to clothing and household items, these women had also had experience in making do. A single pair of men's trousers could provide pants for two small boys: one got the top, including the waistband (gathered in with a piece of rope or twine to size), and the other got knee pants fashioned from the bottom halves of the legs. Coats that the family wore by day became blankets at night; beds materialized from three kitchen chairs, lined up; and kitchens themselves turned into dormitories. In order to avert chaos in one or two rooms that served at once as kitchens, laundries, workrooms, and living and sleeping quarters for large families and perhaps one or two boarders, women had to develop both meticulous housekeeping habits and expert managerial skills. Not only did they have to keep milk out of the meat dishes, but they had to keep soup off the bundles of garments, and toddlers away from hot, heavy pressing irons.

Room for One More

Keeping boarders was one of the most common occupations among married first-generation women, particularly if they had small children to care for. Molly's sister Ida was one of the few women who started out taking in boarders and ended up a real estate operator. When Ida and Sam arrived in America, they went to board with Sam's relatives. Sam's cousin found him work stripping tobacco leaves in a sweatshop. Ida, who had been a midwife in the old country, intended to set herself up in this occupation again. In the meantime, since Sam had a job, she looked for an apartment of their own. She found one on Hester Street, and borrowed money from a Jewish *landsleit* organization to pay for the first month's rent. She spent a few days gathering furniture and from her brother Morris coaxed some odd pieces to put in the three rooms that was now their home.

The apartment was on the sixth floor of a tenement, facing the back. It contained a square kitchen—large by old-country standards—and two other small rooms, each with a window opening onto an airshaft. At first Ida was frightened to go near the windows, and would walk as far away as possible when she passed from one room to another. Compared to what she had come from, the apartment was large and light, and, as far as she was concerned, luxuriously furnished. She had a table and four chairs for the kitchen, and in the bedroom, an iron double bedstead and a chest, both of which she painted white. She used one of her feather comforters for a mattress and the other for a cover. In the remaining room, she placed a wooden chair, a small table and a cot, for she planned to take in a boarder, as the other women in the neighborhood did.

If Ida had not been so clever herself, she probably could have gotten good advice from one of the other women in her building, for ghetto women were not stingy with hints for ways to supplement the family's income. In Anzia Yezierska's novel, *Bread Givers,* one woman tells another how to create a furnished room that will bring in more money:

"Do as I done. Put the spring over four empty herring pails and you'll have a bed fit for the president. Now put a board over the potato barrel, and a clean newspaper over that, and you'll have a table. All you need yet is a soapbox for a chair and you'll have a furnished room complete."

Another landlady, in Yezierska's story "My Own People," goes to great lengths to rent an undesirable room. She is a master of euphemism:

"It ain't so dark. It's only a little shady. Let me turn up the gas for you—you'll quick see everything like sunshine. . . . You can't have Rockefeller's palace for three dollars a month. . . . If the bed ain't so steady, so you got good neighbors. . . . I'll treat you like a mother! You'll have it good by me like in your own home."

A few days after Ida had completed furnishing the apartment, Sam brought home a "greenie" from the shop. This man took his meals with them, and paid three dollars a week for room and board. Shortly after, another boarder was sent to them by the organization that had loaned Ida the rent money. They made room for him by putting a couch in the kitchen, which now became the living room as well. Because he didn't have a private room, this man paid only $2.25 per week. And he was followed by a woman who took supper with them, paying twenty-five cents a night.

Ida and Sam were already affluent by other families' standards. As a midwife Ida received five dollars for a delivery, and sometimes had as many as two a month. As her reputation for cooking spread, people began to ask if they, too, could take their meals at her house. Ida said people also came for the conversation, and to make friends with one another. Talking about her success in those days, Ida recalls:

Suddenly I'm having a restaurant—six or seven people eating at my table. Sometimes I had to serve in shifts. I used to make real Jewish meals, like in the old country, only better because here you could get many things. I would make a lot, and what we didn't use at one meal I'd put covered on the fire escape for the next day. (Of course, only in winter.) In summer I made just enough but there was always left over. You could find everything on Hester Street—herring, beets, cabbage, apples, dried fruits, fresh fish packed in ice like I never saw.

I was making enough so we could put a little money away each week. I was delivering babies but couldn't have one myself. Sam didn't seem to mind, but I did. Anyway, the years passed and by 1911, we had saved enough money so we could buy a building, with a little help. So we're landlords. I took two apartments on the second floor for myself. In the back we had boarders, in the front a small restaurant to accommodate the boarders and a few friends. It was not open to the public, just to people who knew us. Sam gave up his work and we worked together. He helped shop, cook, and clean. And he managed the building, collected the rents, and repaired what he could.

Life was good to us and we bought another building next door two years later. And so it went. But we were killing ourselves, so Sam said, "Ida, give up the babies and the cooking. We can afford to live like people now." So I stopped with the babies, but not the cooking. I enjoyed having a lot of people. Believe me, we had it better than anyone else we knew.

By 1912, we had a piece of property in the country which was also a boardinghouse during the summer. And we began acquiring some land uptown. By the twenties we were already rich. We were lucky. We came at the right time, met good people. I knew how to cook, but without the pushcart women I would have been a failure. They saved food for me, they told me who had what and how much I should offer, they sent me customers. Believe me, I had plenty help. And Sam, too. He said, "Ida, let's buy a building." Me, with a building? I couldn't believe it. In the old country Jews didn't own. So I said, "Sam, buy it. We're in America, everything is different here, everything possible." So here we are.

Ida's success was not a common occurrence; the boarder was. Indeed the boarder was almost an institution in most poor, first-generation East European Jewish homes in America. Jacob Riis, a well-known journalist who covered the ghetto during the period of peak immigration, commented that "for the Jews in the crowded tenements of New York the lodger serves the same purpose as the Irishman's pig: he helps to pay the rent." In *Children of the Tenements* he reports that one woman cared for a "rent baby"—a motherless infant whose father paid seventy-five cents a week for its keep. "The child"—it was never called anything else—was like a lodger.

In *One Foot in America,* Yuri Suhl describes how another motherless boy and his father found meals—and more—at the table of Mrs. Rosenthal. She normally fed from eight to ten boarders, and "if someone brought an eleventh, he would not be turned away. Mrs. Rosenthal would add a chair to the table and a cup of water to the soup pot. Her motto was, 'If there's enough for ten, there is enough for one more.' " Beyond sustenance, Mrs. Rosenthal's meals provided her boarders with a link with the past, a reminder of the old country. After dinner, the boarders—many of them men separated from their families—gathered in the front room where they gossiped, shared news of their families, and discussed the needle trades and developments in the labor movement.

Mrs. Rosenthal's household and countless others like it were institutions that met both social and economic needs in the immigrant community. There was always an abundant supply of greenhorns who needed beds and meals. The boarder became a fixture of most immigrant Jewish families. In fact, the absence of a boarder was taken as a sign that the family was "doing all right."

While in the old country, Jewish households often contained extended families of several generations, in the New World the presence of boarders—strangers—in their midst required certain adjustments in family life. Harry Golden describes his vision of the boarder's social role within the family in a commentary included in the recent republication of *The Spirit of the Ghetto,* a classic of the period written by the gentile journalist Hutchins Hapgood:

> The male boarder occupied a unique and important position in the immigrant culture. Once he moved in, he quickly became a familiar. He even had the authority to spank misbehaving children. Wherever the family went the boarder went, too. He knew the ins and outs, the joys and sorrows, and could often step in between a quarrelling husband and wife.

Golden's version of "Life with a Boarder" seems a bit romanticized. In the same book, Hapgood, who was one of the few outsiders who wrote about the immigrant Jewish community with sensitivity, insight, and a minimum of ethnic bias, points out that the boarder was often taken in at the cost of domestic happiness. It seems likely that the boarder often came *between* the wife and husband, and was himself the cause of the quarrel. The husband-wife-boarder triangle, as well as other problems with boarders, became popular themes of Yiddish plays, novels, and stories around this time.

The *Jewish Daily Forward*'s most widely read column, *"Bintel Brief"* (bundle of letters), frequently carried letters from husbands and wives seeking to restore domestic harmony to a household that had been disrupted by a boarder or from boarders pleading for forgiveness for breaking up marriages. One woeful letter from a husband who had twice been betrayed by his wife when she became involved with a boarder recounts his story:

> A few years ago a brother of mine came to America, too, with a friend of his. I worked in a shop, and as I was no millionaire, my brother and his friend became our board-

ers. Then my trouble began. The friend began earning good money. He began to mix in the household affairs and to buy things for my wife.

This man lost not only his wife to the boarder, but his children, too. In his letter, the husband was not appealing for help—it was too late for that; rather, he wanted to let his wife know how she had ruined him and his life. Hoping to make her feel guilty, he ended:

I hope that my wife will read my letter in the *Forward* and that she will blush with shame.

Perhaps it was from the columns of his own newspaper that *Forward* editor Abraham Cahan drew the inspiration for episodes in *The Rise of David Levinsky*. In this novel, a greenhorn who becomes a millionaire in the garment industry falls in love with his first landlady. Dora will not leave her husband, fearing to lose her children, but Levinsky, something of a romantic, never finds another woman he really wants to marry.

Even though keeping boarders was an extension of their normal household duties, it still put an extra burden on women, many of whom did other wage-earning work as well, either inside or outside the home. Not all women like Ida had a Sam who recognized the enormity of her tasks and helped her out. In Alter Brody's play *Rapunzel,* Rifkah Sorel complains to her daughter Malka that she must be on her feet all day, cooking for hungry boarders, while " 'the only kind of business your father ever did was exchanging stories with the synagogue do-nothings——' "

Etta Byer, who came from Lida, Lithuania, by way of London around the turn of the century, describes what may have been a typical male attitude toward women's work in her memoir, *Transplanted People.* Etta's three brothers lived with her and her husband in their first small apartment. Many friends were always dropping in, so Etta and Joe had no privacy. The brothers helped out with expenses, but not with household tasks, so when Etta came home from the tobacco sweatshop, where she was an expert roller, she had to do all the cooking, washing, and ironing, and clear up the dirty dishes her brothers left behind. Finally, Etta became ill.

> I told Joe I was overworked. They all laughed at me and said that I was crabby. The four men around me were great philosophers, talking about how to improve the world situation; but when a tired little woman asked them to help around the house, they paid no attention.

The situation grew worse. Etta became pregnant but even after she returned home with her new infant, she got no help from the men. When she asked her brothers to fetch coal up from the basement, they refused, saying that was why they paid *her* rent.

> So I took the pail and went myself. In the basement big rats jumped at me. I screamed and I fainted. When I was brought upstairs, I wished I were dead. How could I live with such logical brothers and such a smart husband, all lazy men? When people live together, they have a responsibility toward each other. They must help each other.

Etta could not nurse her infant; he grew ill and died after several months. In her memoir Etta remarks bitterly, "The baby and I did not get the care a cow would get when she brought a calf into the world."

More of the Same

Etta spent a few months away from the shop after giving birth, but many other women in her position barely missed a stride in their wage earning, switching from factory work to home production after they became mothers. The needle trades provided the largest number of jobs for Jewish women. Between 1900 and 1925, for example, about 65 percent of the workers in this industry, male and female, were Jewish. The patterns of production in America were similar to those in Eastern Europe, with the division between home and factory production falling along generational lines. The women who worked in the sweatshops were generally young and single, but after marriage they would join the older generation of homeworkers.

The clothing industry was growing rapidly here. In some American industries, the factory system had become advanced, but sweatshops and home production were still features of the needle trades at the turn of the century. Controlling the trade were German Jewish factory owners who exploited their East European coreligionists as a source of cheap labor. Provided with immediate employment, the East European immigrants became less of a burden on the American community in general, and the German Jewish community in particular. Since Jews had been urban, not rural, dwellers in the old country, and had urban workers' skills, they had fewer problems adjusting to the industrial economy of the large American cities than members of other ethnic groups.

The needle trades produced all types of headgear and millinery, dresses, shirtwaists, skirts, cloaks, suits, and coats, as well as underwear, known as "white goods." The production of artificial flowers and hat trimmings employed many Jewish women as well.

Retailers had been among the first to enter ready-to-wear manufacturing. Some set up shops to produce clothing to sell directly to their store customers, employing designers, cutters, pressers, seamstresses, and finishers. The popularity of ready-made clothing was growing, coincidentally, as immigration from Eastern Europe increased, so Jews who had already had some experience in the needle trades found their skills in demand. As the industry grew, production became more specialized; in the beginning, all work was done in one shop, but it gradually became more expedient to break manufacturing down into a number of tasks, some of which would be given out to contractors. Designing, patternmaking, and cutting usually remained inside the shop, where they could be closely supervised, but other processes—basting, sewing, felling, and finishing—were contracted out.

Competition among contractors was fierce. They were continually seeking ways to reduce their overhead so they could underbid one another. One way to do this was to parcel out work to subcontractors who hired the freshest of greenhorns who were willing to work for the lowest wages. Turnover was fairly rapid, for greenhorns soon learned and they moved up to another level of production, but the subcontractors were usually able to replace them easily.

Contractors picked up bundles of cut garments from "inside shops" and turned them over to subcontractors, who usually had sweatshops in their own homes. There two or more people worked on the bundles, and the family was often pressed into service as well. And bundles were also farmed out to housewives who worked on them in their own homes. The subcontractor himself worked along with his hirelings, suffering from the same long hours and close conditions. Since the margin of profit was very low, he often made little more than those in his employ.

Work was paid by the piece. Women working at home alternated paid tasks with their normal household routine. They would set up their sewing machines, spread out the bundles, and between cleaning, shopping, making meals, and caring for their children and any boarders, they managed somehow to complete their work, often pedaling and stitching far into the night. In one story written about this period, a little girl describes her mother's life:

"She ain't got no friends. She ain't got time she should have 'em. She sews all times. Sooner I lays me und the babies on the bed by night my mamma sews. Und sooner I stands up in mornings my mamma sews. All, *all,* ALL times she sews."

Although most women deplored their long hours and low pay, they were grateful to earn the money their families so desperately needed, and availed themselves of every opportunity to get this type of homework. Contractors and manufacturers were able to play willing homeworkers off against disgruntled factory workers seeking to organize and obtain better wages and working conditions. Despite the fact that homework created a breach in labor solidarity, it operated favorably, in the short run, for women who had to continue to share financial responsibilities with their husbands even after they had children. The development of the factory system and the enactment of anti-sweating laws, while benefiting the shopworkers, most of whom were young, unmarried women, actually penalized homeworkers, for it divided the home from the workplace, and kept women out of occupations that had previously provided them with a source of vital income.

As homework became scarcer, a small proportion of mothers tried to make arrangements for the care of their children so they would be free to work in the shops. Of course, there was little day care available to them: more often, these women relied on a female relative or neighbor to look after their children, or even left younger ones in the care of older siblings.

Whatever their hesitations were about leaving children under less than optimal conditions, many women could not afford to pass up opportunities to work, for production in the garment industry was sporadic and between the busy seasons were long periods of idleness. A scene described by Samuel Ornitz in *Bride of the Sabbath* was probably not unusual: a destitute mother who was nursing an infant when it became "busy by cloaks" had her older son bring the baby to her at work. The boy would carry his sister and a pot containing his mother's dinner up five flights to the factory loft.

> Mamma nursed the baby and ate at the same time. She ate mechanically, too tired to taste the food. Between mouthfuls she kissed the baby's head. When the baby was satisfied, she was too, and handed the boy the baby and the pot. Then, without looking at them again, she went back to work, pedaling like mad.

However crowded and unpleasant the conditions in one's own home, they were worse in sweatshops and subcontractors' homes. A twelve-hour day was not unusual in a subcontractor's place where the "boss" regulated the hours. If a worker couldn't keep up, it was too bad for her, for there was always someone else willing to take her place, under any conditions. In "inside" shops, it was no better. Workers often had to bring their own sewing machines and buy needles and thread from the manufacturer, who sold them at a profit. Sanitation was minimal; some shops had only one toilet for a hundred workers. The task system was introduced to speed up production: the labor was divided into a team operation in which each worker had to keep up with the others. The fastest worker naturally set the pace and drove the others to keep up through constant complaining, using guilt and fear as driving forces. Since workers were paid by the piece, they tried to produce as much as possible, and teams within the shop competed with each other for larger portions of the available work. All of this was, of course, to the advantage of the manufacturer, for he was able to make optimal use of his space and capital, increasing production and thereby his own profit.

Uptown manufacturers set up more factories to wrest control from downtown contractors who, without any capital investment, were becoming successful and threatening to crowd their market. Unlike contractors and subcontractors, they provided machines for their workers, an outlay of cash which, of course, the downtowners, who already operated close to margin, could not afford. Although the development of the factory system thus effectively cut out a good deal of the competition, it also laid the foundation for unionization, for workers were no longer isolated from one another as they had been in the homework and sweatshop system. Crowded together in large numbers they were able to share their complaints about low wages and poor treatment.

The Cost of Survival

Despite the rapid growth of the ready-to-wear clothing industry, there were frequent periods of economic recession and seasonal layoffs. Most immigrant women could never save enough from their meager earnings to tide them over slack periods, and the abolition of homework added to the numbers of unemployed.

Workers who were unable to find legitimate alternatives for making a living were often forced to turn to the streets. The women who became beggars or prostitutes were an embarrassment to the entire Jewish community.

Like the pushcart trundlers, women *schnorrers*—professional beggars—also rented children as props, part of their survival kits. A *New York Times* columnist, Meyer Berger, something of a street historian and sociologist, was intrigued by the ingenuity of the poor, displaced Jewish women who were forced to live by their wits and cunning. He sometimes wrote about their lifestyles:

> There were a great many women schnorrers among the Jews in the old days. Some of them would hire a neighbor's child and take it with them to increase their appeal, particularly in the shopping and market districts. The usual rental for a baby was twenty-five cents a day. Another trick was showing a landlord's dispossess notice, generally faked, to entice larger contributions.

Berger also wrote about a woman named Beckie who used malingering to get herself housed and fed. She probably had some medical knowledge, for she was able to fake artfully the sort of physical disorders that insured a hospital stay.

> Beckie was not hard to look upon, fairly young, a squat little Jewish woman with an appealing expression and eyes which under duress of suffering could be so eloquent as to tear your heartstrings. She had an uncanny way of knowing when a young green doctor would be on the ambulance and in this way she got back many times into the hospital before she was recognized. The ailment she would fake depended on how long she wanted board and lodging. If a long period of time was needed to study obscure symptoms and differential diagnosis, this meant, of course, bed, security and food.

Traditional family ties survived among immigrants in the New World. Like so many others, this family included an unmarried cousin (the woman standing on the left) who came alone to America. **Moishe and Ethel Finesilver and family, Boston, 1912.** *(1)*

Two women pickets on strike with the Ladies' Tailors Union, dressed in the fashion of the day. New York, 1910. (2)

Jewish women were often entrepreneurs, too. Molly Berger and an employee in front of the dressmaking shop she owned with her sister Tillie. Boston, 1914. (3)

Annie Nathan Meyer, one of the founders of Barnard College for Women, was the daughter of a man who objected strongly to higher education for women because "men hate intelligent wives." (4)

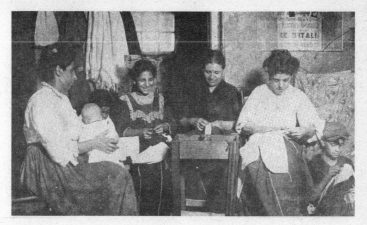

*A typical New York sweatshop at the turn of the century.
The sub-contractor's apartment was both workroom and
living quarters. Often the whole family was pressed
into service. (5)*

*A sub-contractor's sweatshop, New York, 1908. Pattern-
making, draping, and cutting were "inside" operations.
Basting, sewing, and finishing of women's garments were
often sub-contracted "out" and were female occupations. (6)*

(Right) Anzia Yezierska, an immigrant Jewish girl from the Lower East Side who became famous as a writer in the twenties, was known as the "Historian of Hester Street." This photograph was taken just before she was beckoned by Hollywood. (7)

(Below left) Rose Schneiderman, who said, "we not only wanted labor laws and bread, we wanted roses, too," best typifies the Union Woman who devoted her life to bettering conditions for all workers. (8)

(Below right) Sadie American, president of the New York section of the National Council of Jewish Women, was the United States Representative to the International White Slave Traffic Conference, 1910. (9)

(Opposite) A woman carrying home a bundle of pieces to be finished "outside" and then returned to the manufacturer. (10)

Temple Sisterhoods became involved in a wide variety of "charitable" activities during the first two decades of this century. In San Francisco the Temple Emanu-El Sisterhood offered cooking classes and set up residences for young working women who had come here without families. (11) (12)

The YMHA in San Francisco offered classes in nursing skills to Jewish immigrant women. This photograph taken in 1918 shows the first graduates. (13)

*A German Jewish family, the Lowes, outside their
San Francisco restaurant, 1894. (15)*

Two sisters from a San Francisco German Jewish family.
Helen (Nellie) and Ida Greenbaum, c. 1890. *(14)*

A second-generation Jewish girl. The first female in her family to graduate from high school, Brooklyn, New York, 1939. She worked as a bookkeeper in a candy factory and married the boss. (16)

There were others who had to resort to prostitution in order
to stay alive. *Jews Without Money* describes the circumstances
that drove one girl to make her decision:

Rosie worked for years in the sweatshops, saving money to
bring her parents from Europe. Then she fell sick. Her
savings melted. She went to a hospital. She came out, and
could not find a job. She was hungry, feeble, and alone. No
one cared whether she lived or died.

She was ready for the river. A pimp met her. He took her
to a restaurant and fed her her first solid meal. He made
her a practical offer. Rose accepted. She never regretted her
choice; it was easier than being in a sweatshop. She saved
money to send her parents, and was never sick with asthma
again.

Gold also mentions that pimps "infested the dance halls,"
where they lured factory girls into "the life" with fantastic
stories. For this reason, many East Side parents forbade their
daughters to go dancing, but girls who were on their own did
go to the dance halls, and, since they were more likely to be
vulnerable, they fell prey to the pimps. Once they entered the
profession, many were afraid to leave.

Prostitution among Jewish women in America, no longer the
rarity it was in the old country, caused the community great
despair. Prostitutes did not occupy isolated sections of the
ghetto, but the same streets where families lived and children
played. Parents feared for their daughters, and were known to
sit *shiva* (a period of ritual mourning) for those who became
prostitutes. But in some sectors of the community, "respectable" Jews made their peace with prostitutes, who were, after
all, Jews like themselves. As Gold put it, "All these things
happened. They were part of our daily lives, not lurid articles
in a Sunday newspaper." In his novel, the mother is friendly
with the prostitutes who live on their street. Although she disap-
proves of their life-style, she invites them in for tea, protects
them against teasing and taunts, and listens to their tales of woe.

As a novelist, Gold is sympathetic to their plight, seeing them as victims of poverty and capitalism.

Yuri Suhl also treats the phenomenon of the Jewish prostitute matter-of-factly in *One Foot in America.* When Sol, an adolescent in the story, goes to a prostitute for the first time, he finds himself in familiar surroundings. Walking across a newly washed floor spread with newspapers,

> I thought to myself consolingly, the pimp is Jewish, the woman is Jewish, the tenement house is Jewish, the neighborhood is Jewish, so what's there to be afraid of?

And the prostitute herself could have been his mother:

> She tilted her head slightly to one side and regarded me critically. "How old are you, *boytchik?*" she said in a hoarse, grating voice. "I'll betcha you just turned *bar mitzvah* yesterday. . . . Go home and shoot marbles," she said, adding a short, mocking laugh. "He asks me what to do! Today is Sunday. I have no time to fool around with kids. . . . Come back some other time and I'll make up for it. But not on a Sunday, please."

But the prostitutes were not the only indications that Jewish family life in America was disintegrating under the strain of cultural assault and social dislocation. A study by the United Hebrew Charities of family desertion among Jews from 1910 to 1923 reveals some of the main causes: "immorality of husband, or wife, or both; incompatibility of temper; shiftlessness; intemperance; economic conditions including industrial disturbances; financial depression; insufficient wages; illness; discrepancy in ages; interference of relatives; differences in nativity; forced marriages; and immigration of the husband ahead of his family." Husbands who spent a few years here without their families often formed liaisons with Americanized women and then rejected their wives when they arrived, finding their traditional ways and appearance embarrassing.

The number of deserting husbands was so great that the

Forward began publishing a column called "The Gallery of Missing Husbands" in which it printed photographs of the men and worked with the National Desertion Bureau, a Jewish agency set up to locate deserting Jewish husbands. Abandoned wives also wrote letters to the *"Bintel Brief"* describing their plights. In a typical letter, appearing in 1908, a woman appeals to her husband:

> Max! The children and I now say farewell to you. You left us in such a terrible state. You had no compassion for us. For six years I loved you faithfully, took care of you like a loyal servant, never had a happy day with you. Yet I forgive you for everything.
>
> Have you ever asked yourself why you left us? Max, where is your conscience; you used to have sympathy for the forsaken women and used to say their terrible plight was due to the men who left them in dire need. And how did you act? I was a young, educated, decent girl when you took me. You lived with me for six years, during which time I bore you four children. And then you left me.
>
> Of the four children, only two remain, but you have made them living orphans. Who will bring them up? Who will support us? Have you no pity for your own flesh and blood? Consider what you are doing. My tears choke me and I cannot write any more.
>
> Be advised that in several days I am leaving with my two living orphans for Russia. We say farewell to you and beg you to take pity on us and send us enough to live on.

The United Hebrew Charities of New York, which began keeping statistics in 1910 on the proportion of their total relief funds allocated to deserted families, found that over 13 percent of cash relief went to such families in 1910, over 11 percent in 1911, and 9 percent in 1912. With a slight decrease during the war years, the proportion of deserted families obtaining relief remained relatively constant.

In most large cities Jewish orphan asylums were established to care for children who were left not only because one or both parents died, but also because their parents could not afford to keep them, or had to work and couldn't care for them. The *"Bintel Brief"* often carried letters from a parent pleading for someone to take a child, and in later years printed letters from parents looking for children who had been placed in orphanages, as well as from children wishing to locate parents who had abandoned them.

This was unheard of in the old country. If families had difficulties and could not care for their children, neighbors and relatives immediately came to their aid. But in the New World, despite the reforming of communities of *landsleit,* persons from the same community in Eastern Europe, families often felt alone with their problems. Every family had its own troubles, and informal community support systems broke down and were replaced by institutionalized aid offered by strangers. Of course, the higher proportion of broken families in the new country probably accounted for this change: there were many more children who needed to be taken in than there were families who were able to accommodate friends and neighbors in distress.

Illness also caused a disruption of family life. The new immigrants were susceptible to virulent forms of diseases they had not been exposed to before. Although tuberculosis infected some Jews in Eastern Europe, it became so common an affliction in America that it was even called "Jewish asthma." In *Bride of the Sabbath,* Ornitz describes the measures one mother took to protect her children from the disease. In order to get around the New York City Health Department's regulation barring consumptives from factories, she has herself certified a victim of "Jewish asthma" and continues working. She stops taking meals with her children, however, and eats alone, boiling her dishes afterward. She no longer picks up her baby, nor will she kiss her son Saul. Only years after her death does Saul realize that he had done nothing to earn his mother's sudden coldness; she was only trying to spare her children.

Another new problem was the care of the aged. In America households could no longer afford to support members who contributed nothing to their upkeep. While in the old country, many extended families managed financially because they often owned their own houses and some might have had a small garden that yielded a few vegetables and potatoes to supplement the family diet, in America they had to pay rent and buy every grain of food. Although many immigrant families earned more money in America, the standard of living for some was even lower than it had been in Eastern Europe. Some old parents who lived with their children earned their keep by running the household, thus freeing their daughters or daughters-in-law to go out to work; those who were too sick to work became a burden. Homes for the Jewish aged were first established in America to deal with this new problem, though it was difficult both for the aged and their children to accept such institutions. The decision to place parents in homes often divided husbands and wives, sisters and brothers, and even friends. There was a social stigma attached to those who sought this solution, and the ones who were forced to commit their parents were often seen as "heartless opportunists." Children who made this decision suffered as much as their parents, who felt abandoned, for they carried a sense of guilt with them to their graves. Even though economic factors justified this solution on practical grounds, and even though institutional care for the aged was common among other Americans, these Jews felt ambivalent because they had not yet shed entirely old-country standards that condemned their actions.

Jewish homes for wayward girls, also unknown in East European Jewish communities, were established here to help families cope with the problems growing out of the new conditions. There was no doubt that the breakdown of traditions and customs—an internal control system—was eroding family and community life. Even suicide, rare among the Jews of Eastern Europe, became a way out of one's misery. While the idea of America had brought hope to the Jewish immigrants, the reality of America generated a sense of hopelessness for some. Although the immigrants found political freedom and safety from pogroms, threat of destruction, and discriminatory laws, in most instances working conditions and the level of poverty in America were similar to those the Jews thought they were leaving behind.

In Eastern Europe women had, as an extension of their domestic responsibilities, two additional functions: helping to support their families, and transmitting certain elements of Jewish culture. In America they could not continue to perform this second function since their children regarded them as conservative forces, and rejected their teaching and guidance in favor of American ways. In fact, the children reversed the teaching process, and brought the New World home to their parents. The matter of language was one example, as Harry Golden pointed out:

> The system in most households was fixed and simple. The parents spoke Yiddish to the children who answered in English. This system gave rise to the ghetto proverb: "In America the children bring up the parents."

In light of this intergenerational conflict, it is ironic that the women of the immigrant generation have come to be revered as the bearers and conservers of culture—the mythicized "Yiddishe Mommas"—while their real contribution to the immigrant community as breadwinners has gone unnoticed. Because many first-generation women, especially if they were adults when they emigrated, remained tied to the old ways, their grandchildren often remember them only as their babushkaed *bobbas* who seemed isolated from the mainstream of American life. But perhaps the misconceptions perpetuated by the second and third generations can be explained by the fact that these Jews had absorbed Western bourgeois notions of womanhood, and had come to espouse the belief gaining popularity in the late nineteenth and early twentieth centuries that woman's true role was not as wage earner but as keeper of morality. Thus second and third generation men, who went on to achieve great financial success themselves, did not recognize the significant contribution Jewish women had made to the economic survival of their forebears.

5

Weaving the Fabric of Unionism
Jewish Women Move the Movement

We not only wanted labor laws and bread, we wanted roses, too.

—ROSE SCHNEIDERMAN

Both married and single first-generation East European Jewish women assumed, as had been the custom in the old country, partial economic responsibility for the family in America. Some single women who emigrated alone to America sent part of their earnings back "home" to help support the family there or to finance the passage of other members. While Jewish women, married and single, were living in a new environment, their need to earn a living was a familiar experience. But there was a difference. Fortunately, there were many more and varied job opportunities for single women in America.

As in Eastern Europe, females were expected to begin contributing to the family's support at an early age. But despite custom and the family's needs, educational opportunities for poor girls were far better here because education in America was both compulsory and free. Therefore, most girls did attend school for longer than they would have in the old country.

Compulsory education laws, in effect since the mid-1800s, generally required that girls remain in school until they were fourteen (for boys it was sixteen). Even so, since the education of girls was deemed less important than that of boys, and this attitude was, in fact, even reinforced by the American law, many Jewish families violated it without compunction, and girls as young as ten could be found holding down various jobs. Of course, this was true for some of the boys as well. For poverty often interfered with the compulsory education laws and the child labor laws of the Progressive Era (1900–1920). In any case, enforcement of the laws was difficult at best so families dependent on their children's earnings not only disregarded the authorities, but actively circumvented the meager system of enforcement. Jewish families in dire straits, as did other immigrant groups in the same economic predicament, employed many tactics to get around the laws. The purchase of false birth certificates was not uncommon, and many families lied about their children's ages.

In Anzia Yezierska's short story, "My Own People," the mother swears that her twelve-year-old daughter is fourteen and therefore qualified to work. When an inspector catches up with the truant girl and threatens her with arrest, the mother defends her daughter and attacks the system that demands compliance to laws that fail to take into account a family's circumstances:

"If there was enough bread in the house would I need an inspector to tell me to send her to school? If America is so interested in poor people's children, then why don't they give them to eat till they should go to work? What learning can come into a child's head when the stomach is empty?"

This fictional Jewish mother dependent on her daughter's earnings already displays a changed attitude toward the education of girls. For she holds their impoverished situation responsible for the interruption of the girl's schooling, and indeed states that but for that condition, she would have seen that the child remained in school. Despite their extreme poverty, many immigrant Jewish families did make an effort to keep their children in school, even the girls, contrary to Old World attitudes. But the legendary sacrifices Eastern European Jewish parents made were usually for their sons, not their daughters. A complete break away from Old World cultural attitudes toward women did not usually take place among first-generation Jewish émigrés. Furthermore, the old attitude toward the education of girls might have been reinforced in the New World by practicality. For, if professional opportunities were open to males, then it certainly made sense for them to be prepared to take advantage of the expanded possibilities.

There is no doubt that young men were often able to continue their schooling because their sisters went out to work. This was, in fact, the experience of many second-generation Eastern European Jewish females. It was common knowledge that many Jewish males who not only finished secondary school, but went on to college, were subsidized by their sisters. Indeed the rapid social and economic mobility of Jewish males who passed through the American educational system has often been attributed to the Jewish family's support and encouragement. Moreover, this "Jewish ambition" did not go unnoticed by native Americans. In fact, it seemed to stir up some amount of hostility. A gentile journalist writing about the immigrant Jews in New York in 1909 described a common behavioral pattern, but turned an otherwise admirable quality into an attack against the Jewish community:

The odds in life are from birth strongly against the young Jewish-American girl. The chief ambition of the new Jewish family in America is to educate its sons. To do this the girls must go to work at the earliest possible date, and from the population of 350,000 Jews east of the Bowery tens of thousands of young girls go out into the shops. There is no more striking sight in the city than the mass of women that flood east through the narrow streets in a winter's twilight, returning to their homes in the East Side tenements. The exploitation of young women as money-earning machines has reached a development on the East Side of New York probably not equalled anywhere else in the world.

While his observation of a common phenomenon is probably reliable, the Jewish community certainly didn't consider it exploitation of its women, but rather a practical compromise between the family's economic needs and its aspirations.

Although most young unmarried women usually received little family encouragement to go beyond a minimal education, many took advantage of courses offered in the evening school system and by the settlement houses. Most often they first enrolled in vocational training courses to prepare themselves to enter the labor force, or to acquire skills to enable them to get better jobs than they already had. Dressmaking, sewing, and hat-trimming courses were very popular because these skills were in demand on the job market.

After finding work in factories and sweatshops, many young women continued attending classes in English and other subjects. And after learning the new language, some enrolled in courses where they could learn typing, stenography, and bookkeeping—all "middle-class" occupations. In the Jewish community, a bookkeeper, for example, was regarded as a "professional woman." Salesclerking was a valued occupation, too, especially if the stores were located in the "better-class" neighborhoods. Many of the women attending evening classes spent ten or twelve hours working in factories during the day. Self-motivated, they did not need family encouragement, but often they had to be determined enough to resist family opposition, and driven enough to battle against teachers' low expectations of them.

Yezierska's stories and novels are frequently peopled by young Jewish women, in fact like herself, seeking education not only in the interest of getting better jobs, but for their own fulfillment. In one story, a sweatshop girl attending a school for immigrant girls resists the principal who suggests it might be practical for the girl to learn to operate a sewing machine— something the girl already knows how to do. Desirous of receiving a "real education," she retorts: "Us immigrants want to be people—not 'hands'—not slaves of the belly! And it's the chance to think out thoughts that makes people." But the teacher's attitude merely reflected the expectations of the times. Society regarded women as temporary members of the labor force who would eventually fulfill their real purpose in life by becoming wives and mothers. And the overwhelming majority of immigrant Jewish women did marry and have children, but they continued in this period to make an economic contribution to the family in homebound occupations.

Some families, though, did encourage their daughters to get a "proper" education. And many second-generation Jewish girls went on to college and entered the "Jewish professions"—schoolteaching and social work. In fact, by the 1920s, there were a disproportionate number of Jewish girls enrolled in colleges and universities in the urban areas of the United States where many Jewish families settled. Frequently, it was their mothers who became the mediating force between Old World cultural attitudes of the male population toward educating women and the new educational opportunities opening up for women which they wanted their daughters to take advantage of.

Elizabeth Stern, writing about her early life in her memoir, *My Mother and I,* describes the struggles her mother had with her father, an orthodox rabbi, who told his daughter that education would make her an "alien" to the rest of the family. He wanted her to give up her ambition to go beyond grammar school and become "quiet, modest, a good homemaker," the valued traits in a woman. But Elizabeth persisted and her mother resisted. Mrs. Stern's ambition for her daughter at first, however, was to turn her into a lady—perhaps like the German Jewish women "uptown." For despite their extreme poverty, Mrs. Stern managed to find someone to give Elizabeth music lessons—for twenty-five cents, a considerable sum in those days. She justifies her expenditure by saying, " 'In America, to be a gentlewoman, I hear, you must know how to play piano. So you go take lessons.' " Yet, apparently in time her expectations for Elizabeth widen, for when she enters high school her mother relieved her of all household duties so she could concentrate on her studies. Elizabeth eventually went on to college and became a social worker and a writer. And as her father had feared, she turned her back on the community by marrying out of the faith.

While Elizabeth Stern took avid advantage of the opportunities her mother fought for, other Jewish girls who were encouraged to continue their education had internalized the prevailing attitude toward educating women and often felt unworthy of any sacrifices their families were willing to make for them. One young woman who felt guilty because her family had had to deprive itself so she could get an education wrote to the *Jewish Daily Forward* asking for advice:

There are seven people in our family—parents and five children. I am the oldest child, a fourteen-year-old girl. We have been in the country two years and my father, who is a frail man, is the only one working to support the whole family.

I go to school, where I do very well. But since times are hard now and my father earned only five dollars this week, I began to talk about giving up my studies and going to work in order to help my father as much as possible. But my mother didn't even want to hear of it. She wants me to continue my education. She even went out and spent ten dollars on winter clothes for me. But I didn't enjoy the clothes, because I think I am doing the wrong thing. Instead of bringing something into the house, my parents have to spend money on me.

I have a lot of compassion for my parents. My mother is now pregnant, but she still has to take care of the three boarders we have in the house. Mother and Father work very hard and they want to keep me in school.

The editor instructed the girl to obey her parents and stay in school as a kindness to them since they valued her education more than the money. How common this family's attitude was is hard to determine. But the *Jewish Daily Forward* was the most widely read newspaper among poor immigrant Jews and the fact that so many of the letters in the *"Bintel Brief"* column were concerned with the education of girls indicates that it was an issue of some importance to the community, and the stand the *Forward* took represented a significant trend.

In the early period of resettlement in America, most East

European Jewish immigrant families were so poor the girls had to leave day school and go to work. If they were ambitious or serious about their education, they attended evening classes, although for some it was also a form of entertainment, a place to make friends. And in winter the schools provided a pleasant warm atmosphere in contrast to the cold and gloomy apartments in which most of them were housed.

For married women, continuing their education was a more difficult problem. While some husbands may have encouraged their wives to take advantage of educational opportunities, more often they stood in their wives' way. In another letter to the *Forward* a wife complained of her husband's attitude toward her quest for an education:

> Since I do not want my conscience to bother me, I ask you to decide whether a married woman has the right to go to school two evenings a week. My husband thinks I have no right to do this.
>
> I admit that I cannot be satisfied to be just a wife and mother. I am still young and I want to learn and enjoy life. My children and my house are not neglected, but I go to evening high school twice a week. My husband is not pleased when I come home at night and ring the bell, he lets me stand outside a long time intentionally, and doesn't hurry to open the door.
>
> Now he has announced a new decision. Because I send out the laundry to be done, it seems to him that I have too much time for myself, even enough to go to school.
>
> So from now on he will count out every penny for anything I have to buy for the house, so I will not be able to send out the laundry any more. And when I have to do the work myself there won't be any time left for such "foolishness" as going to school. I told him that I'm willing to do my own washing but that I would still be able to find time for study.
>
> When I am alone with my thoughts, I feel I may not be right. Perhaps I should not go to school. I want to say that my husband is an intelligent man and he wanted to marry

a woman who was educated. The fact that he is intelligent makes me more annoyed with him. He is in favor of the emancipation of women, yet in real life he acts contrary to his beliefs.

This husband's behavior reflects a real conflict. While supposedly in agreement with the new enlightened American value of educating women up to the level of men and indeed of "permitting" women to act on their own behalf—in their own interests—he apparently *feels* she is not entitled to either. Perhaps he felt threatened by the idea that his wife might become more educated than he. Common wisdom decreed then that a wife should not know more than her husband and prevailing opinion had it that education made a woman unfit for the limits of family life. Even she admits, in fact, that she finds being a wife and mother not entirely satisfying.

What is more interesting, though, is the *Forward*'s response. The editor supported the woman's position that she had the right to go to school and took the husband to task for desiring to keep his wife enslaved. The *Forward* was in many ways the voice of the non-Orthodox community. It both presented the popular view and led the population toward more up-to-date attitudes. In fact, it was a shaper of thought and political opinion which translated into changing behavior on many levels of Jewish life. The *"Bintel Brief"* column concerned itself with the most common problems. Therefore, letters printed in that column—even if written by the staff, and many knowledgeable people believe they were—reflect not only the problems of the immigrants, but the issues considered of some importance to the community, and changing values and cultural ideals. Women's education seems to be one of the issues considered to be a problem.

Married immigrant Jewish women, to a much lesser degree than single women, availed themselves of educational opportunities open to them. Whether this was due to the community's attitudes or to the pressures of homework, household tasks, and family life cannot be substantiated. Many women, of course, may not have wanted to go to school because they were simply too weary to make the effort, felt uncomfortable in alien surroundings, or may have had to remain home with their children. Jewish men, despite their popular image as ideal family men, were reluctant to become baby-sitters. This was considered their wives' responsibility, and men who were willing to free their wives in the evening often did so at the risk of losing face among their male peers. As one Jewish woman who was attending evening school in 1910 put it, "My husband was a good man, he allowed me to go to school at night, but made me promise not to tell anybody he was home with the children."

Working Girls in Evening Schools, a study conducted in New York City during 1910 and 1911 by Mary Van Kleeck, under the auspices of the Russell Sage Foundation, provides a guide to what was going on among Jewish women during this period. Single working women, or women preparing themselves for the job market, made up the bulk of first-generation Jewish females attending evening school. Foreign-born Jewish women made up the second largest group of those attending evening schools— about 15 percent of the students. As a group, they were exceeded only by women who had been born in America. Even so, approximately 25 percent of the American-born women were the daughters of Jewish immigrants—second-generation Jews. Therefore, according to this study, about 40 percent of the women attending evening schools in New York were Jewish. Although many of the women were taking vocational courses or attending evening trade schools, still the enormously high proportion of Jewish women in the evening school system signifies both their eagerness to advance themselves economically and the extent of their desire to take advantage of educational opportunities available in America that were denied to them in the old country.

Where a Little Education Can Lead

If most first-generation immigrant women seemed to be living in harmony within the confines of the Old World traditions, Van Kleeck's study indicates many were breaking with the customs of the past, and indeed some of them were in open rebellion against its limitations. Many, in fact, like the women of the Bund before them, had become familiar with contemporary issues and were taking public political positions. One Jewish woman, a millinary worker who was interviewed by a Van Kleeck investigator, was not only at ease in discussing working conditions in her trade, but she could also talk about "socialism, women's rights, trade unions, Bernard Shaw, the drama in America, the school system and Russian versus American women." One of the principals of the schools covered by the Van Kleeck study describes the Jewish women who worked in the shops and attended evening school as overall: ". . . eager to learn all they could about America; keen and independent in judgment; and withal, ready to make sacrifices not for themselves alone but for their fellowworkers, to improve the conditions in their trades."

Of course, the infamous conditions in the shops affected all workers, and all workers, males and females, were poorly treated by management. But, in general, accounts of the particular conditions for women in the shops stand out as unrivaled by those of male workers. Girls, for example, were timed when they left the room to go to the toilet. And the "bosses," assuming the timidity and ignorance of the most newly arrived immigrant girls, often took advantage of them in the most obvious ways: first and foremost, they were paid lower wages than the others not because they were less skilled, but because they were unaware what other girls were being paid for the same work. Not that they would have demanded more had they known—they were grateful, in most cases, to be earning any money at all. In one of Yezierska's stories, "Hungry Hearts," about life in the shops, she recounts a common experience of a young woman who is hired readily because there is a scarcity of labor, and is paid less than the others because she doesn't know about pay rates and the employers' game of getting away with what you can. When she's taken on, another woman, wise to the ways, exclaims: " 'Gevalt! All these greenhorn hands tear the bread from our mouths by begging to work so cheap.' " In another of Yezierska's stories, "How I Found America," which describes the pre-union working conditions in the garment trades, the boss tells the women that since the other trades are slack he can find workers who are willing to do their jobs for half the wages, but out of kindness he'll keep them on and lower their pay from seventy-five cents to fifty cents for a dozen shirts. He suggests they work nights to make up the difference in money. One woman, a widow with three children to support, wails:

> "Oi weh! The blood sucker, the thief! How will I give them to eat—my babies—my babies—my hungry little lambs!"

Cheating the workers was the rule of the day in pre-union times. "Mistakes" were often made in computing the amounts due them. The victims rarely complained, both because they were fearful of losing their jobs and because most simply could not understand how the amounts were figured. Clocks could be slowed down during working hours and speeded up during lunch hours. This was bad enough, but even more outrageous conditions existed throughout the industry. The workers were charged for needles and for the cost of electric power to run machines and irons. According to the official history of the International Ladies' Garment Workers' Union, *owners charged workers 20 percent more than they paid for electricity, and 25 percent more than the price of needles and electric belts!* Workers had to rent lockers to hold their hats and coats—and even had to rent their chairs. Fines were imposed for lateness, and if a mistake was made on a garment, the worker was held responsible and fined not at the rate of cost of the piece but at 300 to 400 percent more! In other words, workers not only had to contribute directly to overhead and basic equipment, the overcharges to workers represented a net profit to the bosses.

But this was still not the worst of it. Working conditions were extremely hazardous. The collective weight of the employees who were crowded into the space, and the machinery on the floors, made very real the threat of the floors collapsing. Workers knew, too, that the materials they worked with were flammable and the sewing machines well-oiled. Shop fires were not rare in those days and not even the minimal fire regulations were enforced. Not only was there little regard for the safety of the employees, most were assumed to be untrustworthy. Doors, for example, were often locked after all the workers arrived in the morning, and remained locked until it was time to go home. Girls' handbags were searched as they left. Though perhaps not without reason, for, as Molly Chernikovsky revealed, the workers did sometimes resort to petty thievery. This practice of locking doors, however, increased the risk in case of fire.

In addition to all of this, the amount of time spent in the shops took up the greater portion of most workers' lives. The workday usually started at eight in the morning and was supposed to end at six in the evening, with a half hour off for lunch. On Saturdays, most employees worked from eight in the morning until a quarter to five. Eager as they were to make extra money because of their meager wages most worked overtime during the busy months, if they could. And some workers held second jobs to earn enough to support or help support their families. This was the reality of most workers' lives, male or female. For females, though, there was an added misery men were not subject to.

Trading in The Trade

Many women experienced sexual abuse in the shops. They suffered their humiliation and fear in private for one did not complain publicly about such matters. Anyway, sexual payoffs for the privilege of holding a job were expected and a common enough practice in cases of advancement within the shop. Sexual exploitation of young girls by men in power, even if they were only the foremen who controlled bundle distribution, was often a source of outrage among the female workers. Few could afford to refuse to play by the rules. Elizabeth Hasanovitz, a young Russian Jewish immigrant who became a factory operative and later a union organizer, was one of the few women who recorded her experiences in the garment industry. In her autobiography, *One of Them,* Hasanovitz gives lengthy detailed descriptions of the sexual abuse of women in the shops where she was employed as well as her own sexual experiences with the men she encountered. While some women workers couldn't afford to risk losing their jobs by holding out, Hasanovitz decided she had to resist:

> . . . I wanted to lead my life in purity. I did not want anyone to soil my path. I feared that if life continued as it was, I might be plunged into the dirty slough as many others were, and I decided to prefer death, if it came, rather than allow anything to happen to me.

But she paid dearly for that decision. Out of work for a long time and desperate for money, she finally lands a job. Without a cent, after working two and a half days, she asks for her pay even though it isn't yet due her. Her boss agrees, but attempts to make her "come across" before giving her her wages. Hasanovitz describes the incident:

> When the bookkeeper had my pay made out she left. I still waited for the money. The boss sat at his desk writing. I had no courage to disturb him, so I sat and waited. At last he stood up, straightened himself, and smiled at me.
>
> "So you are in hardship—too bad, too bad."
>
> Then he took my pay, looked at it, fixed his eyes on me and asked: "Is that all you get?"
>
> "No, I get thirteen, but this is only for two days and a half," I said, already regretting to have aroused his pity.
>
> "But my dear girl, that would not be enough for you. Don't you need more than that?" . . . I sat trembling with fear. . . . "Wait a moment; I will give you some more."
>
> But no more had I time to refuse when he grasped me in his arms.
>
> I screamed, and with superhuman strength threw him from me and ran into the hall. . . . How I hated men, all of them without exception! I stood up before the mirror and studied my face, trying to find out if there was anything in it that awakened men's impudent feelings toward me. . . . If only I could discredit that man so that he would never dare insult a working-girl again. If only I could complain

of him in court! But I had no witnesses to testify the truth; with my broken English I could give very little explanation. Besides that, if I were working in a shop and were called to court, the firm might suspect some evil in me and send me away.

So I left him alone and never went to collect my money, although I was in a frightful need.

Although Hasanovitz never solicited sexual attention from anyone—and in fact actively avoided such encounters—she, like many women who have been victimized sexually, was blamed for being an enticer. On one occasion she was fired from a plum job she'd just obtained because the boss's wife accused her of arousing the man's lust. Hasanovitz had noticed that the boss flirted with the girls and was careful never to be alone with him in a room. But one day, unable to avoid it, he cornered her:

"My, what curly hair you have! Is it not beautiful!" he said, beginning to smooth my hair. I blushed and moved away. "Do not be afraid, I will not hurt you," he whispered, his eyes wandering all over me. "What a wonderful form you have. If you were only a few inches taller, you would make a perfect model, wouldn't you?" . . . Again I moved away in indignation, but before I could open my mouth to speak, his wife stood in the open door, her eyes filled with rage. . . . "So you are flirting with an old man—for shame! Now, you get your hat and go. This is no place for you, you sample flirter."

The religious culture of Eastern Europe demanded sexual abstinence before marriage, but regarded women as sexual beings capable of enticing men away from their religious pursuits. Indeed, the culture ensured that the sexes lived very separated existences. In America the men suddenly found themselves in a new close contact with women. The religious laws regulating behavior no longer seemed to apply to the new situation. With the breakdown in the shops of the *shtetl*'s male/female stratification, and with the loosening of religious taboos in the workplace, the old restraints gave way to what many considered the Americanization of sexual attitudes. Women began to be seen as the weaker sex and men tried to prove their masculinity and strength by abusing them. Not all men, of course, intimidated women in the shops physically; some used their power to manipulate them, while others remained neutral. Many men, however, in the new environment felt free to tease, taunt, and degrade women verbally. This may have been the form their contempt for women took—an expression of it—but it was usually explained away as "just having fun with the girls." Some women who accepted this explanation felt flattered because they were the recipients of male attention, while others who could not actively confront this type of abuse learned to ignore it, thus living with it. Abraham Cahan, in *The Rise of David Levinsky,* describes the situation in one of the shops and the women's responses to the sexual slurs by males which often took the form of male "playfulness":

> As a rule, they were ostensibly addressed to some of the other fellows or to nobody in particular, their real target being the nearest girls. These would receive them with gestures of protest or with an exclamation of mild repugnance, or in the majority of cases pass them unnoticed as one does some unavoidable discomfort of toil.

While many women may have tried to come to terms with the sexual conditions prevailing in the shops, once they were organized and union grievances committees set up, charges of sexual abuse were among the major complaints made by female workers to union officials. Rose Schneiderman, an outspoken and effective union organizer, in her memoir *All for One* recounts an incident involving a complaint made by the union representative in a shop. A woman complained about the owner of a shop who "had a habit of pinching the girls whenever he passed them and they wanted it stopped." Schneiderman went to speak with the man and "told him that this business of pinching the girls in the rear was not nice, that the girls resented it." The man replied, "Why, Miss Schneiderman, these girls are like my children."

Whereupon the chairwoman of the committee who was sent to speak to the owner responded, "We'd rather be orphans."

Another woman union organizer, however, felt that the sexual complaints the union was being asked to act upon would antagonize the males and would overwhelm the "real" issues—the horrendous working conditions which affected all the workers. Writing to another female union organizer in 1912, she said:

> Insofar as moral conditions are concerned, well, this should not have been the chief issue in the strike . . . you know as well as I, that there is not a factory today where the same immoral conditions does not exist. You remember factories where we have worked and . . . both of us know that the cloak factories and all the other shops in the city, in New York and Chicago, every one of the men will talk to the girls, take advantage of them if the girl will let them, the foremen and the superintendents will flirt with the girls and this is nothing new to those who know that this exists today everywhere. True that I have seventeen affidavits in my possession now, but I read them over and you find the same old story, that the foreman asked a girl to come into his office and hold hands, etc., etc. This to my mind can be done away with by educating the girls, instead of attacking the company.

The sexual complaints, as this woman saw them, were a female problem that could be solved by educating the females, not the males. The fact that she, a Russian Jewish immigrant, locates the problem where she does—in women's behavior—indicates the continuation of the notion that in sexually charged situations the women are to blame.

Women Are Different

The many aborted attempts made in the late 1800s and early 1900s to unionize the garment industry might have succeeded if the organizers had addressed themselves to the problems of women in the trade, for women were a substantial proportion of the labor force, and Jewish women dominated, in fact, the women's wear industry. Moreover, given the labor history of Jews in Eastern Europe, the Jewish women who entered garment manufacturing were the most likely candidates for unionization. Especially since their attitudes toward labor, social, and communal reform could be characterized as "advanced" when compared to those held by other ethnic groups who came to America during the same period.

Italian women and East European Jewish women, for example, emigrated to America about the same time, tended to live in close proximity to one another, and entered the clothing industry in similar occupations; but they were quite different from each other. Jewish women had a rather different work experience in the old country. They had also been exposed to, and some had even participated in, the Jewish labor movement in Eastern Europe. It might, therefore, be illuminating to see the ways in which these two groups of women differed and how their differences affected their outlook and their relation to the labor union movement.

During the Progressive Era some studies of particular industries and some of the social problems of the lower classes were conducted under the auspices of private foundations and governmental institutions. It was hoped by many of those involved in the studies that reform legislation would grow out of their findings. One of these studies, Mary Van Kleeck's investigation of New York's *Artificial Flower Makers* (1910) provides the material for comparing the differences between Italian and Jewish women workers in the trade. Her findings reveal that Italian women were most concerned with their craftsmanship and their own individual wage problems, and less concerned with the working conditions in the industry and problems that affected and united all workers. In contrast, the Jewish women interviewed had an overall awareness of the labor question. They were more concerned with wages, hours of work, treatment of the workers, and conditions in the shops than with the product of their labor. Jewish women displayed a sense of connection with the working-class community in general, rather than solely with their families or ethnic group. Van Kleeck found, furthermore, that Jewish women faced employment discrimination as a result of their history of involvement with labor organizing, and their reputations as "agitators." Employers, even if Jewish, preferred hiring women of other ethnic groups or native-born women, considered to be more docile and less likely to make trouble.

The Italian women's work attitudes and disinclination to become involved in labor problems probably grew out of the Italian family culture and their own history as farm laborers rather than industrial workers. The Italian family structure and the *padrone* system—the use of and dependency on the family as a unit of labor to be contracted out—mediated against industry unionization. In other words, their more exclusive family-oriented social structure as well as their lack of previous experience as independent members of an industrialized wage-labor force probably accounts for the difference in the Italian women's attitudes toward unionization. In addition, their unfamiliarity with the tenets of trade unionism and their traditional and historical lack of participation in public life probably partially accounts for the initial difficulty that, in fact, the union had in drawing Italian women into the movement.

But there were other reasons also, and the fault lay with the union organizers. As early as 1907, Jewish women tried unsuccessfully to organize the artificial flower makers. The industry was dominated by Italian immigrant women, with Jewish women following next in numbers. Since the original organizers spoke only Yiddish, the effort to unionize was doomed to fail. One of the members of the group that attempted to form the union in 1907 noted that "the only time there was a large turnout for mass meetings was when English and Italian speakers were on the platform." During 1909 and 1910 Jewish women once again tried to organize women in this trade. Now their goal was to unite milliners, wire makers, and flower makers into one union. These three occupations were naturally related—the wire forms and flowers were used to make the hats then in vogue. This attempt at unionization also failed because of language problems. In desperation, the Jewish flower makers renamed the union the Education League of Flower-Makers, hoping it would attract more Italian women. Their first mistake was in planning meetings for Saturday nights. If they had been more familiar with the Italian culture, or had bothered to ask, they would have known that male members of Italian families rigidly controlled the women's activities, and since the culture was family-centered, Italian women were expected to stay at home when they weren't working. Italian women, compared to Jewish women, had an entirely different social and family experience. They were often, for example, actually escorted to and from work by a male member of the family. East European Jewish women were not regarded as being in need of protection. In fact, as we've seen earlier, it was the women who often felt protective of the males in the *shtetl* environment and who frequently continued in that role, serving as buffers, for example, between Jewish men and government officials.

But changes in the ways in which Jewish males viewed Jewish females did take place soon after they got to America. Both the corruption of Jewish life and values and the absorption of American attitudes toward women often resulted in a feeling of contempt for the same survival qualities of women so admired in *shtetl* culture. In the shops this contempt became translated into abusive behavior by Jewish males who began to feel diminished by the strong Jewish woman. Italian men, on the other hand, having experienced a sense of belonging in the old country, may have had less of a desire to assimilate and become Americanized, and therefore may have been more resistant to change. In any case, the American view of women as the weaker sex was not in conflict with the Italian male attitude of protective paternalism. So Italian men, for a much longer period, continued behaving in Old World ways.

Despite these differences in attitudes and culture and despite the Italian family system interfering with attempts to organize Italian women workers, eventually they were drawn into the labor movement. But Jewish women had a head start and spearheaded unionization in the garment industry though they are often blamed for its early failures. The short-term participation of Jewish women in the labor force, where most of them did spend less than five years, is usually held responsible for the length of time it took for the union to grow in strength and power. Jewish women employed in factories were, for the most part, single, and although they were enjoying freedoms that had been unknown in the old country, marriage and children were the primary goal of most. And why not? Life in the factory was *not* a more attractive alternative. Jewish women did have a high rate of early marriage and usually became pregnant quite soon after. This work-marriage-family pattern must have interfered with the growth of the early Jewish labor movement since women made up a substantial proportion of the industry's work force.

Jewish Women Move the Movement

Nonetheless, according to Louis Levine's history of *The Women's Garment Workers,* in 1909–1910 Jewish women were the movers and shakers behind the "Uprising of the 20,000," the largest strike by women in the United States up to that time. This strike by the female shirtwaist makers of New York

> ... laid the foundations of unionism in the dress and waist trade and created the first local with a membership of many thousands. During the first year after the general strike, Local 25 counted over 10,000 members. This inspired the workers in other branches of the industry. It showed that "big" things could be done in the way of organization, that large masses of workers could be marshalled, great powers of resistance called forth, and deep emotions of enthusiasm awakened. It popularized the idea of the general strike. It thus supplied the initial impulse which led to the next stage in the development of the International, to the general strike of the cloakmakers.

There were six Jewish women on the executive committee of Local 25, which was eventually responsible for calling the general strike of the shirtwaist makers on November 22, 1909. Eighty percent of the workers in the trade were women; 70 percent of them were between the ages of sixteen and twenty-five. Sixty-five percent of the women employed in the industry were Jewish, 26 percent were Italian, and 8 percent were native-born Americans. The rest were Polish, German, and other English-speaking foreign-borns.

Actually, it was the management or the mismanagement of the Triangle Waist Company and then the Leiserson shop that was responsible for touching off the "Uprising of the 20,000." Triangle was one of the largest manufacturers of shirtwaists and the largest proportion of its employees was Jewish. Some, at Triangle, had tried to organize the workers several times before. In 1908, in response to the latest attempt at unionization, the owners of the company set up a Triangle Employees Benevolent Association. It was controlled by the firm and only "loyal" employees—those who had resisted the union—were invited to join.

Even so, a problem broke out among the workers within the company's association. In September 1909, as the Jewish holidays were approaching, the workers voted to distribute ten dollars of the association's treasury to each member who had a family to support and was in need. The company refused to go along with the vote although it offered to lend the money to the members. Angered by this, the workers defected and met with representatives of the United Hebrew Trades. The company then fired a number of workers suspected of being sympathetic to unionization, claiming a lack of jobs. At the same time it was found that the company was advertising for other workers. Local 25 of the International Ladies' Garment Workers' Union declared Triangle had locked out its workers and called a strike against the firm on September 27. The Leiserson shop also went on strike.

By the middle of October the strikers' enthusiasm was evaporating. Tired and hungry, the picketers had suffered from all sorts of harassment, abuse, and beatings. Leiserson hired professional thugs to beat up the strikers; Triangle had hired prostitutes to fight and to taunt the pickets; and the police upheld the law by bullying the strikers. Worried about the waning spirit of the strikers, Local 25 and members of the United Hebrew Trades considered calling a general strike of all shirtwaist makers—there were then over 30,000 people employed in the various New York shops. At an executive committee meeting of Local 25 it was decided to call the workers together and put the proposal before them. Before the decision was implemented, a member of the Women's Trade Union League was arrested for helping to picket Leiserson. On November 4, Mary Dreier, president of the New York Women's Trade Union League, was also arrested when she joined the picketing. These arrests focused public attention on the striking workers and may have strengthened the workers' spirit. When the meeting for workers in the trade was held on November 22, 1909, an overflow crowd of thousands converged on Cooper Union.

For hours, the question of whether a general strike should be called was debated between the platform and the audience. Finally, a young Jewish worker in the Leiserson shop, Clara Lemlich, asked for the floor. According to newspaper accounts, some in the audience expressed annoyance—perhaps because she was female, perhaps because she was so young, or perhaps, as one historian has suggested, only because she was known to be an impulsive person. Nevertheless, the chair declared that she had a right to speak. She made her way to the platform and, addressing the audience in Yiddish, said:

> I am a working girl, one of those who are on strike against intolerable conditions. I am tired of listening to speakers who talk in general terms. What we are here for is to decide whether we shall or shall not strike. I offer a resolution that a general strike be declared—now.

The *New York World* reported that "the big gathering was on its feet, everyone shouting an emphatic affirmative, waving hats, canes, handkerchiefs, anything that came handy. For five minutes, perhaps, the tumult continued; then the chairman made himself heard and asked for a seconder of the resolution. Again the big audience leaped to its feet, everyone seconding." The chairman then asked the audience: "Do you mean faith? Will you take the old Jewish oath?" Thousands of hands were raised, and the following prayer recited by everyone:

If I turn traitor to the cause I now pledge,
may this hand wither from the arm I now raise.

Clara Lemlich, on the day this chapter is being written, is still alive. She is living in California, supported partly by a pension she receives from one of the most successful unions in America, and one which owes some of its success to her and the thousands of workers—many of them Jewish women—who became organizers of the union in the many shops where they worked and who fought for what they considered their rights. Louis Levine, the official historian of the ILGWU, in fact credits the women with the strike's success:

Many of the women strikers took upon themselves the task of keeping the banner of the strike waving. In fact, though the principal union officials were men and the direction of the strike was in the hands of men, the women played a preponderant part in carrying it through. It was mainly women who did the picketing, who were arrested and fined, who ran the risk of assault, who suffered ill-treatment from the police and the courts.

He describes the remarkable efforts of some of the women. Esther Lobetkin, for example, a recent immigrant from Russia who was in charge of one of the shops, spent the entire day on the picket lines and then attended the night meetings of the union. She was arrested many times and would yell from the police wagon, "Do not lose courage. We'll win yet." Bessie Switzski and her sister, who picketed in front of a shop that hired "gorillas" to fight off the strikers, returned each day to engage the "gorillas," persisting until the shop came to terms with the union. Levine said in his book, "In every shop there were women like these who influenced others. These hundreds of leaders remained unnamed and unrecorded." A social worker who participated in this strike said of the women activists:

Into the foreground of this great moving picture comes the figure of one girl after another, as their services are needed.

With extraordinary simplicity and eloquence, she will tell any kind of audience, without any false shame, and without self-glorification, the conditions of her work, her wages, and the pinching poverty of her home and the homes of her comrades. Then she withdraws into the background to undertake quietly the danger and humiliation of picket duty or to become a nameless sandwich-girl selling papers on the street, no longer the center of interested attention, but the butt of the most unspeakable abuse.

Despite Their Devotion . . .

Despite the devotion of women to the cause of unionization, the courage they displayed in the face of physical threats, and the fact that the industry was dominated by female workers, women retained their second-class status within the union. The movement itself was biased against women workers. It was felt that they ought to be part of the marginal labor force and, in fact, in the late 1800s, in the very beginning of the labor movement in America, efforts were made to keep women out of certain occupations in order to insure male employment. Discrimination against women is part of the history of the labor movement. This was true in general and it was certainly true of unions in industries dominated by Jews. Moreover, in industries in which Jewish women were, and historically had been, heavily represented, there was an attempt to push them out. For example, a report presented to the International Cigarmakers by the union president (Adolph Strasser) in 1879 suggested ways to control female participation in the industry:

We cannot drive the females out of the trade but we can restrict this daily quota of labor through factory laws. No girl under eighteen should be employed more than eight hours per day; all overwork should be prohibited; while married women should be kept out of factories at least six weeks before and six weeks after confinement.

What Strasser is recommending is the initiation of protective legislation for women: not because they need it, nor because it might be desirable for the female workers, but because it is a way of limiting the entrance of females into the industry, thereby keeping places for men. For, if protective legislation for women resulted in the shrinking of the workday for women, what employer would prefer to hire them? Actually, Strasser was not suggesting women be protected; he was suggesting they be penalized.

While Strasser was attempting to legalize sexual discrimination against women in the tobacco industry, another tactic was being used in the clothing industry. In the late 1800s when the manufacture of clothing became a real industry, women made up the largest proportion of the workers. But with the arrival of both skilled and unskilled males from Eastern Europe, women became marginal. In his *Jewish Labor in the United States,* Melech Epstein describes the changing conditions for women. As men entered the clothing industry, women were pushed out of the skilled and higher-paying jobs, and were reduced to the status of unskilled workers:

> At the end of the 1870s men entered the ladies' garment industry en masse. In 1876 the heavy cutting knife was installed. This gave men a chance to displace the women cutters. A few years later, after mass emigration, men made their first appearance at sewing machines—an occupation formerly reserved for women. Only finishing was left to girls. Production of ladies' cloaks and skirts became overwhelmingly a man's job. The change was brought about by the old-world tailors. Because their wages were no higher than the female workers received, the employers were eager to hire them.

This is but another example of sex discrimination. Many East European Jewish women also had experience as cutters. But employers preferred to hire men for cutting, and once it became a primarily male occupation it became closed off to women entirely. Fathers trained sons, jobs were passed on from one male family member or friend to another. In this way, the supply of trained cutters was limited, thus guaranteeing that wages would be maintained at a certain level. Epstein's rather curious explanation for the male takeover of this occupation is that the introduction of the "heavy" cutting knife was the determinant. What is evident in his analysis is the reflection of contemporary opinion that women are the weaker sex. Yet from descriptions of women in the literature of the late nineteenth and early twentieth century, and from a close look at photographs of East European Jewish immigrants, it is evident that the women in many instances were heavier and probably as strong as the men. And though spared the burden of the cutting knife, these women were *schlepping* heavy bundles of garments on their heads, pushing through the streets vegetable-laden carts weighing hundreds of pounds, and working at foot-pedaled sewing machines fourteen to eighteen hours a day, in addition to caring for their households.

One further example of discrimination against women in organized labor: In the garment industry, the 1890 strikes that led to the agreement of July 23, 1890, between the Cloak Manufacturers' Associations (the owners) and the Operators' and Contractors' Unions—which attempted to regulate wages and provide better working conditions for the workers—specified "that no part of this agreement shall refer or apply to females employed by the Cloak Manufacturers' Association." Employment standards and wages were set by the union for men only.

This trend continued. More surprisingly, women continued to participate in the labor movement despite the overt discrimination against them in the movement itself and despite the sellout of the women by the movement. The famous 1913 "Protocol in the Dress and Waist Industry," the first agreement between labor and management arbitrated by outside parties, institutionalized sexual discrimination against women and formalized sexual division of labor in the garment industry. It insured that the higher-paid jobs were reserved exclusively for males. The Dress and Waist Manufacturers' Association and the International Ladies' Garment Workers' Union agreed to the following:

TERMS OF EMPLOYMENT AND SHOP STANDARDS

A. Wages

Week-Workers. The following shall be the minimum rates for week-workers:

1. *Provisions relating to Cutters, including Apprentices*
   Full-fledged cutters who have heretofore been receiving a minimum of $25 per week, $27.50 (men only).
   Cutters' apprentices are divided into four grades: Grade A, $6.00; Grade B, $12.00; Grade C, $18.00; Grade D, $21.00
2. Drapers (women only), $15.00.
3. Joiners (women only), $13.00.
4. Sample-makers (women only), $15.00.
5. Examiners (women only), $11.50.
6. Finishers (women only), $9.50.
7. Ironers (women), $14.00.
8. Ironers (men), $17.00.
9. Pressers (men), $23.00.
10. Cleaners: Girls under 16, during the first year, $6.00; girls 16 or over, during the first year $7.00; girls under 16, during the second year, $7.00; girls 16 or over, during the second year, $8.50.

At the time of the formalization of the 1913 Protocol, 85 to 90 percent of the workers in the industry were female. Even so, sex discrimination against women was built into the agreement. The lowest-paid male was to earn more than the highest-paid female and the highest-paid jobs were reserved for men only. Moreover, men and women doing the same work were not to be paid equally. Female ironers were to receive $14 and males $17. Surely skill would not have accounted for the difference.

What the Protocol of 1913 accomplished for women was both the institution of a wage differential between the sexes (with women the losers) and age discrimination among females as well.

The union, while looking out for the men, disregarded the interest of the women in an industry dominated by female workers. What makes it even more ironic is that women were central to the establishment of the union both through their organizational efforts and because the two events that won the public over to supporting the union revolved around the women workers: first, the "Uprising of the 20,000" and then the Triangle factory fire. Both of these events are dramatically connected. For the women who struck in 1909–1910 were not only demanding recognition of the union as a power bloc, a shortened work week, regulated year-round employment, and fixed wages, but among their other demands—on which they compromised—were more stringent safety and health regulations and the enforcement of those already on the books. The compromises they were forced to make may very well have resulted in the death of 146 workers in the Triangle Waist Company fire a year later, on Saturday, March 25, 1911.

Victims and Survivors

The Triangle factory occupied the top three floors—the eighth, ninth and tenth—of the Asch Building, located at Greene Street and Washington Place in Greenwich Village. The building was supposed to have been fireproof: It had wooden window frames and floors and wooden trim in the interior, and violated numerous of even those inadequate regulations that did exist. There were two staircases in a building that ought to have had three. The law required that factory doors open out "if practicable" and were not to be "locked, bolted, or fastened during working hours." The Triangle doors were kept locked because management was concerned about employees stealing, and the doors opened in because the stairs and stairwell were so narrow that it wasn't practicable for the doors to open out. The single outside fire escape ended at the second floor of the airshaft between the Triangle building and another. The windows leading to the fire escape were covered by a metal shutter that was closed with fasteners that had rusted, so that precious time was required to open them. The fire escape itself was not designed to support very much weight, certainly not the number of people who climbed onto it at one time during the fire. In addition, there were no fire sprinklers in the building; there was no law that required them. Triangle had never held a fire drill, even though management had been warned, as early as 1909, about hazards on the three floors. P.J. McKeon, a lecturer on fire prevention at Columbia University who had been hired to inspect Triangle when it applied for an increase in its fire insurance, noted that conditions there were very serious. In his book *The Triangle Fire*—the best and most thorough account ever published— Leon Stein sums up McKeon's report:

> He was concerned immediately with the crowding of so many people into the top three floors of the building. . . . He noted that without previous instructions on how to handle themselves in such an emergency a fire would panic the girls.
>
> McKeon found that the door to the Washington Place stairway was "usually kept locked," and was told this was because "it was difficult to keep track of so many girls." He thought he had impressed management with the need to hold fire drills.

McKeon recommended that a fire-prevention expert be called in, and even gave Triangle's management the name of one who did indeed write Triangle offering to act as a consultant. Triangle never replied.

Triangle was the largest shirtwaist factory in New York City, employing between 800 and 900 persons during peak periods. On the day of the fire, 500 employees were working in the factory; 146 persons died as a result of the fire, and an unknown number were injured or maimed for life. The fire had a strong impact on the entire population of the city, bringing together as it did so many of the political issues of the time. But it had an even stronger impact on the East European Jews because there was scarcely a person from the community who did not have a relative or friend or a *landsman* working there that day, or who had not at one time or another been employed by Triangle. Furthermore, most of the Jews employed in the garment industry worked under similar hazardous conditions and identified strongly with the victims. Many workers interviewed after the fire expressed fear and rage and the idea that "there but for the grace of God go I." Fifty thousand people marched in a parade memorializing the victims—all of the victims, those who had been killed and those who had survived.

Some of the survivors had managed to escape by elevator before it gave way. Some found their way to the roof and crossed over to the rooftop of another building. And some few managed to make it down the stairwell before it turned into a roaring hot flue. Most of those who had died had jumped to their death from the windows; others were unable to get to the windows and suffocated or burned to death inside.

Many of the girls leaping to their deaths were already on fire. Nets were held by firemen hoping to catch the women before they hit the ground, but many women jumped two and three together, holding hands or arms entwined so that the force of the combined weight of each falling body was 11,000 pounds by the time it reached the nets. Blankets and tarpaulins were also spread by passersby hoping to save some, but the weight of the bodies tore the blankets from their hands.

Some people on the streets yelled "Jump," while others yelled "Don't jump." Some called for ladders to be hoisted, but when they were, they only reached to the sixth floor and the fire was blazing on eight, nine, and ten. One girl, the edge of her skirt aflame, tried to leap to the ladder, but missed. Some tried to keep their bodies upright during the fall. Some were helped out the windows to death by others who were hoping to save them.

In Ornitz's *Bride of the Sabbath* one of the characters, commenting on the fire, says that the fact that it took place on a Saturday morning "gave the fanatical Orthodox the opportunity to say that it was God's punishment on the girls for breaking the Sabbath."

But Morris Hillquit, a leading socialist lawyer who later became counsel for the ILGWU, attributed the fire and loss of lives to everyone who refused to heed the demands of the striking shirtwaist makers. Speaking at a Cooper Union rally the Friday following the fire, he said:

> The girls who went on strike last year were trying to readjust the conditions under which they were obliged to work. I wonder if there is not some connection between the fire and that strike. I wonder if the magistrates who sent to jail the girls who did picket duty in front of the Triangle shop realized last Sunday that some of the responsibility may be theirs. Had the strike been successful, these girls might have been alive today and the citizenry of New York would have less of a burden upon its conscience.

William Shepherd, the United Press reporter who covered the fire, agreed with Hillquit. He wrote:

> I looked upon the heads of dead bodies and I remembered these girls were the shirtwaist makers. I remembered their great strike of last year in which these same girls had demanded more sanitary conditions and more safety precautions in the shops. These dead bodies were the answer.

While many people agreed with Hillquit and Shepherd, popular opinion laid the blame on Max Blanck and Isaac Harris, the owners of Triangle. It was said that if the owners had cared about their employees the fire would never have happened. Blanck and Harris collected their insurance and were acquitted of the charges brought against them. How Blanck and Harris managed to absolve themselves of the psychological guilt and responsibility for the deaths of 146 people and the ruined lives of many more—their families, friends, and lovers—can only be guessed at. Ornitz suggests that Blanck and Harris turned the accusations against them from a charge of negligence and murder into "just another incident of anti-Semitism." More outrageous than their response, though, was that of an owner of another factory who replied when a fire-prevention expert recommended that fire drills be held, "Let 'em burn. They're a lot of cattle, anyway."

The Triangle fire gave impetus to unionization and helped swing public opinion to the side of the labor movement. Frequent public memorials and fund-raising events were held to benefit the survivors. By most accounts, it was Rose Schneiderman, twenty-nine years old, tiny, red-haired, whose speech after the fire enlisted the sympathy of the uptown bourgeoisie—Jewish and gentile—and resulted in winning their support of the union.

The Women's Trade Union League (which brought workers and social reformers together) called a mass meeting after the fire to protest the factory conditions responsible for the tragedy. The meeting was held on May 2, 1911, at the Metropolitan Opera House, rented for the occasion by Anne Morgan of *the* Morgan family. Every seat was taken. There was a long list of speakers. Many proposals and resolutions were put forth and the audience eventually grew restless. Then Rose Schneiderman was called upon to speak. She walked to the podium, and stood silent for a moment. Holding back tears with difficulty, and in a whisper so that everyone had to lean forward to hear her, she began:

> I would be a traitor to these poor burned bodies, if I came here to talk good fellowship. We have tried you good people of the public and we have found you wanting. The old Inquisition had its rack and its thumbscrews and its instruments of torture with iron teeth. We know what these things are today: the iron teeth are our necessities, the thumbscrews the high-powered and swift machinery close to which we must work, and the rack is here in the fireproof structures that will destroy us the minute they catch fire.
>
> This is not the first time girls have been burned alive in the city. Every week I must learn of the untimely death of one of my sister workers. Every year thousands of us are maimed. The life of men and women is so cheap and prop-

erty is so sacred. There are so many of us for one job it matters little if a hundred forty-three of us are burned to death.

We have tried you, citizens; we are trying you now, and you have a couple of dollars for the sorrowing mothers and daughters and sisters by way of a charity gift. But every time the workers come out in the only way they know to protest against conditions which are unbearable, the strong hand of the law is allowed to press down heavily upon us.

Public officials have only words of warning to us—warning that we must be intensely orderly and must be intensely peaceable, and they have the workhouse just back of all their warnings. The strong hand of the law beats us back when we rise into the conditions that make life bearable.

I can't talk fellowship to you who are gathered here. Too much blood has been spilled. I know from my experience it is up to the working people to save themselves. The only way they can save themselves is by a strong working-class movement.

Rose and Bread and Roses

Rose Schneiderman had been born in 1882, in what was then Russian Poland. In 1889 her father, a tailor, emigrated to New York and in 1890 sent for the rest of the family: Rose, her mother, and her two younger brothers. Rose's father died of flu in 1892, leaving a pregnant wife with no means of support. The United Hebrew Charities came to their aid and when the baby was born, they sent one of the boys to the Hebrew Orphan Asylum in the city, and shortly thereafter committed the other boy to the Hebrew Sheltering Guardian Society, where Rose, too, ended up about a year later. Rose's mother earned the family's keep during her pregnancy and the baby's infancy in the way of the day—she took in sewing and a boarder.

When the baby was weaned, Rose's mother went out to work in a fur factory, and Rose left school to stay home and tend the baby. Her mother, concerned about Rose's education, made the difficult decision to send her to an orphanage, too, so she could be looked after and could attend school. Her mother sent the baby to live with a sister. Within a year, Rose's mother had the two girls living with her again in one small room in someone else's apartment. She not only worked all day, she brought home bundles to sew at night. On weekends the three of them would visit the boys at the Orphanage (they were now together) and spend the time picnicking or visiting a nearby farm.

The Schneidermans' living arrangements were not unusual for a family in their circumstances. Formal institutions were established to service immigrants in need, and informal *landsleit* institutions took on the dimensions of the Old World extended-family system. People who came from similar localities or were employed in the same or allied industries opened their homes to what the outside world might have considered strangers. But Eastern European Jewish immigrants were not strangers to each other. They were bonded compatriots. Every one of them had a friend or relative in need, and both formal and informal systems of self-help grew out of the immigrants' varied needs—economic, social, religious, and psychological. While the Jewish mother is often referred to as the cement that held the family together, the immigrant Jewish community's informal self-help institutions supplied the nourishment that reinforced Jewish identity. Everyone was or had been in similar circumstances. Formal institutions set up by the more affluent German Jewish community in response to the needs of the new Jewish immigrants were often thought of, by the initiators, as the mediator between the Old World culture and Americanization. Instead, surprisingly, they served as catalysts for continued bonding or solidarity among first- and second-generation Eastern European Jews. And the Jewish labor movement was partly the logical outgrowth of both the formal and informal system of self-help extended and enlarged upon in America, but nonetheless historically indigenous to the Jews.

When Rose rejoined her mother, she returned to school for two more years, thus finishing altogether four years of schooling in America. When her mother lost her job, Rose left school to help support the family. She was working at thirteen as an errand girl for a department store. She worked sixty-four hours a week for $2.16. Her mother supplemented the family income by taking in sewing. When Rose was fired from her job the Hebrew Charities found her another as a check girl in a department store for $2.25 a week. Rose's new job was definitely a step up for her because the store was located in a fashionable shopping area. Rose made friends with some of the older women working in the store, enrolled in night school, and also began attending a literary club that met regularly in a nearby settlement house.

So far, her life experience and her aspirations were typical of those of many Jewish immigrant girls of the time. She was romantic, hoped to meet "the right man" and get married. At the end of three years' employment in the department store Rose was earning but $2.75 a week. Rose, knowing many girls working in factories and earning much more than she, spoke to a family friend who made linings for caps. She got Rose a job as an apprentice in the factory where she was employed. As was the requirement of the time, Rose had to buy her own sewing machine and supply the thread. In *All for One* Rose Schniederman recalled that her mother was not pleased with her switch despite the fact that she was earning twice as much as she made in the department store, because her mother felt store employment was a more genteel occupation.

It was also a more comfortable and safer environment. While working at her first job as a cap liner, Rose's sewing machine was destroyed in a factory fire. The employers were, of course, insured, but the workers' own equipment was not. Rose had to replace the machine at her own expense, but this time she bought it on the installment plan, just in case. This incident in her early factory employment may have contributed to the passion of the speech Schneiderman made after the Triangle factory fire, for she, too, had been a victim of fire, though only her machine had been lost, not her life. Rose had also been an active participant in the "Uprising of the 20,000."

But the shirtwaist makers' strike of 1909 was not Rose's first involvement with the union. In 1903 a young anarchist, Bessie Braut, came to work in the shop. She pointed out to Rose that the males in the cap-making industry were organized and were the recipients of privileges not granted to women in the trade. Since the trimmers and liners were all women, Bessie suggested they get together and form a union, too. Upon learning about the possible benefits to workers who were unionized, Rose and two other women from her shop formed a committee and approached the United Cloth Hat and Cap Makers Union, volunteering to organize their shop. Told they needed twenty-five women from several shops in order to obtain a charter, the three of them set to work. They would wait at the doors of different factories, approaching the women as they were leaving for home and talking to them about the need for unionization—convincing them to join and go back to their shops and enlist other women. And they were most effective, for within a few days they had the required number of women and received a charter as Local 23. Rose was elected secretary.

Her first action on behalf of women workers took place in her own shop. Saturday all workers came in for a half day; the men would be paid as they left, but the women had to wait to be paid until four in the afternoon. Rose and some of the women decided to notify the owner that the women expected to be paid at the same time as the men. Rose presented the women's case and the following Saturday their pay was given out at the same time as the men's. Rose Schneiderman was then only twenty-one years old.

By 1904, just a year after joining the union, Rose Schneiderman was elected to the general executive board of the United Cloth Hat and Cap Makers Union. She was the first woman to hold such a position in the entire trade union movement. That year she was one of the leaders of her union's strike, which lasted thirteen weeks. And while it was an unusually bitter winter, Rose was on the picket line every day. During that strike, $6.00 a week was paid to all married male strikers. Women like Rose who were unmarried, but nevertheless had families to support, were not eligible for strike benefits.

She was obviously aware of the need for women to join together, for in 1905 Schneiderman joined the New York Women's Trade Union League and was elected vice-president in 1906. She divided her time between both unions, but in 1908 became a "professional" part-time organizer for the League and gave up her factory job, mostly because an anonymous benefactor (later revealed to be a Jewish woman, Irene Lewisohn) gave the League a "scholarship" for Rose. She was paid what she had been making in the factory working full time. She was to go to school during the day and devote her evenings to organizing for the League. But Rose's interest in the plight of the workers overtook her day life and she was soon involved in representing the League as a field worker—visiting all unions with women members and helping set up classes for women in which the principles of trade unionism were taught.

In addition, Schneiderman worked day and night in most of the apparel industry strikes. During the "Uprising of the 20,000," she went from city to city, speaking and raising funds for the strikers. She was also one of the organizers of the White Goods Workers' Union and was in charge of the Settlements Committee during the general strike of 1913. She was well-known by this time and seemed to be everywhere doing everything; she was fast becoming the labor movement's "token woman." Between 1914 and 1917 Schneiderman traveled from city to city acting as the business agent and general organizer for the ILGWU.

In addition to working directly for the ILGWU, she continued her affiliation with the Women's Trade Union League and in 1918 was elected president and organizer for New York and in 1919 was elected vice-president of the national WTUL. At the same time, Schneiderman was becoming involved in "outside" politics. She participated in the women's suffrage campaign and in 1917 was chairperson of the Industrial Section of the Women's Suffrage Party. In 1920 she became a candidate for the United States Senate on the Farmer-Labor Party ticket. The first Jewish woman to run for Senate, but not the first Jewish woman to become a national political figure, she had been preceded by Ernestine Rose and Emma Goldman. And others followed her.

Rose Schneiderman's interests proliferated and her activities widened as she became a prominent labor figure. During 1920–1929, Rose, who never had a "proper" education—never went to college—was a member of the board of directors of three institutions of higher learning: Brookwood Labor College, Bryn Mawr, and Hudson Shore Summer Schools for working women. In 1926 she was elected president of the national WTUL and served in that capacity until 1950, when the League was phased out. In 1933 she was appointed by President Roosevelt as the only woman member of the Labor Advisory Board of the National Recovery Act and served until 1935, when the Supreme Court declared the NRA unconstitutional. During this time Schneiderman also was elected honorary vice-president of the United Hatters, Cap and Millinery Workers (1934) and continued to hold that office until 1962, when she requested that she not be re-elected because of her age. In 1937 she was appointed secretary of the New York State Department of Labor and remained in that post until 1943.

Although Rose Schneiderman was a dedicated trade unionist all her life and rose to a position of power within the union, and although she often lauded the unions for their success in improving the working conditions for women, she had her complaints, too. In *All for One* she frequently comments on the position of women in the trade union movement and recounts incidents in which women were not treated as equals or competents, consulted on issues involving women's interests, nor even thought to have special gripes. She was contemptuous of the attitudes of the unions toward the New York Women's Trade Union League. She remarked:

The few unions that helped us looked upon us as children look upon their parents. The help they gave us was, first of all, not enough and second, it wasn't given graciously, the way we gave our services to them. There was never any question of our helping when we were needed.

This outlook somewhat sums up the general attitude of the unions toward its women members from the very beginning. The male union leaders were often patronizing and paternalistic. Even when women initiated their own actions, such as the "Uprising of the 20,000," men who were already in leadership positions directed the participants from the backroom, formed the negotiating board, and worked out the settlements. It is no wonder, then, that the women's interests were frequently not served. Moreover, history, which is most frequently written from the top down (and this is true of the history of labor as well), concentrated its attention on the mediators between demands and settlements rather than on the action and the participants. Therefore, much of the credit for the advances made by the union has been assigned to the members of the executive boards instead of to the organizers and activists. Without in any way demeaning Rose Schneiderman's contributions, and they are dazzling, she was not the only woman who made the union her life.

Schneiderman, like so many other women in the trade union movement, merged her professional life with her personal life so that her public and her private existence became one. And while these women managed to function effectively in the factory, the trade union movement, and the world of politics, they did not do so without paying a price. For most of the women who distinguished themselves in the movement remained single all of their lives, which means that they did give up some of the pleasures of a conventional family environment and security as well. Rose Schneiderman, for example, died alone in a nursing home in New York. While it is true she outlived most of her compatriots, still one wonders how she felt about her consignment to a nursing home even though it was self-chosen. Not that marriage and a family ensure commitment and care in one's old age, but there is the promise of it when one marries and these women forwent even that.

The single women who made the union their life by and large led work-oriented, successful, satisfying lives rich with social activities tied to their "professional" activities. Although they were members of the Jewish working class, their friendships included college-educated German Jewish women from the middle class as well as gentile women from the upper middle class, and eventually their relationships and their influence extended to the White House. Eleanor Roosevelt, an active member of the Women's Trade Union League, formed close friendships with many of the trade union women. In Joseph Lash's biography *Eleanor and Franklin* he says that, in fact, "Rose Schneiderman taught Eleanor Roosevelt all she knew about trade unionism."

Eleanor Roosevelt often entertained the union women she knew at Campobello and at Hyde Park. And when the Roosevelts got to Washington, they continued receiving and playing hosts to Rose and lesser-known Jewish women trade unionists. One, a former shop forewoman who was active in both the ILGWU and the Women's Trade Union League, remembers those days at the White House. In an interview with her she recalled that she and a group of women were invited to the White House for a weekend to discuss labor problems. Awakening from a dream in the middle of the night, she looked around her and exclaimed, "Imagine me, Feigele Shapiro, sleeping in Lincoln's bed." This woman had come to America as a young girl and had worked her entire life at a sewing machine, though she was also a labor organizer. She said she refused to be paid for her union work and organizing responsibilities. Many former women labor organizers interviewed proudly proclaimed that they "never received a cent" for their work. Perhaps they considered working for the union part of their social responsibility, or perhaps they could not think of themselves as serious labor careerists.

While many of the union women who remained single may have chosen to do so, still they were regarded by many men to be marriage rejects or failures. In *Union Pioneer,* Abraham Bisno, a labor organizer, discusses the single woman in the labor movement. Despite his radical politics and his disdain for marriage as an example of institutionalized exploitation of women, he still regards them as having a problem not only because they "did not succeed in establishing themselves in homes," but because they "seemed to have felt a need for a personal life in relation to men." But Bisno and most of his male comrades in the union and socialist movements got married even though they "charged those matrimonial relationships with barter and sale." Moreover, contrary to their "liberated" or "revolutionary" attitudes toward marriage and the family, most of them lived very conventional married lives which, in fact, provided them with certain comforts and allowed them certain freedoms. Bisno, in his memoir, for example, writes admiringly of his wife and the matrimonial setup that permitted him to be the political figure and very much the man while his wife remained the homemaker and very much the woman:

> She allowed me to spend night after night in public meetings and very seldom interfered with my being out, took the entire burden of the care of the children and the hard work necessary to keep up the household and the family.

There appears to be a rather wide gap between ideology and reality in the lives of the union and socialist men. For even though they criticized and assaulted the institution of marriage and the family, they structured their relationships along those very lines that they derided. If they married "liberated" women, by and large these women soon fell into the old patterns of behavior and accepted the traditional role of the married Jewish woman in contemporary society.

Most of the Jewish women who remained single and part of the labor movement led rich lives despite the absence of a long-term male relationship. Although they forewent marriage and its attendant security, they managed to set up a community of their own that offered some satisfaction. There is evidence, too, that a small number of Jewish women in the labor movement became involved in same-sex relationships, some of which lasted a lifetime. One of these couples even adopted a child. The intimacy and love between them probably grew out of their intense and time-consuming interest in the same cause. Men were not central to their lives; the union was.

Whether married or single, the common theme uniting East European-derived Jewish women was one of self-sacrifice. The Jewish mother put her children's needs first, and the Jewish labor movement woman put the community and workers' needs first. Since Jewish women were responsible for many of the labor laws that benefited the workers, and in addition provided the bread for their families, let us finally give them their much-deserved roses.

6

The Uptown Lady and the Downtown Woman
Two Kinds of Jews

When the Eastern European immigrants began arriving in large numbers in the major American ports, the American Jewish community of German origin was well-established and prosperous. In New York City, which was the largest Jewish community and immigrant center in the United States, the German Jews resided in the stately mansions of the middle and upper East Side and in the gracious apartments of the upper West Side. The new immigrants from Eastern Europe, on the other hand, settled in the Lower East Side, making it one of the largest Jewish "neighborhoods" in the world. From their geographical distribution in New York City, the two communities rapidly acquired their respective nicknames: the uptown (German) Jews and the downtown (Eastern European) Jews. While a few of the earliest Eastern European immigrants may have begun to move uptown by 1900, essentially the geographical division remained an ethnic one at least until the 1920s.

The worlds of the uptown lady and the downtown woman occasionally overlapped despite the vast differences in social background, economic standing, and cultural bearings between the settled American Jewish woman and her immigrant counterpart. The American Jewish community of German origin felt responsible—and was made to feel responsible—for its unfortunate Eastern European coreligionists who were streaming into American port cities and settling into voluntary ghettos.

Yet German Jews in America initially had opposed the mass immigration of Eastern European Jews to the United States. Immigration, the German Jews claimed, represented a surrender to the anti-Semitic policies of the Russian and Rumanian governments. Moreover, the willingness of the Jews to pick up and leave their countries of origin in the hope of escaping their oppressive conditions encouraged Eastern European governments to view the persecution of their Jewish subjects as the best way to solve their "Jewish problem"—by ridding themselves of their Jews. Finally, ever sensitive to the charges leveled by anti-Semites that Jews were not patriotic citizens and changed nationality at whim, American Jews contended, from their own position of security, that appearing to encourage immigration would lend credence to such anti-Semitic accusations. Central to the attitude of American Jews was the way they viewed the impact of mass immigration upon their own situation. They were convinced that providing for the needs of impoverished immigrants would bankrupt their institutions. More importantly, they feared that they would be identified, as Jews, with the lower-class and (at least in Western terms) uncultured immigrants, and blamed for the latter's social lapses. Their fears were not entirely unfounded, for the period following the Civil War witnessed the rise of social anti-Semitism in America. Jews were not admitted to the best schools and clubs. Exclusive resorts began to advertise openly that they were reserved for gentiles. By the 1890s, even the patrician members of "Our Crowd" were subject to the indignities of social discrimination because of their Jewish origins. Social discrimination against Jews was a product of the rapid upward mobility of the German Jews in the post-Civil War period when American society was becoming more competitive and less open. While Irish immigrants were ostracized as inferiors, German Jewish immigrants were excluded because they were seen as threatening. It was the claim of the wealthiest German Jews to social equality that stimulated social anti-Semitism.

Attempts by established Jews to control the flow of immigration failed. Nevertheless, when faced by the reality of mass Jewish immigration, American Jews responded to the social problems created by immigration by engaging in large-scale philanthropic projects—as no other religio-ethnic group did— to aid the immigrants upon their arrival and to facilitate their rapid assimilation. Before too long, it was hoped, the immigrant Jew from Eastern Europe would wisely choose to resemble his middle-class coreligionist of German origin.

While most Jewish philanthropic organizations were controlled by men, the women of the German Jewish community in America did not leave all contact with the new immigrants to their menfolk. The United Hebrew Charities was the first to aid Eastern European immigrants at the docks and in their period of adjustment. However, through their largest organization, the National Council of Jewish Women, women assumed responsibility for caring for the immigrant women and children, particularly those who were unescorted. In doing so, they had several goals in mind. Genuine concern for the unfortunate was, of course, their primary motivation. No less important, however, was their desire to influence immigrant women and to find useful and rewarding work for themselves. Though they occasionally encountered resistance from the male-dominated Jewish organizations, women, through their immigrant aid work, soon established a claim to serious consideration in the realms of Jewish philanthropy and social work.

The immigrant Jewish girl traveling alone and the immigrant Jewish woman with her worldly possessions tied into bundles and her young children in tow often had their first contact with the women of the American Jewish community as they stepped off the boat. A paid dock worker who spoke Yiddish was first stationed at Ellis Island in 1904. While her salary was subsidized by the Baron de Hirsch Fund, a philanthropic organization established by a prominent European Jewish financier, and by the United Hebrew Charities, the establishment of her position was first proposed by the New York section of the National Council of Jewish Women. Sadie American, the indefatigable president of the New York section, whose immigrant father had,

in gratitude to his adopted country, assumed his unusual surname, described the Council's motivation in a letter soliciting
financial assistance from the Baron de Hirsch Fund: "Many
girls," noted Ms. American, "are misled into immoral lives, and
others are subjected to great dangers because of the lack of some
directing and protecting agency at Ellis Island. . . . It is in order
that there shall be a complete chain of protection that the Council now asks to maintain a woman at Ellis Island . . . and the
Council would be very glad to supervise the work of such a
woman if you so desire . . . and also to engage other women's
organizations in assisting to fully protect and safeguard our
immigrant sisters." Concern for the vulnerability of unescorted
female immigrants thus underlay the Council's initial involvement with immigrant aid. And as Sadie American later noted,
the Council focused on helping girls and women because other
Jewish organizations ignored their special needs.

The aid extended by the Council was extensive and well
organized. From shipping companies and immigration authorities the Council received the names of all immigrant girls and
women aged fourteen to thirty-five, traveling alone or with children. Between 1909 and 1911, years of heavy immigration, assistance at the port of entry was proffered by a paid worker and
a staff of volunteers to 19,377 girls, 4,020 women, and 6,427
children. It was the Council's workers who often cut through
red tape and facilitated the entry of the immigrant woman who
had difficulty establishing her identity. In one case, a twenty-
two-year-old woman, Chaya Blocker by name, had arrived at
Ellis Island with a falsified passport under an assumed name,
perhaps because she had left her native country illegally. She
asked to be released to her fiancé. After speaking with him, the
Council worker discovered that the couple were, in fact, married, but the marriage certificate was in the woman's real name,
thus conflicting with her passport. By explaining the situation
to the inspector and producing the marriage certificate from the
woman's valises, the Council worker rapidly secured Chaya's
admission to the United States.

Besides their role as interpreters, the Council workers also
explained Eastern European living conditions to government

officials to prevent them from declaring immigrant girls fee-
bleminded (and hence unacceptable as immigrants) when the
girls' responses to questions were unintelligible to those who
were ignorant of their background and culture. In addition, the
Council workers searched for lost funds wired to immigrant
girls, sent telegrams and letters to locate their relatives, deci-
phered addresses, and found suitable lodgings for girls with no
relatives waiting to receive them. After World War I, the Council's Department of Immigrant Aid published a monthly bulletin, "The Immigrant," and a pamphlet entitled *What Every
Emigrant Should Know.* So renowned was the activity of the
Council that when Sadie American visited Rome in 1914 she
was asked to meet, and did meet, the Secretary of Immigration
of the Italian government to advise him as to what should be
done to aid Italian women immigrants.

Soothing the trauma of immigration for children was another
task assumed by the Council women. They found clothes for
and spent time with immigrant children who were detained
temporarily in the hospital at Ellis Island with such afflictions
as ringworm. Their intervention often extended beyond the
purely routine administrative tasks of most organized philanthropy. Typical of the personal dimension which the Council
workers brought to their task is the following case, from
November 1909, reported in the Council representative's own
words:

Ettel Eisenberg, forty-eight years old, came with her married daughter and children. While visiting the hospital, I
noticed the little girl, eleven years old, was crying bitterly.
She thought that her mother left her and went to Buffalo,
their destination. I was told that she kept on crying about
twenty-four hours. I spoke to the child and explained to her
that I saw her mother on the Island and that she is waiting
for her return from the hospital. I will arrange that the
mother can go to see her in the hospital. It took me quite
some time to calm the child. She could have lost her reason
if there wasn't someone to assure her that her mother is
here and she will be admitted together with her. The child

returned from the hospital about two days later and was admitted.

The Council's immigrant aid did not end at the docks but continued until immigrant women could make it on their own. The home visit became the primary method for assuring the successful adjustment of the Council's clients to American conditions. In 1911 a total of 7,466 home visits were made by Council volunteers to the homes of newly established immigrant women in New York, Boston, Baltimore, and Philadelphia. The home visit was designed to ascertain whatever problems the immigrant women were experiencing and resolve them, even when those problems involved interfamily relations. One home visitor, for example, brought to a rapid conclusion the exploitation of one young girl by the aunt with whom she boarded. The aunt had demanded that every cent the girl earned be applied to her board and prepaid passage, and had threatened her with deportation if she failed to comply. The home visitor could also channel immigrant women to the other services which the Council provided: vocational training, English classes for mothers, social clubs, and medical aid.

Because of her vulnerability, important decisions were not to be left to the judgment of the immigrant girl herself. For she might be swayed by momentary passion or lack the necessary information to make a rational choice. The Council worker's intervention sometimes extended even to the choice of a husband. In 1911, for example, the Council's paid representative at the docks, Betty Meirovitz, had second thoughts about permitting a young immigrant woman to be released to her male pen pal with whom she had fallen in love at first sight upon her arrival at Ellis Island. As Sadie American recounted the story to the Council's convention that year,

It was a little too quick to suit Mrs. Meirovitz, and the girl was allowed to land only on condition they were immediately married. . . . Then Mrs. Meirovitz got worried. . . . We found that he came from a little place in Pennsylvania. We had a correspondent there and so we wrote to

the mayor . . . Miss Schoenfeld came into the office and
. . . said: "I know somebody in that town!" She wrote to
her friend and we got back word that the man was all right.

By 1917 American immigration authorities would turn over all
girls arriving to be met by their fiancés to National Council
representatives, who would take them to City Hall for a civil
ceremony described as "for their protection."

It was this expression of the need to protect the immigrant
woman that strikes us today as paternalistic and patronizing.
These attitudes, however, were characteristic of much social
work of the time. By virtue of needing assistance, the client
forfeited her or his right to independence and self-determina-
tion. For the Council's Department of Immigrant Aid did not
limit its sphere of activity to Ellis Island. Immigrant aid included welcoming the immigrant girl, seeing that she reached
a proper home, guarding her against wrong, assisting her to find
work, providing wholesome amusement, and placing her in
touch with Americanizing agencies. Starting with the assumption that women and girls encountered special problems in
housing and employment, Council women developed a network
of activities and institutions to facilitate the immigrant woman's
adaptation to American life and to ensure that no evil befell her.

To the single girl traveling alone, the Council was most protective—probably overprotective. They were placed temporarily
in the custody of the Clara de Hirsch Home, administered by
the Council and subsidized by the Baron de Hirsch Fund. The
girls stayed an average of a few days while their prospective
homes with relatives and family friends were checked out. However, if their future lodgings were found wanting, the Home
located positions for the girls as domestics. Solicitous attention
to the living arrangements of the new immigrants continued
even after their initial placement. When three months had
elapsed, Council workers checked up to find out whether the girl
was well established and earning sufficient money to maintain
herself. As the Home reported to the trustees of the Baron de
Hirsch Fund,

In thus taking kindly charge of the girl, we feel that she gains a better foothold in this country. She escapes many pitfalls, and is not taken advantage of by the runner of the employment bureaus or by agents soliciting for illicit purposes.

The White Slavery Issue

The concern for the vulnerability of the impoverished immigrant Jewish girl was not excessive, once its cause is made clear. What really bothered the women of the National Council was the growing incidence of prostitution in the immigrant Jewish community. Indeed, the issue of white slavery agitated the Jewish community as a whole. For the Jewish establishment the involvement of Jews as pimps and procurers preying upon unattached immigrant girls was the major issue. Knowing that anti-Semites were quite prepared to publicize—and exaggerate—the number of Jews in the white slave traffic strengthened their feeling of communal responsibility to clean up this blot on the honor of American Jewry. The members of the National Council shared this sense of moral indignation and outraged pride, but there was another dimension to their involvement with the issue. As women, they sympathized with the prostitutes, whom they saw as the victims of the most vicious of male predators, both Jewish and non-Jewish.

As early as the late 1890s the already well-established German Jewish community in America became aware of the growing number of immigrant Jewish unwed mothers and the presence of prostitution among Jewish girls and women. By 1906, no longer able to wish away these problems, the National Council of Jewish Women, with a $10,000 donation from Therese Loeb Schiff, quietly took over the management of a Home for Wayward Girls on Staten Island. Realizing that the establishment of an institution designed to ameliorate a problem was publicly admitting its existence, and fearful of the consequences this might have on Jews in a period of rising anti-Semitism, the Council was careful to avoid drawing attention to the fact that the home was established specifically to aid immigrant girls. In a letter to the board of directors of the Baron de Hirsch Fund soliciting additional financial support for the Home, Sadie American pointed out:

> In our reports we do not call the work of Lakeview work for immigrants, as we consider this an unwise thing to do, but the facts are that only 20 percent of our inmates have been native born and only an additional 10 percent have been here over five years.

Of course, it is apparent that Sadie American was using the existence of anti-immigrant sentiment—which could easily be generalized into anti-Semitism—to secure money for the Home. In fact, she used a sophisticated form of political blackmail. Anti-Semitism was a real factor to be considered. For by November 1909, with the publication in *McClure's* magazine of an article, "The Daughters of the Poor," by George Kibbe Turner, the extent of Jewish involvement in prostitution became a serious public issue. While the article was overtly racist, Turner's underlying motive was exposure of the real connection between vice in the Jewish quarter of New York and Tammany Hall politics. But what overshadowed the political intent and content of the article was the detailed, though undocumented, description of a large-scale international business in women—Jewish women—controlled by Jewish men. Now, there is little doubt that the article contained some truth, but at that time spokesmen for both the uptown and downtown Jewish communities reacted defensively, attempting to deny it all. The downtown Yiddish press questioned the accuracy of Turner's article and noted the absence of hard evidence to support the charges. The uptown Jewish community was somewhat less defensive, being less directly involved. However, its official stance was that prostitution was "but rare among us," as Dr. Judah L. Magnes expressed it in an address he gave as rabbi at the fashionable Temple Emmanuel after the article appeared. A paid investigator was hired by the Kehillah (a Jewish communal organization of New York established by a coalition of uptown and downtown Jews in 1910) to look into the charges. He reported that he could find no evidence that organizations of Jews were responsible for the traffic in girls and women.

Despite these denials, there was some evidence that prostitution among Jewish women was not the rarity the voices of the community claimed it was. Rather, it appears that it was indeed a fact of life among immigrant Jews. For example, at about the same time that the controversy about Jewish prostitution became a public issue, the *Jewish Daily Forward* printed a letter in the *"Bintel Brief"* column from an ex-prostitute, describing how she, through the traditional marriage broker, ended up in "the life." Now a respectable woman with an offer of marriage, she was appealing to the *Forward* for advice about whether or not she should reveal her past to the man who wanted to marry her. What is striking in the *Forward*'s response (they advised the woman to tell the truth with the comment, "whatever will be, will be") is their acknowledgement that "letters from victims of 'white slavery' come to our attention quite often but we do not publish them. We are disgusted by this plague on society, and dislike bringing it to the attention of our readers."

Furthermore, had the charges been merely a fabrication there would have been no need to hold, in London in 1910, a Jewish International Conference on the Suppression of Traffic in Girls and Women, with Sadie American as the American delegate. The National Council of Jewish Women was, in fact, the only American Jewish organization to send a delegate both to that conference, which was convened by the British Jewish Association for the Protection of Girls and Women, and to the International White Slave Traffic Conference, also held in 1910 in Madrid.

The Council's participation in the struggle against white slavery was recognized as important and effective in countering the charges of rampant Jewish trafficking in women. As Sadie American remarked of the Madrid conference, "Underneath it all, like powder ready for the match, was the fear that the whole conference would be turned into . . . denunciation of the Jew because of the Jewish traffickers of whom there were too many, no matter how few they might be." That conference did not degenerate into an anti-Semitic session partly because of the

Council's efforts. Claude Montefiore, a prominent British Jew and head of the European delegation to the Madrid conference, publicly commented that Sadie American's presence had been exceedingly helpful. In general, he added, "it is remarkable how we have been able, by the very fact of our work being widely known and respected, to check and suppress any symptoms of anti-Semitism."

But Sadie American and the National Council were not trying merely to combat anti-Semitism through their concern with the issue of white slavery. They were trying to suppress Jewish involvement in the white slave traffic to the benefit of its women victims. In her opening speech at the London Conference, Sadie American tried to remove the blame from the victim of white slavery by attacking the double standard of sexual conduct prevalent at the time. Expressing ideas current among women involved in social reform, and particularly with the issue of prostitution, Ms. American maintained that the problem had always existed and that

unless at this Conference we lay the foundation of an education inculcating a single standard of morals, which shall raise men up to the standard demanded of women . . . we shall continue to have white slaves. When we learn to speak of a male prostitute in the same way socially as a female prostitute, then we shall have made a small beginning.

Moreover, on another occasion, she declared,

There are forces in girls as in men, sexual forces which are stronger than they are; and there are girls who cannot help themselves and will become prostitutes and for them nothing can be done until the world treats the whole question of prostitution differently from what it has; and if we recognize this we will not always condemn the woman of the streets.

She also disputed the Jewish community's denial of the problem by advising the conference members that she had been told by one of the members of the National Vigilance Committee that 30,000 prostitutes a year were being brought to the United States and that a large number of them were Jewish. She produced maps showing the towns and cities where prostitution was rife, and described the work the National Council was doing in those localities. The Council had a protective network of contacts in over 250 cities to whom they supplied the names of single immigrant girls about to arrive in their areas. This communication insured that the immigrant girls would be met by a Council affiliate in order to thwart potential abductors. The Council also had discussed with shipping companies in Hamburg and Bremen, the main ports of embarkation, the need to provide safeguards for female passengers. All of these precautions today seem unbelievable, but according to reports of the period, single immigrant Jewish girls *were* abducted into prostitution. They were also tricked by promises of marriage that never came about, fake marriages, false employment brokers who met trains and boats, pimps who hung around ballrooms offering friendship and affection. These were the most common traps, so the reports and official investigations show. Maude E. Miner's study of prostitution, carried out over a period of about eight years beginning in 1907, indicated that only about 25 percent of the girls "claimed that men had definitely brought them into prostitution." Miner, then secretary of the New York Probation and Protective Association, a governmental agency, added that "so generally did I find women associated with procurers and men living on their earnings, that I am convinced that practically every girl in prostitution has been exploited at some time by a trafficker."

Of course, Miner's study did not consist primarily of Jewish women, and she came in contact only with prostitutes who had been arrested. Statistics do show, however, that about 17 percent of arrested prostitutes in Manhattan from 1913 to 1930 were Jewish. In those years about one-third of the population in New York City was Jewish. Therefore, the number of arrested Jewish prostitutes recorded was proportionately less than the Jewish proportion of the population. Still, the Jewish community's self-righteous denial that prostitution had ever been or was now a significant social problem among the Jews was a reflection both of their idealization of Jewish women as well as of their insecurity in the face of anti-Semitism. Jewish women were recognized as sexual beings, but had always been held up as the moral pillars of family life.

Outside the Jewish community the Jewish prostitute herself was sometimes idealized by non-Jews—she was the turned-on tart. And she commanded a higher price than others, especially if she happened to have red hair. In San Francisco, at the turn of the century at least, the redheaded Jewish whore was all the rage, perhaps because she was seen as exotic. Nell Kimbrell, in her autobiography *Her Life as an American Madam,* states that "a redheaded Jew girl was supposed to be just pure fire and smoke." Reminiscing about "the life," Kimbrell talks about the "big Jewish madam" of San Francisco, Idoform Kate, who had herself been a whore. The proprietor of about twenty establishments, she stocked "each one with a genuine Jewish redhead, swore the hair was natural, and each girl a pious Jewess saving to bring a husband, mother, and father to the U.S.A." Kimbrell also verifies the existence of an underground railroad of Eastern European Jews who

bring in girls attracted by promises of honest jobs and so are lured into the trade, but I never dealt much with them. At least not until the rage for redheaded Jew girls took on the town. Most of the Jew girls were snappy but willing, and a great many of them soon became madams [another instance of upward Jewish mobility, probably resented within the trade]. They learn quickly, and they gave a john the act he was impressing them, driving them mad with his abilities as a man.

Encountering Resistance

Despite the Council's many activities on behalf of immigrant women and children and despite occasional instances of public recognition of the usefulness of individual Jewish women or of their organizations, the efforts of Jewish women to be recognized for their contributions to Jewish social work and philanthropy often met with resistance from the male leaders of the establishment. Even the immigrant aid activity of the National Council of Jewish Women was not universally welcomed. As Sadie American commented,

> There is no problem upon which the men in New York City would be so delighted to have the women out of, as this problem [of immigrant aid] because they have immense faith in their own ability to handle it, and have not such immense faith in the women's ability; in fact, they fear that the women will make a mistake and hurt all the Jews.

As the field of social work was increasingly professionalized, volunteer women, who had devoted themselves to the day-to-day matters of home visiting and interviewing of prospective clients, were dismissed scornfully by male professionals as "ladies bountiful," ignorant of the scientific bases of social work. This despite the fact that such organizations as the National Council had recognized the need to incorporate new "scientific" techniques into its programs and had realized that fundamental social problems could not be solved by philanthropy alone, and therefore had come to support progressive social welfare legislation, such as a minimum wage and unemployment compensation.

It seems that the contempt for the woman volunteer derives as much from her status as female as from her status as volunteer. For accompanying the professionalization of social work was the rise to prominence in the field of trained men, who saw their leadership as necessary to win popular respect for the new profession. From their perspective, as long as social work was regarded as woman's work, it would lack status and significance. Besides, the men who transformed Jewish social work from an avocation into a profession assumed that "leader" and "male" were synonymous. It is no surprise that male professionals tended to call upon other male professionals to appear as experts and discourse on the state of the field at conferences and conventions.

Jewish women did not accept their exclusion from leadership circles with equanimity. Sadie American was not atypical in her drive for funding on behalf of the National Council's Immigrant Aid Department and in her spirited defense of the immigrant woman and the Council volunteer. Minnie Low, prominent in Chicago's Jewish circles and president of the National Council of Jewish Charities (and the only woman on its executive committee of eighteen) was another fighter, this time for recognition of women in the social work profession. Noticing that the program for a Conference of Jewish Social Workers, to be held in Baltimore in May 1915, included no female speakers, she wrote a letter to David Bressler, the president of the National Association of Jewish Social Workers. "While you very graciously accord women the opportunity of being session chairmen," she pointed out, "you have not accorded a place to any woman—North, East, South, or West—on the program proper. According to your present program, there are thirty-one speakers named—all of your own sex. I am afraid that women count for very little as social workers in this world, judging by the opinion of you gentlemen in the East. . . ." Moreover, she concluded sweetly with the tentative suggestion, "I wonder if one of your three men on the program [dealing with industrial disputes] could not be replaced by [Belle Moskowitz a prominent social worker and later manager for Alfred Smith's campaign]."

Bressler's reply strikes a familiar chord. He was surprised at the tone of Miss Low's letter: "One might almost be led to believe from what you say that our Executive Committee deliberately went out of its way to slight the women social workers. As a matter of fact, we did not think in specific terms of men or women. When it came to making up the program, we thought of social workers. We selected the names in accordance with our best judgment. . . ." And the unstated conclusion: The best social workers just happened, in their view, to be men. Bressler softened the blow somewhat, for he conceded, "There are no doubt a great many able women in Jewish social work, but unfortunately we do not number them in our membership." Besides, he added, "we appointed three women social workers as session chairmen; a fair proportion, I think." Low's letter did put Bressler on the defensive, and he promised to have Belle Moskowitz appear on the program in some capacity.

After World War I, during which American Jewish women had followed the pattern of American women in general and had assumed greater social responsibilities and entered fields previously closed to them, the insistence on recognition of their achievements grew stronger. They were not ready to retire graciously from such fields of endeavor as overseas relief and immigrant aid, or from paid employment. As an article appearing in 1924 in *The Jewish Woman*, the organ of the National Council, declared, women had become firmly entrenched in jobs and demanded the right to stay in them. Rebekah Kohut had stated the case earlier for female volunteer organizations. At the Council's 1920 convention she proclaimed

> that the National Council of Jewish Woman . . . not only deserves, but demands recognition as an important body of women in all organizations that shall need their services in the future. . . . It begs to call to . . . attention . . . the relatively unimportant recognition and opportunity given to the Council during the war period to function . . . through boards like the Jewish Welfare Board and the Joint Distribution Committee [two major philanthropic agencies]. . . .

She concluded with the demand that the Council be included in the fund-raising campaign of the Joint Distribution Committee and that not less than $100,000 be appropriated to the Council for its philanthropic endeavors.

Within the Zionist movement as well, the women of Hadassah, who were often referred to as "diaper Zionists," served notice that they would not allow themselves to be manipulated and exploited solely as volunteer labor. Their opinions would have to be considered on political issues as well. In fact, their stance resulted in an open break with the male leadership of the Zionist Organization of America (ZOA). At the 1923 convention of the ZOA, the national board members of Hadassah stood behind Louis Brandeis, the American Zionist leader, in his conflict over policy with the supporters of Chaim Weizmann, the president of the World Zionist Organization. As a result, they were removed from their leadership positions by the president of the ZOA. The Hadassah women did not acquiesce quietly to this maneuver. Rather, they withdrew from the ZOA and staked a claim to independence by affiliating separately with the World Zionist Organization.

It can hardly be said that American Jewish women prevailed in their battle to achieve parity in funding and equal status as leaders within the American Jewish community. That battle has yet to be won. But under the leadership of German Jewish women they had begun, in the first few decades of this century, to recognize and proclaim their self-worth and their ability to understand and articulate the problems of women better than the male leadership of American Jewry.

Conflict of Cultures

The struggle of the uptown women to win from the male Jewish establishment recognition of women's leadership abilities and social contributions went unnoticed by their immigrant clients. Despite the sympathy and concern the German Jewish women expressed for their Eastern European sisters, even for the victims of white slavery, the immigrant women could not help but view their uptown coreligionists with mixed feelings. The uptown lady was, after all, the social worker, upon whom the immigrant woman often found herself dependent for largesse. No matter the noble sentiments that may have motivated her activity—and those too were suspect—the uptown lady was an intruder, sometimes welcome but more often not, in the lives of the immigrant women.

The chasm of ethnic and class differences stretching between the German Jews and the Eastern European immigrants was difficult to bridge. Jewish immigrants with socialist leanings were particularly wary of the motives of the German Jewish women philanthropists. When the National Council began its work with immigrants, Cahan's socialist *Jewish Daily Forward* trumpeted sarcastically: "Rich Jewish aristocratic women from

uptown will shower favors upon and seek remedies for downtown Jews." The Council women, suggested the *Forward,* gave
aid "with their hands bedecked with diamonds more to show
their alabaster fingers with well-manicured nails than really to
save the unfortunates."

It was easy for immigrant Jews to find reason to mistrust
the German Jews, both men and women. The uptown *Yahudim* (Jews), as they were called by their immigrant coreligionists in formal Hebrew rather than familiar Yiddish to mock
their pretensions to social superiority, saw the Eastern European immigrants as culturally inferior and socially backward.
They viewed their religious traditionalism and European customs at best as distasteful. Certainly those customs and beliefs
merited neither respect nor understanding. It is ironic, of
course, that it is the Eastern European immigrant Jews and
their children—and not the German Jews—who have contributed so many talents to American literature, popular music, and the entertainment field in the twentieth century. With
no social standing to jeopardize and everything to gain, they
took risks in the new and marginal entertainment industries.
And the intensity of cultural conflict and alienation they experienced as "new Americans" became material for serious literary creation.

The negative attitudes toward immigrant Jewish culture were
shared by women as well as men within the German Jewish
community. Even the women of the National Council assumed
that the cultured woman was a rare find in immigrant settlements. In 1896 they discussed the possibility of recruiting those

few who have the leisure, refinement, and education . . .
which would guarantee them as desirable members of our
organization. The cultured Russian American Jewesses
must feel the isolation of their position keenly. Cut off, in
a measure by intellectual superiority from the majority of
their expatriated fellow-countrymen and by social distinctions from their equals, we should ask them to join with us
in furthering our common cause. . . .

This tentative invitation to the elite of the immigrant Jewish women was viewed smugly by the Council women as a measure of their own tolerance and good nature. For they concluded with satisfaction, "Let us who often suffer from exclusion be not exclusive."

Nor were the Council women alone in their attitudes. In fact, they were rather tolerant for their class and social situation. It was not uncommon even for a German Jew who fancied himself liberal—such as the prolific writer and academic Ludwig Lewisohn—to describe an immigrant relative (by marriage, one would imagine) in his memoirs in highly unflattering terms:

> My aunt . . . though a woman of some kindly qualities, was a Jewess of the Eastern tradition, narrow-minded, given over to the clattering ritual of pots and pans—"meaty" and "milky"—and very ignorant.

Kashruth—the rules of keeping Kosher—loomed large as a symbol of cultural backwardness for German Jews, most of whom were adherents of Reform Judaism, which by the mid-nineteenth century had pronounced *kashruth* as incompatible with the enlightened spirit of the age. The fact that keeping kosher was an important cultural as well as religious value to most immigrants was ignored by their upper-class benefactors. The Clara de Hirsch Home for Girls, for example, did not provide kosher food for its immigrant residents until 1913. This lack of sensitivity to immigrant sensibilities—and this is only one example of many—could only serve to antagonize the immigrants, who felt, and rightly so, that their culture and freedom of choice were being denied.

Immigrant Jewish writers reflect the perception, widespread among immigrant Jews, that they were looked down upon by the uptowners. Whenever immigrant novelists portrayed upper-class German Jews, they drew portraits of the ultimate snob, self-satisfied and shallow. Perhaps in that way they were able to avenge themselves and their community upon their generous, but fault-finding, benefactors. For the portraits—more precisely caricatures—of the German Jews were etched in sarcasm and a kind of reverse snobbery. The German Jews are depicted as socially aspiring parvenus whose sense of superiority is rooted in their inability to perceive that culture transcends class lines. Shalom Asch's Mrs. Hirsch, in his novel *East River,* embodies the smugness that the immigrants felt characterized her type. She opposes her son's friendship with an immigrant youth and particularly his plan to visit his friend downtown: "But after all," she admonishes, "to visit him at his home, to spend so much time in that awful neighborhood! They are Eastern European Jews, I understand, from Poland. I'm sure they have very little culture. . . . There is nothing you can learn there. . . ."

The charity woman also fell victim to the acid pen of the immigrant writer. She was better known to immigrant families than the men who determined policy in Jewish welfare agencies, for it was she who came into immigrant homes to investigate eligibility for aid and to look for evidence of moral failings. It was she who passed judgment on the way immigrant parents were adapting to American customs and rearing their children. No wonder then that the figure of the female social worker, volunteer or professional, became a stock character in immigrant literature. In *Hungry Hearts* Anzia Yezierska took careful aim at the "friendly visitors" from charitable agencies who arrived, unannounced and inauspiciously, when families receiving aid were enjoying a rare luxury such as fresh eggs or cake. These charity ladies did not refrain from deploring the ostentatious style of living followed by their immigrant clients. In one scene the friendly visitor departed only to return with inspectors who accused an immigrant Jew, Shmendrik by name, of deceiving the agency. Thereupon the heroine, Sophie, expresses the rage and frustration of impoverished immigrants dependent upon the benevolence of fellow Jews who loudly proclaim their social and cultural superiority but reveal, to their immigrant clients at least, their moral inferiority. She shouts,

"You call yourselves Americans. You dare call yourselves Jews? . . . This man Shmendrik . . . who you made to shame like a beggar—he is the one Jew from whom the Jews can be proud. He gives all he is—all he has—as God gives. He *is* charity. But you—you are the greed—the shame of the Jews! Allrightniks, fat bellies in fur coats! What do you give from yourselves?"

A passage of this sort gives expression to the immigrants' perception of the superiority of their concept of charity, and of their Judaism, over the bureaucratic philanthropy and attenuated, assimilated Judaism of the *Yahudim.*

Why is so much of the resentment immigrant Jews felt and expressed in literary forms directed at the German Jewish women rather than at the male leaders of the community? There are several possible explanations which we might explore. First is the issue of accessibility. If immigrants had any face-to-face contact whatever with uptown Jews, it was more likely to be with women than with men, for women were more involved in the day-to-day activities of social work, settlement house service, and "friendly visiting." In these contacts, it was the women who expressed in ways both subtle and direct the disdain the entire German Jewish community felt for the Eastern European immigrants. Jacob Schiff and other uptown leaders were simply too remote to attack, except as political personages whose policies could be opposed. Moreover, given both American and Jewish cultural stereotypes, women were simply easier to mock than men. For women had no power and could be taken less seriously.

Too, it was in the sphere of personal relations that discrimination was felt most keenly, and women were considered to hold dominion over that sphere. Men were simply too busy with more important worldly affairs. Thus, it is uptown women who are portrayed as discouraging friendship and romance between their children and the children of immigrants. It is they who are depicted as gossips, carping during their teas and luncheons about the ill-mannered and ignorant immigrants who were being coddled by charity boards. " 'I've been quite worried about the future of our girls,' " one of Yezierska's obese society matrons muses at a luncheon. " 'Are we using all our knowledge and wisdom to help them face life? Face the conditions in which they are born and to which they must adjust themselves? You all know the besetting vices of the working class are discontent and love of pleasure. Have we the right to give our girls luxuries they can't afford when they're out of our care?' "

All of these biting literary characterizations of German Jewish women notwithstanding, the reality of the relationships between uptown and downtown women is far more complex and ambiguous—on both sides—than might be supposed. With all the disdain that uptown women felt for the immigrant women's lack of social graces and middle-class culture, they did come to the aid of their poorer coreligionists, often with generosity of spirit and with a genuine sense of caring. Furthermore, some American Jewish women were moved by their confrontation with the rich Jewish culture of the immigrants to a reexamination of their own Jewish identity. Emma Lazarus was not alone in coming to the realization, through her empathy with the plight of the immigrants, that the Jews were a people, not merely members of a religious denomination. Concern for and activity on behalf of the immigrants was also important to the development of Henrietta Szold from rabbi's daughter to indomitable Zionist leader. With their vibrant ethnic culture the immigrants challenged the idea propagated by Reform Judaism that Jewish identity was purely a religious matter.

For their part, immigrant women may have resented the contempt of some uptown volunteer social workers. They may have confused the middle-class German Jewish woman whom they encountered with the wealthy German Jewish socialite— both appeared rich to ghetto dwellers. They may also have mocked what they saw as the shallow Christianized Judaism of many of the uptown ladies. But their resentment and mockery were mixed with envy and admiration. After all, the immigrant women wanted to be real Americans too, just like the Jewish women of German descent. They wanted to take advantage of whatever opportunities America offered to leave their poverty behind and move up—and away from the ghetto—into the middle class. It seems most likely that their model for the American lady was the German Jewish woman. While the middle-class gentile American woman may have been the ultimate ideal of

Americanization, the German Jewish woman was not as remote to the immigrant Jew. With a bit of social mobility the Jewish woman of Eastern European origin *could* (and in the 1920s and 1930s *did*) mingle with German Jewish women in such organizations as the National Council of Jewish Women and Hadassah.

Certainly, the immigrant Jewish woman had few other models to emulate. The non-Jews whom she met in the ghettos of America's cities were newcomers like herself—Irish, Italian, and gentile Eastern European working-class women, many of whom were of peasant origin. In other words, the very type of non-Jew upon whom she had always looked down. The uptown women were also but two or three generations removed from their immigrant origins. They were the hope of what was to come for American Jewish women. And, in fact, the first area of settlement—in New York City, the tenement slums of the Lower East Side—was abandoned by immigrant Jews and their children as soon as finances permitted. By 1930 the Lower East Side had a Jewish population of only 121,000 in comparison with 353,000 only fourteen years before. From the immigrant ghettos Jews moved to the more comfortable apartment buildings and modest two-family houses of what is commonly called by sociologists the second area of settlement. The most successful immigrants skipped the second area of settlement altogether and settled alongside prosperous German Jews in the more luxurious apartment houses of major American cities and after World War II in suburban developments—both traditionally labeled areas of third settlement. Only the most recent immigrants and those who had stumbled in the race for upward mobility remained behind in the tenements. Most of the daughters of the immigrants eventually followed their German Jewish benefactors uptown and into the middle class.

7

Pearls around the Neck, A Stone upon the Heart
The Changing Image of the Jewish Woman in Literature

In Europe her name was Malke, and Malke in Hebrew means queen. . . . Malke was close by, a friend, a mother, a provider. . . . I wondered if her husband was a man of learning, and why they had changed her name to Molly. Malke was a queen; Molly didn't mean anything.

—YURI SUHL, *One Foot in America*

The period of the great immigration of Jews to America, which spanned approximately four decades, was not static. By 1930, just after the last major wave of Eastern European Jews reached here, *shtetl* values of the older settlers had already clashed with the realities of life in America. The experiences of later arrivals both recapitulated and were modified by those of their predecessors. What jobs were available, at what age the immigrant came, whether or not *mishpochah* (family) were waiting to greet the newcomers, what institutions and organizations had already been formed to accommodate them—all of these factors, as well as personality and character traits, contributed to the ease or difficulties with which immigrants found their way and made their separate and collective lives in the New World. The impact on individuals of the tension between preserving the old ways and adjusting to the demands of Americanization cannot be adequately assessed, though the *"Bintel Brief"*—the letters preserved from the advice column of the *Jewish Daily Forward* and published in English translation in 1971—does yield a store of information on the troubles of acculturation.

If the *"Bintel Brief"* is a repository of daily problems, the literature produced by first- and second-generation writers reflected something more: the struggle for assimilation and the aspiration to join the middle class, not only economically but culturally. It was impossible to be transported to the New World without being transformed.

It is true that questions are raised by scholars today about the efficacy of the "melting pot" and the submersion of ethnic identity. By itself, of course, the literature produced by the Jews in America cannot provide quantified measurement of what life was actually like; nor can it answer finally whether integration into the available social and economic American patterns signaled true assimilation.

Of the whole of Jewish literary works produced in America from the turn of the century to World War II, we touch here only on some of those dealing with how Jews perceived the problems generated by new opportunities and situations, and the accompanying changes in the expectations of themselves and one another. In one sense, the most immediate impact of dislocation was on men, who were faced with displacement of their traditional idealized roles as scholars and pontificators of wisdom and Talmudic law, and who had to cope with secularized—mostly economic—modes of success and failure. In literature, as character types become stock figures and certain conflict situations become standardized, we find a significant gauge of the concerns, conflicts, and aspirations of the community. For instance, two stereotypes that emerge in American Jewish fiction by the turn of the century are the pious scholar and the *nouveau riche*. Both these types exaggerate certain traits and appear in literature more frequently than they did in the actual population. Nonetheless, as exaggerations, they dramatize a crisis within the Jewish community—the conflict between tradition and the new ways. The figure of the reflective, otherworldly scholar struggling to survive in the harsh grind of the sweatshop and bemoaning his children's apostasy, serves as a metaphor for the tensions inherent in new conditions. Even the "secularized" factory workers could identify with the feeling of isolation from the core values of the *shtetl*. And the figure of the ostentatious, overdressed "allrightnik" flaunting his riches before the impoverished "greeners" points up the dilemma between safeguarding a mode of life that had historically sustained Jewish separateness and the lure of "making it" in America and putting on the cloak of Americanism.

That these characters—the success and the scholar—were generalized as polar opposites reveals the perception of the writers and their readers toward what surfaced for them—consciously or unconsciously—as one of the major strains of their transplantation as a people.

For East European women, the expectation in America that men would bear the economic burden for the family had dramatic implications. Their own status and position in the community was increasingly to be associated with and to derive from the drive toward success and assimilation of their husbands. If their men rose in the world and wanted to disassociate themselves from the lower class, the women had to make striking adjustments. They were to become American middle-class women (or what they conceived of as American and middle class), a role that differed from their usual one in both its traditional image of women and required behavior. Eastern European women had to transform many of the personal qualities that had distinguished them for generations. Nothing in their previous experience molded them for the part of the "lady." Their mothers had been accustomed to sharing in the support of the family and being "out" in the world, and had developed personalities in keeping with these functions. They were robust and direct, energetic and independent. Female charm, in the recognized American sense, was not one of their virtues. As

Hutchins Hapgood, a journalist who observed the New York ghetto around the turn of the century, put it in *The Spirit of the Ghetto*. Jewish women

> lack the subtle charm of the American woman, who is full of feminine devices, complicated flirtatiousness, who in her dress and personal appearance seeks the plastic epigram, and in her talk and relation to the world an indirect suggestive delicacy.

In order to become assimilated, Jewish women would not only have to abandon their places in the work force; they would also have to undergo a radical transformation in personality and appearance in order to make up for their deficiency of "feminine devices" and "delicacy."

This transformation—how it was brought about and how women reacted to it—is complex and difficult to trace. While it is relatively easy to measure the outward signs of assimilation into the middle class—economic standards, schooling, demographic movement, and cultural participation—it is more difficult to determine the effects of these changes in psychological terms. How did Jewish women change in the same generation and between generations, how did their husbands and children feel about them, and how indeed did they feel about themselves?

Literature provides a rich resource for answering such questions—if not absolutely, at least as a perspective from which to view a people's way of defining itself. In the fictional representation of reality, there is often a good deal of information about intangible matters such as cultural ideas and assumptions, matters which are especially important in attempting to understand the process of assimilation. The critical focal points of writers reflect back to readers the shifting images of themselves. While the images may not correlate directly with what was happening to individuals, they do reveal a group picture of life—even if the poses have been deliberately struck and exaggerated to preserve not how life actually looked but how the participants wanted it to be recognized as looking.

The Jewish Woman in America

Sleep Faster, We Need the Pillows

Fortunately, East European Jews began to record their experiences in America soon after their arrival. The publication of Abraham Cahan's *Yekl, A Tale of the New York Ghetto* in 1896 marked the beginning of popular American Jewish fiction. Many of the early novels and stories are merely loosely fictionalized semi-autobiographical works written not for the larger American audience beyond the ghetto, but as communications for a given circumscribed group. As such, they reveal the continuity as well as the already evident disruption of *shtetl* values. In stories about the period of earliest immigration from Eastern Europe, when women's wage earning was still vital to the family, the energetic women who used their skills and ingenuity to help support their families are cast as admirable characters. For example, in Cahan's *Yekl,* Gitl, a young woman who comes to join her husband, begins work immediately. She cooks for boarders, managing to produce dishes that win high praise even before she has mastered the intricacies of the unfamiliar American cooking range. As portrayed by Cahan, Gitl is far steadier than Yekl, who, in his rush to become a "real American," loses his sense of ethics and fails to meet his family responsibilities. He throws Gitl over for a woman who is more "up-to-date," but Gitl survives and remarries, this time to a man who appreciates her fine qualities.

Observers looking back on this period recall women protecting their families against the repercussions of their husbands' impracticality. In some cases, these were men who had no prior commercial experience, although the proportion of male immigrants who had actually pursued Talmudic scholarship as a full-time occupation was doubtless smaller than their representation in literature would have us believe. Nevertheless, fictional women frequently had to intervene in situations where their husbands found themselves at a loss. Mrs. Davidowsky in Shalom Asch's novel, *East River* (1946), is typical of these characters. She has to restrain her husband from extending too much credit to patrons of their small grocery, for the neighborhood is a poor one, and she knows that creditors will not be so lenient with them as they are to their customers. Like many fictional characters (and real women) at this time, Mrs. Davidowsky controls the flow of cash, keeps the books, and generally has a more realistic sense of the state of their business than her husband.

In first-generation families, the women, whether they earned money themselves or not, usually also managed the household finances, collecting the wages of various members of the family and parceling out funds for rent, food, clothing, and other necessities. Edna Sheklow recalls that her mother made important decisions about matters like moving and buying and selling businesses without consulting her husband, who was busy making and trying to market various inventions. In her memoir, *So Talently My Children* (1966), she describes the vicissitudes of a fund the children had started to buy their mother a new coat, a hoard which the mother uses as revolving cash to take care of emergencies. By the end of one month, she has managed to turn up a surplus of $7.96, utilizing a method of cash flow management that many a CPA could profit by. Although her English is faulty, her arithmetic seems to be infallible.

> From The Coat money I took six dollars for buy the boys' two pairs shoes. To the dollar it was left, I put from the electric was lower this month, another two dollars, and from the last time when I used The Coat money to pay for the library books the children lost. I found the books when I cleaned under the stove, and the library returned the money, no questions asked. From this money, I paid the fine the books were overdue and to what was left, I put the remainder from last month's rent, he [the landlord] took off you [her husband] fixed the pipe under the sink he didn't have to call a plumber. . . .

Women like Edna Sheklow's mother were simply recreating an Old World household pattern that made family finances women's responsibility.

None of Their Business

This pattern changed, however, as a number of Jewish men began to make financial gains, some of them so rapidly and so successfully that their exploits became a cause for amazement and a source of legend. But even before their financial stability was assured, many Jewish men discouraged their wives from working, for they had observed that in America ladies remained at home. This attitude appears in stories of the early period. In *Little Aliens,* Myra Kelly's book of stories about the Jewish ghetto published in 1910, one man declares that his wife " 'shall never no more work on no factories. She shall stay on the house und take care of the baby und be Jewish ladies.' " His daughter must not work either, but must attend school " 'for learn . . . all them things what makes American ladies.' "

As men became the sole breadwinners, they consolidated their domination over their families as well. Not surprisingly, there is evidence that men resented women's retaining whatever share of power they had traditionally held, despite the fact that many men were still depicted as somewhat shortsighted and impractical. Nonetheless, women who held on to the old attitudes and attempted to maintain control of financial matters were seen, at least in literature, as domineering and emasculating—or as laughable.

In *The Rise of David Levinsky* (1917), Abraham Cahan's prophetic novel about a garment manufacturer's precipitous success, we see the problem being played out. Cahan, a socialist and the founder of *The Jewish Daily Forward,* was a close, critical observer of assimilative processes within the Jewish community. Though he sympathized with the struggles of impoverished immigrants, he did not always understand the plight of women in particular and how difficult it was for them to adjust to their new roles. Like the rest of the Jewish community, Cahan changed his attitude toward women's economic function. Twenty years before *David Levinsky,* in *Yekl,* Cahan admires the energetic and adaptable Gitl for her contributions to the family's support, but in the 1917 novel he presents the wife of the tailor Chaikin as a dominating shrew because she, too, wants to insure her family's economic well-being by acting as her husband's business agent. Cahan adds a satirical twist to his portrait by making her absurd. The woman in fact knows even less about business than her husband does.

David Levinsky, who needs the skilled but tractable tailor Chaikin as a partner in his new garment manufacturing firm, has little patience with the tailor's wife. In the novel, Levinsky describes the scene that ensues when he brings the Chaikins a check representing their first income:

I had barely closed the door behind me when I whipped out the check, and, dangling it before Mrs. Chaikin, I said radiantly:

"Good evening. Guess what it is!" . . . I let her see the figures, which she could scarcely make out. Then her husband took a look at the check. He did know something about figures, so he read the sum aloud. Instead of hailing it with joy, as I had expected her to do, she said to me, glumly:

"And how do we know that you did not receive more?"

"But that was the bill," her husband put in.

"I'm not asking you, am I?" she disciplined him.

"But it is the amount of the bill," I said, with a smile.

"And how do we know that it is?" she demanded. "It's you who write the bills, and it's you who get the checks. What do we know?"

"Mrs. Chaikin! Mrs. Chaikin!" I remonstrated. "Why should you be so suspicious? Can't you see that I am the most devoted friend you people ever had? God has blessed us; we are making a success of our business; so we must be devoted to one another, while you here imagine all kinds of nonsense."

"A woman will be a woman," Chaikin muttered, with his sheepish smile.

The unfeigned ardor of my plea produced an impression

on Mrs. Chaikin. Still, she insisted upon receiving her husband's share of the profits at once in spot cash. . . .

Explaining to her that they must reinvest their profits in the business in order to make it grow, Levinsky appeases her temporarily. Eventually, however, she persuades her husband to abandon Levinsky and go into business on his own. When Chaikin fails, she tries to convince Levinsky to take her husband back into partnership, arguing that, by rights, part of Levinsky's now flourishing business belongs to Chaikin. But Levinsky will accept him only as an employee.

Cahan's portrayal of Mrs. Chaikin reflects the impingement on the Jewish community of the prevailing American attitude: women do not belong in business. He tries to justify this position by proving that women are temperamentally and mentally unsuited to commercial matters. In keeping with this, he shows novelistic approval for women who embody qualities more aligned with American cultural ideals for womanhood, portraying sympathetically female characters who accept their domestic role and do not attempt to interfere in business. In the novel, Levinsky falls in love with Dora Margolis, a beautiful, sensitive woman who has the misfortune to be married to a crude businessman who fails to appreciate her. Levinsky is charmed by Dora's refined sensibilities and eagerness to learn. Dora has perfected her English by poring over her daughter's schoolbooks, and when Levinsky comes to call on the Margolises, Dora and her children sit with the men for a while, chatting and showing off their newly acquired language. Then Margolis, deciding it is time to talk business with Levinsky, turns to Dora and says brusquely, " 'Well, we have had enough of that. Leave us alone, Dora. Go to the parlor and take the kids along.' " Unlike Mrs. Chaikin, Dora obeys her husband without protest. Her departure symbolizes an important moment for Jewish women in America. It marks their abdication of a long-held position of power. Cahan faults Margolis not for excluding his wife, but for failing to appreciate her "womanly" qualities. He seems to set Dora up as a model for all Jewish women, who should strive for cultural accomplishments as one of the highest expressions of true womanhood.

The bias against women in business is also apparent in the stories of Montague Glass, who chronicles the financial adventures of a typical garment-center partnership in *Potash and Perlmutter* (1909) and *Abe and Mawruss* (1911). The wives of the two manufacturers rarely appear at "the store" where the men conduct their wholesale dress business. The women remain at home, shadowy creatures who are expected to run their households and whose opinions are sought only in matters of etiquette. When Abe Potash's wife ventures to make a suggestion about the business, Morris Perlmutter objects: " 'Is your wife running this business, Abe, or are we?' "

In Glass's stories, women have limited roles in the business world, acceptable only as bookkeepers or as models. In *Potash and Perlmutter* the two men are confronted with a "lady buyer" from an out-of-town store. They find themselves at a loss about how to entertain her. Glass describes Miss Atkinson:

> To be sure, she was neither young nor handsome, but she had all the charm that self-reliance and ability give to a woman . . . "A good, smart business head she's got," Morris said to himself.

Glass's condescending tone reflects the assumption that any woman must first be evaluated on the basis of her sexual qualifications (a test Miss Atkinson barely passes because she is charming but not beautiful), criteria that would not, of course, be applied to a man in the same position. Morris is surprised to discover that Miss Atkinson is competent because he seems to assume that if a woman is to get on in business, she must transcend some sort of innate gender limitations and succeed in spite of them. The attitude of Glass and his two characters represents a significant shift from the belief common among East European Jews that women were entirely competent— indeed, relied upon—to operate in the commercial world, and indicates an acceptance of the American scheme of male financial domination.

A Man's Place

If Jewish women were to be ladies, however, their husbands would have to become adequate breadwinners. Many women found themselves out of the labor market—either by choice or because of unfavorable conditions—before their husbands were fully prepared to cope with the realities of supporting a family by themselves. Although in the old country women expected little money from their husbands, particularly if the men spent a good deal of time studying, in America they felt justified in making higher demands.

Nevertheless, women's expectations of their husbands changed only gradually. At first, many women clung to the Old World system of values, and did not want their husbands to work at degrading tasks, preferring to go to the sweatshops themselves. This attitude is displayed by one of the characters in Asch's novel, *The Mother,* published in 1930 but set in the early days of immigration. Sarah Rifke weeps bitterly when her husband goes off to work for the first time. " 'Alas! That I have lived to see this day when Anshel, the celebrated Reader of Scripture, must become a sewer of shirts like a common woman!' " Sarah Rifke believes it is still her duty to be supportive of her husband's piety, as she was in the old country. But in Alter Brody's play, *Rapunzel* (1928), Rifkah Sorel complains to her daughter Malka, " 'The only kind of business your father ever did was exchanging stories with the synagogue do-nothings——.' " When the father comes home with a piece of wood for Malka (who is blind) to touch, Rifkah rails:

> "Did you hear what a loving father you have, Malka? He brought you a piece of wood from the park. Maybe if he had gone out and brought some bread for his children like other fathers, you wouldn't be blind now."

Rifkah Sorel is questioning not necessarily the value of piety, but rather the viability of a life devoted to religious observance in the midst of a society that is not organized to support it. The Talmudic scholars, of course, argued that in the land of the Golden Calf, piety was needed more than ever. In Anzia Yezierska's novel, *Bread Givers* (1925), Reb Smolinsky claims that all the Jews of the neighborhood should support him.

> "Am I not their light? The whole world would be in thick darkness if not for men like me who give their lives to spread the light of the Holy Torah."

And if not the community, then at least his family:

> "Has a father no rights in America? Didn't I bring my children into the world? Shouldn't they at least support their old father when he's getting older? Why should my children think only of themselves? Here I give up my whole life, working day and night, to spread the light of the Holy Torah. Don't my children owe me at least a living?"

But his daughter Sara has different ideas:

> "What have you ever done for your wife and children, but crush them and break them? I ran away from home because I hated you, I couldn't bear the sight of you."

One of the few women writers of the immigrant period, Yezierska was more outspoken than most of the male writers on many issues, particularly the hypocrisy of Jewish patriarchy. She was clearly writing from her own experience, for in an autobiographical piece, "How I Found America" (1920), she describes her father as "a Hebrew scholar and dreamer who was always too much up in the air to come down to such sordid thoughts as bread and rent." The burden of support fell on the rest of the family; like many other Jewish immigrants, Yezierska herself began working as a child, and her mother took in boarders.

Yezierska felt that a man who lived entirely off the labor of his wife and children was being unfair to them, no matter what his spiritual qualifications. In her novels, she takes a critical tone toward impractical men like her father. But she also censures the misguided wives who encourage men to remain parasites by revering them, indulging their tastes (literally, giving them the food from their own mouths), and failing to demand that the men go out to work.

Enforced Leisure

If women are no longer needed to help support the family—indeed, their working indicates financial ineptness on the part of their husbands—then what is their socially accepted function? Upon them devolve, in Thorstein Veblen's terminology, the duties of "vicarious leisure and consumption." They must continue to run their households, but they must do so in a manner that reflects the wealth of their husbands. The more leisure (obtained by being freed from domestic tasks by servants) they have, the more they enhance their husbands' reputation. Their role as ladies must complement their husbands' financial position; by conducting themselves properly, they become assets.

Jewish women received innumerable subtle social cues to guide them into their "proper" role as ladies and to reinforce appropriate behavior. Nevertheless, the transformation of these women from *balebostes* to ladies did not progress smoothly: many of the expectations and duties of the new role conflicted with those of the old. Whereas the old role had certain built-in community validations, the new one had no reassuring precedents.

One of the most pervasive female stereotypes in the literature of this transitional period is the foolish, overdecorated wife of the parvenu. She is a caricature of a "real" lady, her pretensions to refinement laughable, and her shallowness and materialism contemptible. While reflecting disdain, this characterization gives no hint of the feelings of insecurity, inferiority, and frustration that lay beneath those be-jeweled exteriors.

A typical character appears in Michael Gold's *Jews Without Money* (1930):

> Mrs. Cohen, a fat, middle-aged woman, lay on a sofa. She glittered like an ice-cream parlor. Her tubby legs rested on a red pillow. Her bleached yellow head blazed with diamond combs and rested on a pillow of green.
>
> She wore a purple silk waist, hung with yards of tapestry and lace. Diamonds shone from her ears; diamond rings sparkled from every finger. She looked like some vulgar, pretentious prostitute, but was only the typical wife of a Jewish *nouveau riche*.
>
> "Ach, what a headache! How I have to suffer with these headaches! The doctor says it is because I eat too much, but I only eat as much as my friends. But maybe it's because last night I ate a big ten-course dinner at Lorber's that cost three-fifty. I should not eat in restaurants. My cook's food is better for me; I am of a very nervous nature. She is a good cook; a wonderful cook; we pay her eighty dollars a month, and our grocery and butcher bill is almost one hundred and fifty a month. In a good house one should have a good cook. This house cost my husband twenty thousand to build. It is the most expensive house in Borough Park. What did you pay for your waist?"
>
> "Two dollars," my mother stammered.
>
> "Pfui, I thought so!" said the aristocrat. "For so little money one can only buy rags. My waists never cost me less than thirty or forty dollars; and my shoes twelve dollars; and my hats from fifty dollars up. One must dress well in our position. . . .
>
> [We] left Mrs. Cohen on her martyr's sofa, alone with her headache and her dull, dollar-sign fantasies.

Gold allows Mrs. Cohen no margin: She seems to be completely selfish, parasitic, and arrogant. He had nothing but contempt for what he regarded as the evils of capitalism, but he confused Mrs. Cohen with her husband. *She* was not an active participant in the system which oppressed families like Gold's and the other poor immigrants he knew, but the passive inheritor of it.

Abraham Cahan seems to have been more aware of the position of women as chattels, understanding that they had no direct access to wealth (or even a livelihood), but could obtain it only through marriage. His perceptiveness is evident in a scene in *The Rise of David Levinsky,* as Levinsky watches a crowd of women greeting the "husband-train" arriving at a Catskill Mountain resort.

There were a large number of handsome, well-groomed women in expensive dresses and diamonds, and some of these were being kissed by puny but successful-looking men. "They married them for their money," I said to myself. An absurd-looking shirtwaist manufacturer of my acquaintance, a man with the face of a squirrel, swooped down upon a large matron of dazzling animal beauty who had come in an automobile. He introduced me to her with a beaming air of triumph. "I can afford a machine and a beautiful wife," his radiant squirrel face seemed to say. He was parading the fact that this tempting female had married him in spite of his ugliness. He was mutely boasting as much of his own homeliness as of her coarse beauty.

Prosperity was picking the cream of the "bride market" for her favorite sons.

The emphasis on material acquisition among these newly prosperous Jews is often explained in terms of their former hardships. One commentator, Ruth Glazer, describing what she calls "The Bronx Style" in which "[everywhere] straight lines are abhorred," attributes extravagant taste in clothing and furniture to years of deprivation. Housewives buy thick mattresses and heavily upholstered sofas to blot out memories of folding cots and hard-backed chairs. The rococo abounds: "[even] the draperies fall in little puddles on the floor in the prevailing manner indicating (1) opulence—'Let it be a little longer'—(2) superlative housewifery—'Her floors are so clean you could eat off them.' "

What we have witnessed is the movement from one phase to another in the treatment of women in fiction. From lives lived at stage center they have been removed to the periphery, where their primary role is to adorn men's lives. Whether women actually thought of themselves as existing virtually offstage and whether men thought of them that way is doubtful. The family continued to be the central American Jewish experience, and in the family the mother usually set the standard for the quality of that experience. Many families remained far too poor to lay waste their powers in getting and spending—just the getting and making do with what they got exhausted the energies not only of the parents but of the children as well. Nor were all Jews equally involved in the processes and fevers of assimilation. Quite a number who became wealthy did not leave the ghetto, preferring instead to remain where a network of institutions and organizations enabled them to be engaged in what they considered a proper Jewish life. But literature often looks to the good story, to sources of conflict and tension, for its themes. And Jews who were on their way up socially and economically, Jews who were in transition, were ripe subjects for literature.

But the works we have turned to as source material should also not be considered as removed from actuality by the desire of writers to draw upon the more dramatic elements of life. Without a basis in reality, at least to the extent that it touches a responsive chord in readers, literature would be an empty exercise. In the treatment of American Jewish women who were edged into the consumer society by the dynamics of assimilation and prosperity, writers were revealing their critical attitudes toward these women, but they were also showing, perhaps without quite realizing it, that these women hadn't entirely benefited from their forced idleness.

Particularly after World War I many Jewish families were enjoying a prosperous life and a new life-style. The domains of men and women had become sharply defined: men were to earn the money, women were to spend it.

In the proportion of Jewish families that became more entrenched in middle-class life, the separate functions of husbands and wives drove them apart. In Thyra Winslow's story, "A Cycle of Manhattan" (1923), an immigrant couple, Mr. and Mrs. Rosenheimer, become increasingly alienated from one another. Rosenheimer the greenhorn is transformed into Ross the flourishing manufacturer. The more prosperous he becomes, the more preoccupied he is with business matters.

> He never took much part in the family life. . . . He was not interested in "women's doings," and could ignore whole evenings of conversation about people and clothes. His business was the one thing he cared to talk about—his family knew nothing about business. . . . So, unconsciously, he drew apart more and more.

As a result of their exclusion from the financial realm, women who had once been independent became progressively less autonomous. Although they had themselves once controlled the family monies, or remembered that their mothers had done so, they were reduced to asking permission of, or at least consulting at length with, their husbands before making any major expenditures. The asking may have been merely symbolic, for most of the men were probably pleased to be able to make generous provisions for their families, thereby enhancing their own status. Nevertheless, the gesture had to be made. As Winslow describes Mr. Rosenheimer, "[He] paid bills with a little grumbling. He handed out money when necessary. He greeted all luxuries with something about 'hard times.' He accepted all innovations with apparent disregard."

Out of necessity, Rosenheimer's wife and daughters become manipulative. Winslow recounts several schemes they devise to coax him into spending more than he thinks he wants to for larger, more elaborate quarters, automobiles, and other fashionable items. Their most compelling arguments are based on telling him what a "man in his position" ought to do. They can advise him, but he retains the ultimate authority, and Mrs. Rosenheimer never challenges him directly. Men like Rosenheimer denied their families nothing; nevertheless, the bargaining process must have been demeaning to their wives (and, to a lesser degree, to their daughters).

The Woman in White

Appearance and manner rapidly distinguished the lady from other women. In order to fit her model, East European Jewish women had to learn the details of American taste, fashion, and etiquette. But the renovation of dress and carriage often created internal crises in them, for many of the new ways conflicted with deep-set customs, both cultural and religious. Moreover, the ideal now being presented grew out of a concept of women quite different from the one that had prevailed in Eastern Europe.

Family pressures and broader social forces molded women who might otherwise have been reluctant to change. In the earliest days of immigration, it became apparent that women who could not create at least a veneer of Americanization ran the risk of being rejected by their husbands. Gitl's experience in Cahan's *Yekl* was probably not unusual. The moment she steps off the boat, Jake (Yekl) begins to criticize Gitl's appearance. She has gained weight; her clothing and wig are dowdy.

She was naturally dark of complexion and the nine or ten days spent at sea had covered her face with a deep bronze, which combined with her prominent cheekbones, inky little eyes, and, above all, the smooth black wig, to lend her resemblance to a squaw.

Gitl also earns Jake's disfavor by clinging to orthodox customs. She protests against shedding her wig, and against riding a horsecar on the Sabbath. Many immigrant women, especially those who were older when they arrived, resisted pressure to change, but Hutchins Hapgood observed,

If she is young when she comes to America, she soon lays aside her wig, and sometimes assumes the rakish American hat, prides herself on her bad English, and grows slack in the observance of Jewish holidays and the dietary regulations of the Talmud.

Shedding their wigs became for women, as trimming their beards was for men, the outward symbol of concession to American godlessness, a step that was often regarded in the literature as a great spiritual loss to the Jew involved. But many women feared that their husbands would desert them if they refused, a fate they adjudged, apparently, to be more severe than the wrath of God.

The image of the lady permeated American notions of womanhood, cutting across ethnic and class lines, even to women toiling in the sweatshops and scrubbing tenement floors. These women could not remain oblivious to the image, for their husbands and children brought it to their attention. In the Reznikoff *Family Chronicle* (1929), for example, Nathan urges Sarah Yetta to use the profits from their barely flourishing millinery business to buy clothes for herself instead of sending money to her family in the old country. " 'We must have decent clothes, for you know the saying, According to your clothing people greet you when they meet you.* I can't dress up and have my fiancée go about in old clothes. I want you to be better dressed than I.' "

Children, too, brought home from school notions of what "real American" families were like. Female teachers set standards which all children applied to their mothers, and girls in particular applied to themselves. As Samuel Ornitz describes one little girl in his memoir *Bride of the Sabbath* (1951):

*Another version of the same proverb gives the meaning an ironic twist: "You are ushered in according to your dress; shown out according to your brains."

The immaculacy of her teachers entranced the child, angels not humans, who need not go to the "twilight" (the delicate ghetto way of saying toilet) like mortal Jews. By contrast the women of her own world looked revolting, unkempt drudges chained to a washtub or stove by a brood of kids, always on edge from the need to perform daily the miracle of loaves and fishes.

When they visited their classmates, ghetto children also caught glimpses of women so exotic they hardly seemed like mothers. Elizabeth Stern recalls one such meeting in *My Mother and I* (1917). She had thought her mother the best of all the women in the ghetto, but

> [all] my standards fell before the vision of the strange mother I saw at the party given by my classmate. I could not believe that the woman who opened the door to my knock was my friend's mother. A woman in *white!* Why, mothers dressed in brown and black, I always knew. And this mother sang to us. She romped through the two-step with us, and judged the forfeits. I always thought mothers never "enjoyed," just worked. This strange mother opened a new window to me in the possibility of women's lives. To my eyes my mother's life appeared all at once as something to be pitied—to be questioned.

For younger women like Stern, becoming the "woman in white" seemed a real possibility, a reason to fight their way out of the ghetto. But for older women whose immediate struggle for survival outweighed all other considerations, this ideal, if it was responded to at all, more than likely engendered feelings of inadequacy and self-hatred. These feelings persisted even when practical matters no longer prevented them from paying more attention to themselves.

The American woman knew how to dress well and decorate her home in the latest style. According to fictional accounts, Jewish women who did not want to stand out began going regularly to beauty parlors, tried to diet, polished their English, and even tried to change their voices and inflections. Mrs. Rosenheimer in "A Cycle of Manhattan," for example, failed in her efforts to lose weight, but

> [her] voice had toned down, during the years. . . . When talking with those she considered important, she even tried to put an elegant swing into her sentences. Usually, though, her voice was accented, ordinary, uninteresting. She still made errors and sometimes quite a lot of sing-song crept in.

Mrs. Moscowitz, an immigrant in Meyer Levin's *The Old Bunch* (1937), was "up to date and you would never see a Yiddish newspaper in her hands." She scorns the "greenhorns" who resist fashion or forbid their children to follow it. Her flat is elegantly decorated at the height of the twenties mode with deep sofas, Spanish shawls, and luminous fringed lampshades.

The American lady was also attuned to subtle nuances of etiquette, so that she could complement her husband's business or professional skills with her own social expertise as hostess, companion, and authority on manners. In Glass's *Abe and Mawruss,* Abe and Mawruss compare the social development of their respective wives. Discussing the selection of an appropriate wedding gift for one of their customers, Abe tells Mawruss:

> "You draw the check and get your Minnie to buy it. She's an up-to-date woman, Mawruss, while my Rosie is a back number. She don't know nothing but to keep a good house, Mawruss. Sterling silver bumbum dishes she don't know, Mawruss. If I took her advice, you wouldn't get no bumbum dish. Nut-picks, Mawruss, from the five-and-ten cent store, that's what you'd got." [*sic*]

The skills of the lady, as Abe points out, must extend beyond simple cooking and cleaning.

Of all the descriptions of the processes of assimilation in American Jewish literature, Winslow's "Cycle of Manhattan" is one of the most minutely detailed; she is particularly painstaking with regard to her female characters. Within a year after Mrs. Rosenheimer's arrival in America, she has discarded her *sheitel* (wig) and begun to wear American clothes. She "made the innovation in a spirit of fear, but when no doom overtook her and she found in a few weeks how 'stylish' she looked, she never regretted the change. She was wearing curled bangs, good as the next one, before long." Mrs. Rosenheimer's mother retains her *sheitel* and her old ways (confirming Hapgood's observation), feeling increasingly useless and out of place as the size of their dwellings, the splendor of their furnishings, and the efficiency of their staff increases in proportion to Mr. Rosenheimer's earnings. As each Rosenheimer daughter comes of age, she demands a new car, new quarters in a different neighborhood, and decorations dictated by the fashion of the moment. When each sister discards the items chosen as fit and proper by the one before her, she declares that *her* values are absolute and timeless, legitimizing them by reference to some vaguely identified aristocracy. But Winslow implies, by the repetition, that it is ludicrous to regard the vagaries of fashion as absolutes. In her final ironic scene, the Rosenheimer son proudly brings his family to the charming studio he has just "discovered"—the ghetto tenement where the family lived when they first came to America.

In *My Sister Goldie* (1968) Sara Sandberg also recalls the speed with which taste changed in the twenties, and the frantic efforts many Jewish matrons made to keep up with it. Her Aunt Dora never missed an opportunity to criticize her sister's (Sara's mother's) failures to keep up with fashion. Viewing the Sandbergs' new apartment, she comments:

> "It seems so funny to see all this fancy French furniture —when the whole world is now using English!"
> Mother looked stricken.
> "All my French furniture like yours"—Aunt Dora twisted the knife—"I gave to the Salvation Army. It's too bad," she said pointedly, "you don't ask me, like you used to, before you went to all this expense to furnish a home that it's already passé."

It was with such matters that a "lady" was to be concerned.

The Price of Privacy

Although Jews were moving out of first-settlement areas like the Lower East Side (by 1920 only one third remained there), the new neighborhoods were often as homogeneously Jewish as the ghetto. The social patterns in the wealthier ones imposed a sense of separation that had generally been absent before. Need for one another compelled ghetto inhabitants to become socially intimate. In more spacious flats and apartment buildings, relationships with other families became more formalized and less intense.

In stories about the movement "uptown," there are numerous examples of "downtown" women who felt uncomfortable in their new surroundings. When Sarah Rifke, in Asch's *The Mother,* becomes ill shortly after moving, she is reluctant to ask her new neighbors for help because she feels they are "not her kind. How could she possibly impose on them! She was a mere stranger to them." In Konrad Bercovici's story "The Newly Rich Goldsteins" (1919), the family moves to Riverside Drive (a part of New York that became popular among wealthy Jews during the first few decades of this century), and "Mrs. Goldstein wandered about the rooms as if in a prison." Both she and her daughters feel so ill at ease that the family finally moves back downtown. One of Yezierska's characters, Hannah Breineh in the story "The Fat of the Land" (1920), is not so fortunate. She, too, feels out of place when she and her children become transplanted; she is nervous around her servants, embarrassed to be caught eating in the kitchen (but she dislikes the dining room), and has trouble with the doorman in her elegant apartment building. But when she tries to return to her downtown friends, she no longer feels at home with them. Caught between two worlds, she becomes a victim of her own wealth.

After the Rosenheimers' second move uptown in "A Cycle of Manhattan," Mrs. Rosenheimer realizes that what she misses is the neighborhood chatter.

> Here in the Bronx you had to be "dressed" all the time. In
> Seventy-seventh Street you could go out in the morning in
> your housedress with a basket and spend a pleasant hour
> or so bargaining with the shopkeepers and talking with
> friends, always meeting little groups you knew. . . .

But "allrightniks" considered it gauche to bargain; the butcher
store had become a showcase for displaying one's wealth, so that
a woman would be embarrassed to ask for inexpensive cuts of
meat or quibble over prices when the other matrons around her
were ordering finer cuts and paying what was asked without
question.

Mrs. Rosenheimer feels isolated from her neighbors, but it is
not until the family's fourth move, to the newly fashionable
Harlem, that she decides to conform to the standards of behavior of the women around her.

> The neighbors seemed so cold and distant. As if she wanted
> to know them! Wasn't her husband the owner of a factory
> —with more money than any of them, more than likely?
> Yet they minced by her, as if they thought so much of
> themselves. Well, she could put on airs, too!

According to Winslow, snobbery became contagious. Women
created distance between one another out of defensiveness,
creating barriers in response to those they perceived to be
erected against them.

After making generous donations to several charities, Mrs.
Rosenheimer is asked to join their committees. She shuns organizations primarily run by gentiles who, she thinks, are critical
of her, but she begins to feel comfortable with other Jewish
women in her situation. "She was proud to know women who
a few years ago would have ignored her." But she has only
acquaintances, no intimates. In stories such as "A Cycle of
Manhattan," Jewish women begin to find substitutes for the
ghetto friendships they have relinquished; they are not, however, joined by mutual trust and support, but kept apart by
suspicion and competition.

Hours To Spend like Money

The wives of these *nouveaux riches* often felt uncomfortable, too, because they had been catapulted into lives that had no traditional and supportive underpinnings. They were dispossessed as wage earners by their husbands, and as housekeepers by their servants. Uneducated in the pursuit of culture and the performance of organized philanthropy (the "higher" forms of leisure in which women born into the upper classes found respite from their *ennui*), these newly made ladies found themselves with a great deal of unused time and energy. They could not find outlets in careers, however, for the American ideal of the lady, coupled with Jewish tradition, dictated that a woman's first duty was to her home—at least formally, even if she turned its actual running over to servants. This ideal filtered down even to women who could not afford all the accoutrements of an upper-middle-class life-style, and it was this conception of the woman's role, combined with a labor market unfavorable to women, which discouraged them from seeking work outside the home.

The lack of education and the onus of involuntary leisure were, incidentally, problems that Jewish women shared with middle-class gentile women during this period. Leah Morton, a second-generation Jewish woman who was herself trained as a social worker, noted this fact in a mixed grcup of women she encountered. These were not college graduates. They were

not rich women, not society women. Their husbands were middle-class Americans. But they did not, any of them, do one thing more for their homes, their marriage, than lend their bodies to them. Their interests were quite outside. They were not even interested in "culture," in clubs for reading or studying. They lived for pleasure. [Out of ten women] two had children . . . and [one] woman's child was, fortunately, in boarding school.

It was not that these women were pleasure-loving that amazed me, though. It was that here were women with leisure, who did not even know it, who slept life away. The only thing that was actually real to them was bridge. It was dreadful to watch their faces at bridge, pinched and hard and bitter in defeat. Twelve years ago [she is writing in 1926] to be a bridge fan meant having a career.

Without the bustle of ghetto life, wealthy Jewish women had to learn ways to distract themselves from the emptiness of their days. Mrs. Rosenheimer's routine was probably typical of women of her class: she spent the mornings directing her household, and the afternoons driving or shopping with her daughters. It is impossible to determine whether or not most women found this sort of life satisfactory, although one is inclined to think not, for in fiction, memoirs, and journals of this period, there are numerous references to symptoms of malaise.

Some observers, like Michael Gold writing about Mrs. Cohen, assumed these women were merely hypochondriacs. Chune Gottesfeld, in his autobiography, *Tales of the Old World and the New* (1964), recalls talking to a doctor who treated

rich patients with fancied ailments—women who have become nervous through sheer idleness, not knowing what to do with themselves. They are easily helped. He sends them to the mountains, where they busy themselves with playing cards or indulging in amorous adventures, and they come back hale and hearty. Their doctors are acclaimed as miracle workers.

These women were viewed more sympathetically by organizations like the National Council of Jewish Women, which had first gained strength by recruiting German Jewish women of leisure in the 1890s, and who now turned to their East European sisters. The Council saw itself charged with two distinct but equally important functions: to bring help to those who needed it, and to provide an outlet for the energies of middle-class women. In the pages of its monthly publication, *The Jewish Woman,* the role of this type of woman was frequently discussed. One writer in the October 1926 issue described her as someone who "attended 'modern' lectures, discussed 'modern' problems, spoke knowingly of the 'vital things of life' and came home with an empty heart and a ruffled temper." The solution this writer suggests is that the woman put meaning into her life by recommitting herself to Judaism.

Rose Brenner, who devoted most of her life to the presidency of the National Council, was quoted in *The Jewish Woman* in 1925 as saying, "We see it as a religious duty to secure for every Jewish woman in this land the opportunity for a freer, fuller, happier life, which membership in the Council, and only that, can afford her." Council members would be rewarded with the "consciousness of living a bigger, fuller, and more purposeful life," pursuing activities which, presumably, their husbands— and society—could not fail to approve. However narrow women's sphere, the Council urged them to exploit their power: "Woman's present-day position in home, church and state is such all over the world that her united purpose would wield the destiny of our times. The care of the race is woman's business." In response to the plight of the middle-class Jewish woman, the Council was drawing on the ideology of nineteenth-century American reformism—that social work was an extension of women's traditional concern with nurturance and morality. Although the care of the race was not new to Jewish women, participation in organized philanthropy was. In Eastern Europe, charity had largely been administered by men, so it was now men who, although they were eager for their wives to become Americanized, were reluctant to concede that their wives' charitable work was imbued with the same high purpose as their own. This issue arises between one couple in Isidor Schneider's *From the Kingdom of Necessity* (1935). Rachel is preparing to attend a Women's Auxiliary meeting, and Morris grumbles,

> "Don't you gossip enough all day? Must you sew it up with a holy thread at night?"
> "In the Lord's House," said Rachel, "we don't gossip any more than you men do. What a fine kosher pig's knuckle you are to stand here before me and talk about gossiping in the Lord's House! Do you think we don't know what you men talk about between prayers!"

Morris's brother Joe contributes the observation that a women's meeting is like a "synod of matchmakers"; Rachel and Morris resume their debate.

"In the synagogue we talk about more important matters than you would understand," said Morris. "Nowadays, when women step in where they shouldn't, I suppose it will become a sin to be pious."

Joe interjects that men's gossip is about more important things than women's.

Unmeltable Women

Some immigrant women never made the transition from the East European role to the American one. American customs and ideas had no impact on them. These women looked upon their Americanized friends and families with amazement, distaste, and awe. Many of them were, of course, mortified when their children broke with old religious customs. Some watched in silence; others admonished and criticized the younger generation, trying to force them to conserve the rituals the elders considered so important. These women could never accept a life of ease, but insisted on cooking, cleaning, and caring for children even when servants were hired to do these tasks. First-generation women had had much less opportunity than men to learn English, for they had either never worked outside the home or had left the work force after a few years to marry or raise children. Because they spoke and understood only Yiddish, they felt uncomfortable in new social situations, and often confined themselves to the family. This was especially true for older women who moved with their married children to suburbs where they could find few *landsleit* to befriend.

In *My Mother and I*, Stern recalls that her mother could not become accustomed to her home. She was unused to "sitting" in the living room, and was surprised to find her old copper fish pot used to hold leaves. She thought it unusual to use a kitchen only for cooking, and felt alien and lonely in a house with a maid for company, but no neighbors. As Stern describes it,

> [In] this short visit of hers, for the first time mother saw me as that which I had always wished to be, an American woman at the head of an American home. But our home is a home which, try as I may, we cannot make home to mother. She has seen come to realization those things which she helped me to attain, and she cannot share, nor even understand them.

Stern and her mother disagreed with regard not only to housekeeping practices but to child rearing. She contrasts her philosophy with her mother's:

> Little son [her child] has been taught that he must play without demanding help or attention from adults about him, that "son must help himself." In Soho [the ghetto] little boys are spanked and scolded and carried and physicked and loved and fed all day and night. . . . Mother called to little son a quaint love name, and he turned to her with his bright smile, understanding her love tone. Then he quietly turned away from her to his toys again. . . . Perhaps she was thinking of what she had thought to find him, like one of the children of her own motherhood, dear burdens that one bore night and day. . . . Here was her grandchild, they were together, it was true. And her grandchild had no need of her. She felt alien, unnecessary.

Some of the theories about child rearing that were popular when Stern was writing in 1917 did not support the protective, closely attentive practices common among first-generation women. While Stern marked the differences between her mother and herself, she seemed to accept them as inevitable, and did not attempt to convince her mother to change.

Not all children who were trying to assimilate were as tolerant as Stern of their parents' "old-fashioned" ways, finding them embarrassing in front of "real American" friends. An incident in Asch's novel *The Mother* reflects this attitude. Sarah Rifke's son Solomon is married in an elaborate ceremony held in a fancy hall.

> [Sarah Rifke] felt it her sacred duty to deport herself at the wedding in the good old way, as it was done in the town where she was born and raised, to serve the guests at table, and to coax them to eat heartily of everything. But Solomon would have none of it. He was filled with mortification because of her and under his breath sternly bade her under no circumstances to move from her place.

In Yezierska's story "Fat of the Land," Fanny is ashamed of her mother. She argues with her brothers about taking their mother to the theater.

> "You know mother. She'll spill the beans that we come from Delancey Street the minute we introduce her anywhere. Must I always have the black shadow of my past trailing after me?" . . .
>
> "I've tried harder than all of you to do my duty. I've *lived* with her. . . . I've borne the shame of mother while you've bought her off with a present and a treat here and there. God knows how hard I tried to civilize her so as not to have to blush with shame when I take her anywhere. I dressed her in the most stylish Paris models, but Delancey Street sticks out from every inch of her. Whenever she opens her mouth, I'm done for. You fellows had your chance to rise in the world because a man is free to go as high as he can reach up to; but I, with all my style and pep, can't get a man my equal because a girl is always judged by her mother."

Although Fanny thought she was singularly cursed, a second-generation man admits that he, too, felt ashamed of his "old-world" mother. In *The Story of My Psychoanalysis* (1950), John Knight relates that when the other men at his midwestern university invited their mothers to act as chaperones at fraternity dances, he would always make excuses for his mother, saying that she lived too far away to come. But, he comments, "I am sure I blamed Mother more than she deserved for her failure to become completely Americanized." His analyst points out that although Knight held his mother responsible for the fact that she did not become self-sufficient by learning English, at least part of her failure was due to the fact that he and the rest of the family did not really help her to become acclimatized. " 'Was there really any reason why you and the other children couldn't have tutored her, or hired a teacher for her? After all, with the work of caring for a household, a large family, and a demanding husband, you couldn't expect her to attend school, too.' " Knight agrees, " 'We were so dependent ourselves that we couldn't organize any project that would make our mother really independent.' " He comes to realize, further, that he adjudged his mother as "overly sentimental" because of socially imposed criteria.

In novels, unassimilated women adapted to their alien situations in various ways. In Charles Angoff's *Journey to the Dawn* (1951), for example, Alte Bobbe (old Grandmother) remains a matriarchal figure within the family whose members continue to seek her counsel in all important decisions. Although she never compromises on her principles, her refusal to capitulate to American mores does not vitiate her power. She never becomes a family oddity to be ignored or derided.

When first-generation women were rejected by their children, they often became, in consequence, isolated and withdrawn. Knight's mother, for example,

felt that the children lacked a sincere interest in her culture. This reinforced her own unsureness about maintaining contact with the Old World. When she realized that I had finally developed a mature and genuine desire to know her entire life story, she poured out her autobiography and the complete genealogy of her large family and my father's. It has made her happy to find that her early life has meaning for me.

In *The Old Bunch* Levin describes the situation of a rejected mother which did not resolve itself so happily. The first-generation Mrs. Greenstein lives in continual conflict with her daughter Estelle. She fears that Estelle will marry a "goy," and is appalled by Estelle's open displays of sexuality. When Estelle has her hair "bobbed," her mother tells her not to come home. Estelle finally moves out to escape her mother's interference. Mrs. Greenstein, who has never learned English and fears even the telephone, withdraws into a peculiar state; in a grotesque depiction of motherhood, she exaggerates her menial functions but refuses to relate on a personal level to her husband and son.

> Lately she had taken the role of servant altogether upon herself. She spent her whole time alone in the kitchen, coming out only to work for them. She had even placed a cot in the kitchen, and there she slept. At meals, she would bring food to the table and retreat.

She suffers from the delusion that her husband has taken to visiting prostitutes and explodes at him:

> "Yes, look at me! This is what you have done to me! Is the old scarecrow lacking in beauty for you? My greenhorn Yiddish is not stylish enough for you! Go, go to the parlors, my beau, perhaps you will find your own daughter there for a dollar!"

In Mrs. Greenstein's mad ravings, there is the haunting undertone of truth, of the crisis of spiritual and psychological loss which many women suffered, even in the midst of newly won affluence.

The President of America

The daughters of immigrants, the women of the second generation, raised in the American milieu, had different values and expectations from their mothers'. While first-generation Jews had tended to look upon marriage matter-of-factly, viewing it primarily as an economic and social arrangement, their children espoused romantic notions, looking to marriage for individual satisfaction on an emotional and spiritual level. As part of the postwar drive to keep women in the home, they in particular were urged to find fulfillment through companionship with their mates. In the twenties, the question became not *whether* but *how* they would marry.

The stories and novels of Anzia Yezierska, written during this transitional period, work out many variations on these themes. There is Shenah Pessah, in "Wings," a story in *Hungry Hearts* (1920), who insists on independence. Her uncle and a match-maker urge her to marry a widowed fish peddler with several children. They claim that since she is old (twenty-three) and has no dowry, she should consider this a good opportunity. Shenah Pessah retorts:

"Don't you worry yourself for me. . . . Don't take pity on my years. I'm living in America, not in Russia. I'm not hanging on anybody's neck to support me. In America, if a girl earns her living, she can be fifty years old and without a man, and nobody pities her."

And when her friend Sadie Kranz urges her to use some of her wages to buy clothes so she can catch a husband, she explains that she has another goal in mind.

"Married? You know how it burns in every girl to get herself married—that's how it burns in me to work myself up for a person."
"Ut! [Sadie replies.] For what you need to work yourself up. Better marry yourself up to a rich feller and you're fixed for life!"

In *Bread Givers,* Sara Smolinsky argues with her mother,

"But won't you be proud of me when I work myself up for a schoolteacher in America?"
"I'd be happier to see you get married. What's a school-

teacher? Old maids—all of them. It's good enough for *Goyim,* but not for you."

Sara's mother takes the traditional Jewish view that women have a duty to marry, while Sadie Kranz looks upon marriage in more practical terms. She sees that it is difficult for women to support themselves, and that marriage is a preferable alternative. But Sara and Shenah Pessah are optimistic and ambitious; they have a strong sense of individuality and believe that American democracy will place no impediment in their paths.

Several of Yezierska's characters see another advantage to democracy: infinite possibilities for marriage. In the story "The Miracle," in *Hungry Hearts,* a young woman writes to her friend in the old country, "America is a lover's land. . . . In America millionaires fall in love with the poorest girls. Matchmakers are out of style and a girl can get herself married to a man without worries for a dowry." (Her optimism was undoubtedly fired by the examples of Rose Pastor and Anna Strunsky, immigrant women who married millionaire socialists, James Stokes and William Walling.)

The right to choose their own mates was very important to Yezierska's characters. They vociferously opposed arranged matches. When Sara protests her father's choice for a husband in *Bread Givers,* Reb Smolinsky expresses his disgust with her romantic notions. " 'But Max Goldstein, such a golden young man, he isn't good enough for you yet? You're yet blowing from yourself? Who do you think you are? Whom do you want? The President of America, maybe?' " Sara refuses to yield; the marriages her father has forced upon her three sisters have all turned out disastrously. The eldest daughter, not particularly attractive, he matches to a widowed fishman with three young children. Bessie assumes the drudgery of helping her husband behind the fish counter and looking after her hostile, caterwauling, ready-made family. Reb Smolinsky approves of the shoe clerk brought home by Mashah, the most attractive of the sisters. But he turns out to be a four-flusher who spends nearly all his pay on himself, leaving Mashah and their children in rags. The third sister is married off to a wealthy clothing manufacturer from Los Angeles. While she lives a life of material ease, she misses her family and finds the existence of the California *nouveau riche* to be spiritually impoverished.

Among East European Jews the primary condition for marriage was not sexual attraction but conformance with what was socially and economically suitable. Nevertheless, many matches, arranged with care and wisdom, resulted in long-lived, satisfying marriages between two well-suited partners. Thus Jewish parents tended to look upon romantic love as a frivolous American invention, and retained their faith in the matchmaking services of the *shadchen*. But their children insisted on freely choosing marriage partners. One young woman commented that going to a matchmaker was "like going on the slave market." However, because these young women were not economically independent, their "free" choices could not be made without financial considerations. As commentator Isaac Goldberg remarked in his introduction to *Six Plays of the Yiddish Theatre* (1916),

> The modern Jewish girl is feminist enough to see the degrading commercialism inherent in the *shadchen's* trade and to recognize the insult to her individualism which is thus implied. At the same time this type is not yet so numerous but that, in the chase after doctors and lawyers which distinguishes so many who should be above the purchase of husbands, the *shadchen* still finds employment.

Shadchens did not become obsolete, but merely changed their functions to adapt to new attitudes. Instead of arranging marriages between a bride and a groom who were wed sight unseen, the *shadchen* introduced prospective mates, allowing for the possibility that one or the other might find the choice unsuitable and reject the match.

If a daughter rejected the services of the *shadchen* altogether, her parents would resort to trying to influence her "free" choice in various ways, usually encouraging her to marry a young man who showed financial promise. In one of Yezierska's stories, an ambitious first-generation mother describes her plans for her daughter: " 'I'm going to take her to the swellest hotel in Long Branch where come the richest of the rich American Jews. . . . There ain't no money I wouldn't spend to give my Sadie a chance to marry herself good.' "

In America, criteria for marriages among Jews changed. The strict considerations of *yichus*—family reputation and scholarly achievements combined with wealth—which had determined alliances in the old country yielded to somewhat more flexible standards here. In Cahan's *Yekl,* when Bernstein, an educated man, expresses his desire to marry Gitl after Yekl has thrown her over, a neighbor observes that such a match would have been impossible in the old country, since Gitl comes from an undistinguished family. According to the neighbor, Gitl should consider herself fortunate to be getting " 'a learned man, who is a blessing both for God and people.' " Despite his own status, Bernstein is less concerned with Gitl's background than her character.

Women of the second generation looked for prospective husbands with professional training rather than religious scholarship, and both men and women considered wealth to be important. Although formal dowries were no longer customary, marriages were still informally contracted on a financial basis. A young man who wanted to go into business for himself looked for a wife who had a wealthy father, or who had garnered a bit of capital from her own earnings. A young woman with no ready cash but with wage-earning skills might find herself a professional-in-training, whom she would support until he was ready to practice. A young woman with neither cash nor skills might have to settle for an older man, perhaps a widower with several children. If she had cultural accomplishments, however, she might be able to find a man of means whose wealth she could complement with her ladylike qualities.

Gentlemen Prefer Blondes

Among the criteria for matchmaking formally recognized in the old country, physical appearance had received little consideration. Since young people might not even have seen each other before the wedding, few marriages were based on attraction alone. But in America, as young people began choosing their own mates, appearance became a significant factor. It was particularly important in the "marriage arenas"—resorts and hotels—where parents dragged their children in hopes of finding them prize catches. In the stories of Tashrak (pen name of Israel J. Zevin) about a marriage broker who has successfully adapted his old-country occupation to the new conditions, Shulem the Shadchen gives this advice to women:

> Once there was a time when men were afraid to marry girls who dressed too swell, thinking they will continue doing so even after they are married. They were right. But things have changed and nowadays the young men don't think so anymore. In fact, it looks to me, they have stopped thinking altogether, they just fall in love with a yard and a quarter of silk, half a can of powder and a pair of fancy stockings.
> . . . I say to every girl who intends to get a husband, "Dress well," and I say to every married woman who wants to keep her husband happy, "keep on dressing."

Young women contrived their appearances to reflect their parents' money and their own good taste and breeding. As Tashrak implies, the considerations of modesty and moderation which had circumscribed displays of wealth in the old country were no longer operative.

Second-generation Jewish women also began to try to create another effect: looking "American"—that is, conforming to what was conceived of as a gentile or Anglo-Saxon appearance. Partly they were acting out of a generalized rejection of all things Jewish, and partly they were responding to a real or implied preference for gentile women on the part of Jewish men who tended either to seek Jewish wives who "looked" American or actually married gentile women. The reverse process was not so prevalent among Jewish women; probably because their independence and mobility was more limited than the men's, Jewish women tended to be less exogamous than men, a trend that has continued to the present.

Immigrant and second-generation literature abounds in examples of self-hatred among Jewish women. Those who "looked" gentile were delighted with their good fortune, for they would be more attractive to Jewish men. In Ornitz's *Bride of the Sabbath,* for example, Pauline is proud of not being "Jewish-looking." She and the other girls in her circle ridicule big-bosomed women for having "Jewish figures." Similarly, in Winslow's "Cycle of Manhattan," the Rosenheimer family is pleased that everyone takes their daughter Dorothy for a gentile. She emphasizes this quality by affecting a tailored, tweedy style of dress reminiscent of a British country gentlewoman.

Jewish women who did not "naturally" look gentile often became displeased with their appearances, a phenomenon which was at least partly responsible for the rapid growth of plastic surgery in the late twenties. In her memoir, *My Sister Goldie,* Sandberg recalls one young plastic surgeon who made the rounds of Jewish resorts looking for potential patients. Although by profession he was the most eligible of bachelors, he danced only with the least attractive young women, thus drawing the notice of all the mothers in attendance. They finally discovered that his motives were professional, not social. Sandberg also recounts how her sister tried to convince her to have her nose "fixed."

"There isn't a thing in the world wrong with your looks! I think your freckles are very appealing. Lots of movie stars have them. And it's the style now to be flat-chested. It's just that your nose is a little too long. And that's your own fault. If it was me, I would have had a plastic surgery job the second they started doing them."

"I know a girl who did . . .—and she hasn't been out of the house since." [Sara replies.]

"Why don't you look at the girls who came out raving beauties?"

"Sure—but some of them still can't breathe."

Literature also reveals that this self-hatred among Jewish women was not without its external causes. As Jewish men imbibed Anglo-Saxon standards of beauty, they rejected Jewish physical characteristics. Edward Dahlberg, in his autobiography *Because I Was Flesh* (1963), admits that he was embarrassed by his mother because "I doted on the short up-turned gentile nose and imagined myself the singular victim of nature in having a mother with a nose that was a social misfortune." In *Bride of the Sabbath,* Ornitz describes how Saul begins to feel repelled by Becky's face, with its

> heavy eyebrows, kinkily curlicued like a Negro's, and especially, a too-aquiline Jewish nose. Now, usually, a nose is Jewish only to Jewish eyes or to a Gentile when he knows one is a Jew. Were Becky French, say, he would admire her aristocratic Gallic nose.

As Ornitz implies, there is nothing inherently superior in a gentile appearance, yet it had profound connotations. Jewish men preferred gentile women in the business world as well as in social situations. Irving Davidowsky, a dress manufacturer in Asch's *East River,* wants Mary, a young Irish woman, rather than the Jewish Rachel, to be his model. He feels that Mary's slender figure shows off his "numbers" more favorably than Rachel's fuller one. David Levinsky, in Cahan's novel, also chooses American girls "of Anglo-Saxon origin" for his models, not only because they have the proper type of figure, but because,

> [in] selecting my model-girls, I preferred a good-looking face and good manners, and, if possible, good grammar. Experience had taught me that refinement in a model was helpful in making a sale, even in the case of the least refined customers. Indeed, it is even more effectual than a tempting complexion.

To Levinsky and others, ladylike qualities were closely related to, if not identical with, gentile characteristics.

One of the most revealing examinations of the mystique of the gentile woman occurs in Ben Hecht's scathing novel, *A Jew in*

Love (1931). The protagonist, Jo Boshere, who is the son of immigrants, becomes a noted publisher. At the height of his career, he finds himself married to a heavyset, matronly, red-haired Jewish woman who no longer appeals to him. He sends her off on a series of world cruises and takes up with a mistress, also Jewish, but a poet whose bohemianism offsets the handicap of her religious background. Both wife and mistress are patient and supportive, virtues Boshere perversely rejects when he falls in love with the elusive Tillie Marmon, "a very stylish looking young woman, twenty-six years old, a blonde with a strong pink and white face animated by a trace of Anglo-Saxon gawkiness." Tillie's attraction for Boshere lies in her inaccessibility; winning her symbolizes, for him, the ultimate triumph of the Jew in American society.

Boshere's rival for Tillie is George, a film director to whom Tillie is hopelessly attached and who epitomizes, in Boshere's eyes, the power of the Anglo-Saxon male. George is "a tall blond man, full of that porcine aplomb and nordic bounce he particularly detested."* By rejecting George in favor of Boshere, Tillie confirms his worth, even his superiority; the Jew prevails against the Anglo-Saxon, and takes his woman.

Because of the prevalence of the gentile image, Jewish women felt compelled to divest themselves not only of their Jewish appearance, but of habits and mannerisms that marked them as well. Sonya, in Yezierska's 1923 novel, *Salome of the Tenements* (based on the story of Rose Pastor Stokes, who had married a millionaire), perceives the futility of attempting to transform herself into a gentile. Hoping to catch a wealthy man, John Manning, she secures beautiful clothing and decorates her room, but she realizes that she will have to change *inside* as well. She reflects, "I myself am unprepared. With all my brains I haven't the sense to get cold in the heart and clear in the head

---

*This curious ambivalence, the attraction toward gentile women and repulsion toward gentile men, persists. In Saul Bellow's story, "A Father-to-Be" (1955), the protagonist, Rogin, finds himself repulsed by a fellow passenger in the subway, a middle-aged man whose clear skin, blue eyes, and Roman nose remind him of no one so much as his fiancée Joan, whom he finds extremely beautiful.

like the American-born women of ice. . . . I'm burning up trying to catch on to life—and I wish I were dead." Sonya and Manning do marry, but they are unable to reconcile their profound cultural differences, and eventually separate.

A Girl Is Not To Think

Statistics show that Jewish women were more likely than their gentile counterparts to attend college in the twenties and thirties, although the literature of this period reveals that the parents—and often the young women themselves—did not take their daughters' education too seriously. It is impossible to determine how many Jewish women pursued an education with professional goals in mind, and how many simply saw it as a matrimonial asset. Some parents who could easily have afforded to send their daughters to college apparently refused to do so, disapproving of any commitment that might distract them from the pursuit of matrimony, while others felt that a daughter's education enhanced their own social position, since it showed that they could provide cultural opportunities for their children.

In Winslow's "Cycle of Manhattan," the Rosenheimers could well afford to educate all of their children, but only their son Irwin (*né* Irving) attends college. Yetta, the oldest daughter, sees no point in going, since she does not want to work or have a profession.

> No one tried to persuade her to keep on going. Her father was slightly of the opinion that too much learning wasn't good for a girl anyhow. Men didn't like "smart" girls and Yetta was growing up. If she had wanted to go to school, he might have consented, but she didn't.

Several years later, her younger sister, after graduating from high school, takes "a few harmless courses which gave her something to do, though they didn't satisfy her." Given the large number of Jewish women who did attend college during this period, Winslow's picture of this upper-middle-class Jewish family may be somewhat atypical. Since Mr. Rosenheimer's attitude was not uncommon, young women would have had to have more determination than Yetta and her sister did in order to receive an education.

The Old Bunch, Meyer Levin's novel about coming of age in Chicago in the late twenties and early thirties, also reveals the Jewish double standard about education. Most of the young people Levin portrays come from working-class or lower-middle-class first-generation families. Nearly all the men become professionals—doctors, lawyers, dentists—while few of the women go on past high school. Celia, who comes from one of the wealthier families, goes to business college to learn typing and stenography—like Winslow's character, "just for something to do." Celia's friend Estelle, who comes from one of the poorer families, attends because she knows she may very likely have to earn her own living. Aline considers training to become a teacher but rejects the idea when she realizes she will probably marry soon after she begins to teach. (In many places at that time married women were prohibited by law—as well as custom—from working as teachers.) Aline and Estelle decide to go to college as a way to meet men. Since they hope to marry college graduates, they want to be able to keep up with them. They must be the equals of the men they marry, they reason, "or the marriage would never be successful."

Even if they practiced no profession, education was important for middle-class wives, since they had the role of "culture-bearer" in the family, while their husbands were to concentrate on earning a living. Women's accomplishments made them more marriageable, but ironically, the more educated and refined they were, the less satisfaction they might find with husbands who, although rich, had no interests outside their businesses or professions.

In literature there are numerous examples of young women who felt torn between marrying poor men for love—for emotional and spiritual satisfaction—or rich men for security. Most first-generation parents thought that security should be the primary consideration, viewing the desire for companionship as romantic nonsense. There is an unusual reversal to this pattern in *The Rise of David Levinsky.* Dora looks to her daughter Lucy to fulfill her own unsatisfied dreams for married happiness, so she is bitterly disappointed when Lucy weds an older, wealthy man, apparently just for his money. Tessie, in Daniel Fuchs's *Summer in Williamsburg* (1934), also opts for security, but her compromise backfires. She feels nothing but repulsion toward her husband, Schausser, a traveling salesman. He, on the other hand, is so oblivious to Tessie's behavior that he is perfectly satisfied. Sitting in his living room one night after returning home from the road, "he looked at the piano, the etchings on the wall, and the furniture. It was all his. He owned it, together with his refined wife who knew all about fixing up elegant homes. On the road he told all his friends about her." He starts to make love to Tessie, who cringes inwardly, finding him crude. She tries to fend him off, saying " 'So soon after dinner?' " and begins to play the piano. But Schausser's cultural attention span is limited.

Herman Panken, plumbing contractor, and Sidonie Levine, schoolteacher, form a similar mésalliance in Schneider's *From the Kingdom of Necessity,* but in this case, both parties seem to be fully conscious of the role each is to play, and they strike a bargain that is evidently mutually satisfactory.

She constantly stopped him when he spoke, to tidy up his pronunciation and grammar. . . . The fact that Sidonie was an intellectual, admired writers and artists, always carried a book around with her in an elegant leather cover, did not distress Herman. He could not conceive of anything that could not be bought; and, he had the money. She wanted culture. Well, culture too resolved itself into commodities —a grand piano, oriental rugs, an encyclopedia and sets of the classics, subscriptions to the opera and the symphony society, antiques and oil paintings. He knew his charming Sidonie. She was a practical woman. The commodities of culture were what she wanted along with other articles not classified as culture, such as an automobile and a summer cottage. These Herman was in a more likely position to provide a wife than any of the other men she knew. Herman himself was the one doubtful piece of furnishing, but she did not apparently despair of giving him a passable finish.

Sidonie makes Herman join clubs and attend night school. She arranges to have one of her more artistic friends give him lessons in "culture." Although Herman quits after a while, Sidonie finally decides to marry him anyway, and they set about acquiring an apartment full of "culture." Herman's money complements Sidonie's taste perfectly.

The tone Fuchs and Schneider take toward these women is mocking and contemptuous. According to them, Tessie and Sidonie have betrayed themselves by marrying for security. But they ignore the social and economic factors which made such decisions nearly inevitable for women. Like many second-generation Jews writing in the thirties, they made a blanket critique of the tendency among their coreligionists to abandon the transcendent Jewish tradition for materialistic and Philistine values.

For these writers, the artist or intellectual who retained his integrity despite financial hardship or social disapproval became a symbol of hope for the Jew in America, inheriting the mantle of the East European Talmudic scholar. In the old country, of course, such figures were never women; in America the female artist or intellectual was rare in literature and in fact. Both Jewish and American cultures saw the woman in relation to a husband and children, not as a subject in herself, engaged only with her art and deserving of community support. She not only shared with men the struggle against Philistinism, but had to push against the limitations society imposed on women as well. The writers Yezierska portrays in her work struggle alone, penniless, and often without friends. They frequent no literary cafés, participate in no circle of fellow-artists and writers. Another writer of the thirties, Tess Slesinger, describes a more successful woman writer in her 1935 short story, "Time, the Present," but this woman, too, feels isolated. In addition, she is self-conscious about being unmarried, a state which she has been made to feel is anomalous.

In the literature of the thirties, women were much more likely to be indirectly connected with artistic, intellectual, or political circles as the helpmates of male figures. Like the Talmudic scholars, these men often depended for their survival on women who, believing in the importance of their work, were willing to support them. Asch was aware of this analogy when he created the character of Dvoryelè, Sarah Rifke's daughter in *The Mother.* Dvoryelè had, of course, a superb role model in her mother; from her she learned to fulfill herself through the achievements of others, a sacrifice whose bitter outcome she was yet to taste. Dvoryelè falls in love with Haskel, a sculptor. He plays the *bon vivant,* spending Dvoryelè's factory wages on theater tickets and restaurants, much as her father had squandered her mother's meager earnings on herring and other delicacies in the *shtetl.* While Haskel chisels away at his marble, Dvoryelè cleans up his studio, much as her mother stood over the washtub while her father cantillated the psalms. But it is Sarah Rifke who expresses her disappointment that Dvoryelè, like herself, must work even after she is married. She had hoped for something better for her daughter.

"So you are still working, daughter! Married and working! What a life!" . . .

"But you too work, mother! And aren't you married?" . . .

"I work for my children," exclaimed [Sarah Rifke] in extenuation.

"Well, I work for my husband," countered Dvoryelè. "Didn't you work for your husband?"

Sarah Rifke tries to warn Dvoryelè of what she herself has come to suspect: that ultimately, there is no reward for sacrifice. But Dvoryelè cannot hear. She becomes, literally, Haskel's inspiration, sitting naked in the winter-lit studio as he copies her in stone. The sculpture receives acclaim, but Haskel begins to feel tied down and becomes restless. His friends accuse Dvoryelè of failing to inspire him.

Tess Slesinger describes a similar situation in left-wing intellectual and political circles in her novel, *The Unpossessed* (1934). Despite their idealism, the men are insensitive to the plight of the women around them. They espouse notions of free love, generally to their own advantage and to the detriment of the women who love them and who are made to feel insecure by this unwelcome "liberty." In high-minded theoretical discussions, they criticize traditional female roles, but offer women no real alternatives. They take for granted female succor and ministrations, but refuse to accept women as intellectual equals. In utopian narrow-mindedness, they declare the world an unfit place to bring children into, thus denying women the satisfactions—however problematic they may be—of motherhood. Maggie Flinders, the protagonist of *The Unpossessed,* has a strong desire for children, but when she becomes pregnant, her husband convinces her to have an abortion. She regrets her decision, however, and at the novel's end, she reflects that "she had stripped and revealed herself not as a woman at all, but as a creature who would not be a woman, and could not be a man."

In other novels of this period, women who eschew the role of the self-abnegating female are portrayed as selfish and emasculating—"spiritual heavies." They are the forerunners of the stereotypical Jewish Princesses of the fifties and sixties who "drag men down" with their insatiable desire for attention and their crass materialism.

For the most part, however, literature shows an increasing acceptance of American-style role divisions, and of the new mythology growing up around marriage and the home. Marriage was to be a partnership, a source of companionship, and the private home, filled with modern comforts and created and tended by women, was to be men's refuge from the workaday world. The redefinition of desirable "womanly" traits during the periods of early immigration and resettlement may tell us more about how images are filtered through a culture and reinforced by its literature than about the actuality of Jewish women's lives. Novels and stories may have served, intentionally or not, as propaganda, or at least as corrective and prescriptive guides for assimilation. Like advertising, popular literature often serves as a vehicle for expressing social expectations, either by implicitly criticizing those who fall below certain standards or by suggesting norms of behavior that readers attempt to emulate. The images that are created, then, act in concert with actual circumstances. In the case of Jewish women, particularly those of East European origin, literature was an important guidepost on the road to assimilation, directing them into a domestic role when they found education and employment opportunities to be limited.

The middle-class dream filtered down even to the poorest working girl, who saw marriage and a home as a way to escape from the daily grind. Albert Halper captures the essence of this dream in *The Chute* (1937), his novel about a poor immigrant family in Chicago. Rae, the daughter, has lived all her life in two rooms behind the family's struggling candy store. Her fantasy of married life is to have

> her own kitchen, a bedroom fixed up with nice curtains and drapes, and maybe a neat living room with a suite which they [she and her husband-to-be] could pick out together, when they could afford it. Then she would invite a few girls from the shop for bridge occasionally, the girls could bring their husbands or fellows, and she could serve inexpensive drinks and a cake.

For women of all classes and all educational levels, marriage was the prevailing social expectation in the twenties and thirties. It was the unusual woman who went against the tide.

8

From Veneration to Vituperation
Jewish Women Today

It was not that she had not loved her babies, her children.
The love—the passion of tending—had risen with the need
like a torrent; and like a torrent drowned and immolated
all else. But when the need was done—oh, the power that
was lost in the painful damming back and drying up of
what still surged, but had nowhere to go. Only the thin
pulsing left that could not quiet, suffering over lives one
felt, but could no longer hold nor help.

—TILLIE OLSEN, *Tell Me a Riddle*

One of the ironic by-products of the twin processes—
assimilation and its reverse, the forthright assertion of Jewish
identity—is the confidence with which certain Jewish novelists
are willing to hold their culture up for scrutiny to the American
public at large, while at the same time taking the risk of ridicul-
ing it. The stock figures that have resulted are very different
from the gently ridiculed but deeply loved characters who peopled the world of Sholem Aleichem or the later, fantasy-ridden
creations of I. B. Singer.

Of these contemporary stock figures, none loom as large in

American culture in general as the "Jewish Mother" and the "Jewish American Princess." These stereotypes single out certain qualities in women, characterize them in the first place as unattractive and in the second, as specifically Jewish. In this section, we mean to take a look at some of the fiction (primarily post-World War II) in which Mother and Princess have been personified, as well as some of the nonfiction which has attempted to study their reality. Do Mother and Princess exist as described in fiction? What do they signify? Would they have to be invented if they did not exist?

Overbearing fathers and spoiled sons have often been treated in fiction, too, after all, but they have not been so conveniently labeled as types. And even before the Jewish Mother emerged as a full-blown literary creation, mothers had come in for their share of castigation. The supercharged accusation of "Momism" (that forgotten epithet), widely popularized in the 1950s by the non-Jewish writer Philip Wylie, was supposed to locate a symptom of what was wrong with American life generally. It did not, of course, refer to Jews specifically but to "moms" in general.

But in the 1960s, certain Jewish writers preempted the Momism type. The Jewish Mother became, as Erica Jong's heroine is to say wistfully in *Fear of Flying* (1974), "a real literary property," along with her daughter, the Jewish Princess.

The stereotypical Jewish Mother overdoes her job. We are told that she hovers over her children, preventing them from achieving autonomy by interfering, cajoling, advising, and manipulating. Whether she is actually holding the spoon and urging them to take "just one more bite," or operating through guilt—that most exquisite instrument of remote control—she is seen as ubiquitous and eternal, from the first diaper change through the last word on the doctoral thesis. Her children's achievements belong to her, for she has lived her life for—and through—her children. They succeed not to please themselves but to satisfy her, the fear of her displeasure intensifying their own anxieties about failing. Her domination extends over her husband as well; indeed, she seems to possess unlimited strength and boldness. There are no matters on which she does not presume expertise, no affairs in which she does not claim the prerogative to meddle.

The Jewish Mother has become both a comic and literary convention. She is usually a woman of the second generation, portrayed by certain novelists and comedians, most often male (who are ambivalent about their Jewish background), of the third generation. Although there are scattered references to the particular style of Jewish mothering over the entire range of American Jewish literature, the full-blown negative stereotype does not appear until the sixties, when authors began creating maternal figures who were not only distinctive and laughable, but targets for the bitterest forms of denunciation and vituperation. The composite picture evoked by the words "Jewish Mother" probably refers most directly to characters in three books: Bruce Jay Friedman's *A Mother's Kisses* (1964); Dan Greenburg's *How To Be a Jewish Mother* (1964); and finally, Philip Roth's *Portnoy's Complaint* (1969). By the time Roth got around to writing this novel, he saw the Jewish Mother problem as one so common that it deserved inclusion in the psychoanalytic lexicon. In the novel's epigraph, he gives a mock definition of "Portnoy's Complaint": a "disorder" many of whose "symptoms can be traced to the bonds obtaining in the mother-child relationship."

While the Jewish Mother is known for her unwelcome devotion to others, the stereotypical Jewish American Princess cares for no one but herself. First described by second-generation authors looking at third-generation women—Herman Wouk in *Marjorie Morningstar* (1955)—and then by male third-generation authors observing their female contemporaries, the Princess is spoiled and materialistic, self-centered and assertive.

There is a countercurrent in literature that deals with sons, who, interestingly enough, when they write about their favored position in the family and the benefices bestowed on them, turn this situation into an attack on their mothers. Their heroism lies in the damage inflicted on them by the domineering mother and their struggle to overcome it. The blame for their problems rests outside of themselves.

But the Jewish daughter is given no such hedge. She has been shaped, to be sure, by her overwhelming mother and her doting father, but she is nevertheless held fully accountable for herself. What we have, then, is a picture of a young woman who manipulates the world for her own selfish ends. She belongs, through the perspective of those who wrote about her, to *nouveau riche* middle-class parents. (Either the Jewish poor had ceased to exist, or they had ceased having children, to judge by the dominance in this sort of literature of the Princess model.) Accustomed to being treated like royalty in her family, she expects the same sort of consideration from the world at large. She is condemned as being sexually exploitative, but probably her most offensive characteristic is her refusal to defer easily to male authority, an unforgivable sin in the American pantheon of feminine virtues. The stereotype of the Jewish American Princess is intrinsically critical: it regards her as demanding everything and giving nothing; her assertiveness is viewed as an instrument of emasculation. Further, the stereotype is circular: The Jewish Mother desperately wants her daughter to marry, and marry well; the daughter expects the "right" man to fall at her feet. Thus both mother and daughter are seen as exemplifying the most superficial and materialistic social values.

Dedication or Over-Involvement?

How accurate are these representations? Are Jewish women, for instance, more intensive mothers than their gentile counterparts? Sociologists report that Jewish women tend to resemble closely other American women of the same age and class. Slightly more educated, on the average, than non-Jewish women of the same class, they tend to have fewer children. Since their husbands' income allows them to remain outside of the labor force, they have more time to devote to home and family than their non-middle-class mothers did. But according to some sociologists, rather than reinvesting this time in their children or their homes, Jewish women are more likely to pursue outside activities. The women described in these studies do not fit the popular image of the all-absorbing Jewish Mother who dominates her children. Sociologists also differ with those who suggest that the Jewish woman wields power over her husband as well.

In popular literature, the Jewish man is frequently portrayed as an impotent *schmuck* who has no authority in his own home, but meekly goes along with his wife, handing over to her his hard-earned money and acceding to her opinions. According to sociologist Albert Gordon's *Jews in Transition* (1949), in fact, in Jewish families "there is a minimum of superordination or subordination in the relationship between husband and wife." In *The Jewish Wife* (1969), a popularized study based on interviews with Jewish women, Barbara Wyden and Gwen Schwartz report that Jewish women commonly see their marriages as partnerships, each partner having a separate but equally valued sphere.

This picture suggests that Jews are no different from other Americans, and that Jewish mothers are not the matriarchal tyrants literature sets them up to be. The studies imply that Jewish families are not home breweries for neuroses, but all-American nests in which Jewish children are raised in the accepted middle-class fashion.

Wyden and Schwartz imply that Jewish women hold more power within their families than other women do because their husbands frequently consult with them and seek advice and support for their business decisions. The relationship is not, however reciprocal; women rarely consult with their husbands on domestic matters, and the husbands are not, apparently, prompted to offer help or interference. (Curiously, Albert Gordon in *Jews in Transition* states that "as the economic status of the family improved, the wife had less to say and do about the husband's business.") This lack of reciprocity is probably due to two factors: Traditionally, Jewish men were never involved in home affairs, while wives were frequently involved in business, so women retain their role vestigially as advisers. In addition, because prevalent social attitudes tend to accord more importance to business affairs than to housekeeping ones, men would have less to gain, in terms of status or power, from involvement in domestic matters than women would from financial ones. Although Jewish women's domestic reign is absolute, it holds sway over a sector the rest of society tends to regard as trivial, boring, or even (to men) stifling and entrapping. Because what American society values most is making money, maternal dominance, Philip Slater points out in *The Temporary Society* (1968), "tends to be highly diluted . . . by male occupational success." Indeed, the low esteem with which the domestic realm is regarded receives its most vivid cultural expression in the stereotype of the Jewish Mother.

While Marshall Sklare, the sociologist, implies in his book *America's Jews* (1972) that most second-generation women adapted well to their domestic position, there is evidence that a sizable minority of Jewish women were unable to strike such a balance. Some developed an exaggerated concern with their appearances and with material possessions. In "Profile of a Doll" (1967) the psychiatrist Alexander Grinstein describes female patients of his who have become almost entirely self-absorbed. The wives of business and professional men, these Jewish women, most of them somewhat educated, are preoccupied with their looks, fashion, and possessions, areas in which they compete with other women. While they seem superficially involved with their children and with current theories of child psychology, Grinstein detects indifference beneath. These women pass most of their time shopping, playing cards, and doing some club work.

In treatment, Grinstein reports, these women speak vaguely and reveal childish fears and fantasies. He contends that they suffer from identity conflicts with their mothers, whose behavior and personality traits second-generation women feel compelled to reject, but at the same time have not avoided internalizing.

Their own crudeness and inappropriateness in their dress, the excrescence of harshness in their behavior toward their children, the loudness in their manner, the lack of accepted values—all speak for an identification with some of their mothers' striking primitive *[sic]* characteristics. Their sense of identity is thus seriously disturbed and they are constantly dissatisfied with themselves in the role that they are playing. . . . It is as though one can see the middle European ghetto community living within the "modern personality" of these women, like Williamsburg in the middle of the New York metropolis.

It is difficult to know how accurate studies of women's attitudes have been. Only recently have women begun to talk about their real desires. Grinstein simply accepts uncritically the changes in women's roles from one generation to the next, without evaluating them or comparing them in terms of their ability to provide women with self-esteem or opportunities for self-expression or satisfaction. Grinstein as a psychiatrist admits that the problems of the "doll" elude therapeutic solutions. His therapeutic model, however, fails to take into account social factors, or the biases which assume a norm of acceptable behavior for women that women themselves have begun to question and reject. The pejorative view, for instance, of the "career girl," which has begun to give way only in recent years, was one that damned women for wanting to participate equally with men in the economic sphere, while at the same time the leisure of the middle-class married woman and her participation in the consumer culture was regarded as frivolous. Moreover, women who had chosen to become wives and mothers were often criticized for being too involved with their children, their appearance, and their domestic responsibilities. Thus, the socially sanctioned role of the "good wife and mother," while supposedly valued, was actually being held in some contempt, and those who performed their duties conscientiously were often criticized as "overly" everything and neurotic as well.

In her study "Mrs. Portnoy's Complaint: Depression in Middle-Aged Women" (1971), the sociologist Pauline Bart does look for social explanations for the psychological problems of Jewish women. Bart reports that she found a disproportionate number of Jewish women among middle-aged female patients suffering from maternal role loss, and attributes this anomaly to the fact that the maternal role is more highly emphasized in the Jewish culture than elsewhere. Women who have been intensely involved with their children suffer from the "empty nest syndrome" when their children leave home. The more involved the mother, the more vulnerable she is to this type of depression. As Bart explains,

> The traditional woman bases her self-esteem on a role, motherhood, that she must finally relinquish. Some do this with ease; some others, especially those with inflexible personalities, cannot. But the problem is not hers alone; society has provided no guidelines for her, no rites of passage. There is no *bar mitzvah* for menopause. The empty nest, then, may prompt the extreme feelings of worthlessness and uselessness that characterize depressives. One can think of these women as overcommitted to the maternal role and then, in middle age, suffering the unintended consequences of this commitment.

The woman whose children are grown up, the "retired mother," is in a problematic position. Her "work" is over, but the practical rituals of motherhood are so large a part of her day-to-day life that it is difficult for her to give her children up to adulthood and acknowledge their independent existence. She cannot relinquish her hold on her children, for she has no substitute work.

The sadness of these women is intensified by the stereotypical perception of their behavior, which ridicules and denigrates the Jewish Mother. While the close protectiveness of the ghetto mother may no longer be necessary, its vestiges in contemporary Jewish mothering must be understood in their historical context. Jewish mothering is no spontaneous eruption, but a holdover from a culture in which it was necessary and acceptable— indeed, highly regarded. This mothering now appears to be exaggerated because the Jewish woman has lost most of her other social functions, and because it does not fit in with American notions about mothers. The stereotype has separated Jewish women from their own history. The result has been that, internalizing the negative characteristics of the stereotype, Jewish mothers have become their own worst attackers.

Martha Wolfenstein, in her study, "Two Types of Jewish Mothers" (1955), was one of the first psychologists to recognize the link between the behavior of American Jewish women and that of their immigrant foremothers. She pointed out that the harsh conditions of the *shtetl* and the ghetto engendered maternal protectiveness; only by the standards of a more well-established society does such behavior appear to be overprotectiveness. The "Jewish Mother" stereotype was created by third-generation Jewish writers who felt comfortably Americanized enough to be able to shrug off the heavy emotional clothing of the ghetto.

Despite the objections of the children, it is this type of mothering, some social scientists assert, that is responsible for the fact that Jews have a lower rate of impairing mental illness (psychosis) than Protestants or Catholics, although they do have a higher rate of nondebilitating illness (neurosis). This fact is pointed out by Zena Blau Smith, in her article, "In Defense of Jewish Mothers" (1967). She adds that while Jewish mothers may encourage their children to be physically and emotionally dependent, they also foster intellectual independence. Because their lives are closely tied to their mothers, Jewish children are less likely to depend on peer group support and approval, and therefore tend to be less conforming and more original—at least intellectually.

Matthew Besdine, a clinical psychologist, also praises "Jewish Mothering" (1970). Distinguishing degrees of maternal attention, he establishes a scale of mothering ranging from "negligible" to "Jocasta-type," models of mothering that have been derived from investigating the whole Western tradition rather than the specifically Jewish. Philip Roth's character Sophie Portnoy is a Jocasta, according to Besdine's scale, but her style is an exaggeration, atypical of that of most Jewish mothers, whom Besdine describes as "dedicated." But even Sophie Portnoy wasn't all bad, Besdine comments, for while her

> Jocasta mothering gave her son, Portnoy, the sexual hang-ups, guilt, impotence, fear of love, etc., it is also responsible for the extraordinary development of his talents and gifts. The intensity, quantity and quality of Sophie's deep interest in her son developed the positive aspects of his intellectual and creative abilities.

Although most Jewish mothers are deeply interested in their children, they are not usually so intensely constricting as Sophie Portnoy was. Nevertheless, according to the measurements of social scientists, there seems to be at least some validity to the Jewish Mother stereotype: Jewish women do possess, to a certain extent at any rate, some of the positive qualities imputed to them—creative boldness (*chutzpah* by our definition), free expression of emotion—including love and anger, interference in children's problems and concern about their difficulties, high expectations for children, pride in their abilities, respect for originality, and reward for their achievements. So what's bad? This behavior carried to extremes—which is just what the stereotype really is.

And these are the traits that have characterized Jewish women throughout history. Traits that enabled Jewish women to keep their families together in the *shtetl* and to ease their transition to the New World are the very same ones the processes of assimilation—the attempt to transform the *baleboste* into the lady—were bent on exorcising. And, according to psychologists like Blau and Besdine, these characteristics have coalesced into a type of mothering which, far from being deleterious, may in fact have resulted in rewarding society as well as the Jewish community. For, after all, there *is* a low crime rate among Jews in America, and a low infant mortality rate, to cite just two positive features.

What can be said is that Jewish women have traditional concepts of mothering that may in certain ways differ from the expectations of American mothers of Anglo-Saxon background as a result of their varied history. Though no hard and fast generalization can be made, Anglo-Saxon mothers in the United States may have been more prepared for the separation and independence of their children by circumstances that favored physical and social mobility. Immigrant Jewish mothers and those born in America into an immigrant atmosphere have been inclined to prolong close supervision of their children, in contrast to the tendency in the American cultural pattern to grant autonomy at an early age. These mothers may also strive to maintain physical and emotional contact longer, based on a concept of their parental role that derives from the prevailing conditions of their European origins. Locked in by legal restraints and customs and hedged in by official hostility and the traditional anti-Semitism of the nations they dwelt in, Jewish mothers believed family and group survival was dependent on closeness and cohesion. These differing conditions produced different child-rearing precepts and practices. While the Jewish mother saw a real need for her family to remain intact, and felt that it was vital to keep it that way, the American mother was better prepared for her children's departure from the family nest, both physically and figuratively.

What remains to be examined is why third-generation male writers, through the medium of literary stereotype, have ignored these historical and psychological factors and have turned Jewish women's mothering behavior into negative traits for which they attack second-generation mothers with a lack of comprehension and appreciation.

Matricide in Print

While Portnoy's complaint, and the complaint of his male contemporaries, is ostensibly psychological in nature, it reveals itself, on closer examination, to be primarily cultural. By the third generation, Jewish men were attempting to live out the cherished American myth of masculine independence, starring the lone hero who needs only minimal nurturing before he sets out for the frontier (without, needless to say, a package of *babka* and a few pieces of chicken: "In case you get hungry, you'll have something."). His mother deserves no special honor; in fact, her ministering might be some sort of trap, an encumbrance, an impediment to the masculine mission. Jewish men, anxious to break loose from the constraints imposed on them by their culture, particularly as it was defined by their mothers, were now among the most vociferous detractors of motherhood. The critic Samuel Bellman notes that

it is the Jewish writers and entertainers who have taken special pains to point out how out of phase Mother is with the needs, wants and personalities of the children. Imagine a book entitled, *How To Be an American Mother*. What would there be to write about?

The Jewish male rejection of their mothers is, however, a recent development, a visible by-product of the efforts to assimilate. Indeed, many of the early novelists unashamedly portrayed mothers as highly sympathetic characters whose strength and ministrations were welcomed by their families struggling to survive in a baffling new environment. For example, Sarah Rifke in Asch's *The Mother* is a strong, self-sacrificing practical woman, the mainstay of a poor immigrant family, and, according to Asch, the epitome of Jewish womanhood.

Maternal comfort was also welcomed by the small boys in Henry Roth's *Call It Sleep* (1934) and S. J. Wilson's *Hurray for Me* (published in 1964, but set in the thirties). These novels are honest—if painful—accounts of the terror felt by two little boys facing the ghetto. Although Henry Roth's story is set a decade or two before Wilson's, in both novels the power of the mother —her importance as nurturer, protector, and buffer against the outside world—is emphasized. To these children there was no question that they needed and wanted strong mothers, mothers who would hold and caress them, who had time and patience for them, and who would explain the mysteries of the outside world while shielding them from its dangers. Henry Roth and S. J. Wilson do not seem to see the maternal bond as a source of control or guilt, but as a channel through which ideas, jokes, admonishments, and observations flow lovingly, joyously, and freely—in both directions. Nor do they seem to think that the Jewish mother must be destroyed (at least in psychological terms) in order for Jewish sons to achieve autonomy. Even though in both novels the attachment of the boys to their mothers is colored by Oedipal overtones, Oedipal attachment, as Blau and Besdine point out, need not be destructive; it is a question of degree—of determining at what point nurturing becomes smothering.

If anything, these two novels may exaggerate the actual attentions of Jewish mothers: the *felt* involvement may have been disproportionate to the amount of time and energy that these poor first- and second-generation women had to devote to their children. Alfred Kazin's description of *his* mother in his memoir, *A Walker in the City* (1951), suggests that children may have derived as much comfort from the presence and personalities of their mothers as from direct care. In a chapter called "The Kitchen," he give this account:

> The kitchen gave a special character to our lives: my mother's character. All my memories of that kitchen are dominated by the nearness of my mother sitting all day long at her sewing machine, by the clacking of the treadle against the linoleum floor, by the patient twist of her right shoulder as she automatically pushed at the wheel with one hand or lifted the foot to free the needle where it had got stuck in a thick piece of material. The kitchen was her life. Year by year, as I began to take in her fantastic capacity for labor and her anxious zeal, I realized it was ourselves she kept stitched together. . . . From my mother's kitchen I gained my first picture of life as a white, overheated, starkly lit workshop redolent with Jewish cooking, crowded with women in housedresses, strewn with fashion magazines, patterns, dress material, spools of thread—and at whose center, so lashed to her machine that bolts of energy seemed to dance out of her hands and feet as she worked, my mother stamped the treadle hard against the floor, hard, hard, and silently, grimly at war, beat out the first rhythm of the world for me.

Mrs. Kazin is formidable—but not frightening, not overwhelming. Kazin's description implies that strong women are not necessarily threatening, not even to little boys.

The contemporary Jewish Mother stereotype undermines the positive quality of the energy Kazin valued in his mother. The stereotyped Jewish Mother appears strong not only in an absolute sense, but also vis-à-vis the Jewish father who carried over the male deference of a nonmacho tradition, while also trying to adjust to American ways. The Jewish children of these transi-

tional fathers perceived them as somehow inadequate when
compared to the fathers of American children that were typified
in books or, later, in movies. The Jewish fathers were viewed as
being different because they did not possess the "manly" qualities that were assumed to belong to American men as a birth-
right. And, conversely, the strength and drive of their mothers
—behavior traits associated with masculinity in America—were
seen negatively and despairingly.

In *Portnoy's Complaint* a good part of Alexander's embarrassment arises from the fact that the division of sex roles in his
family doesn't fit the American pattern:

> If my father had only been my mother! And my mother my
> father! But what a mix-up of sexes in our house. Who
> should by rights be advancing on me retreating, and who
> should be retreating, advancing! . . . Filling the patriarchal
> vacuum. Oh! Thank God! Thank God! at least *he* had the
> cock and balls.

In fantasy, Alexander urges his father:

> Tell her, tell her: . . . "the way it works, in case you ain't
> heard, is that I am the man around here, *and I call the
> shots.*" And slug her if you have to. Deck her, Jake! Surely
> that's what a goy would do, would he not? . . . Poppa, why
> do we have to have such guilty deference to women, you
> and me—when we don't!

In traditional Jewish culture, of course, there was no shame
attached to a man's gentleness—or to a woman's strength. But
in America, this distribution of sexual attributes is unorthodox,
and may upset the sexual balance of power. To assimilation-
minded Alex, his father's passivity and his mother's aggressive-
ness seem intolerable.

But let us suppose for a moment that Alexander's fantasy
comes true, that his father and mother change places, that the
mother is feminine, the father is masculine, according to the
American notion. What then? Herbert Gold describes just such

a situation in *Fathers* (1967), his "novel in the form of a memoir." Gold's father is strong, confident, and aggressive, and his mother, deferential and somewhat retiring. Pa Gold works long hours running the family produce store (where his wife also puts in time, between household duties). No stranger to physical labor, this Jewish man rises at dawn to drive to market, where he hoists crates of vegetables with the strongest of *goyim*. No victim of immigrant insecurity, he meets gangsters' threats head on, and lets no anti-Semitic slur pass by unchallenged.

Gold's complaint? His father is remote, a stranger. He doesn't really care, doesn't understand his son. He *shleps* his boy to the *shvitz,* only to abandon him for the card table. Finally, when Gold himself is an adult, no longer threatening his father with the yawning abyss of childish needs, his father comes to his aid, at least for one compassionate moment. And Gold's mother? Despite the fact that she is no lady of leisure, she is as dependent and obedient as an American wife is expected to be. Never one to overwhelm her children or her husband by displays of excessive competence, she once even drives the family car into a river. Still, she manages to make her son Herbert feel guilty.

So here we have the complete reversal in roles and behavior by Gold's mother and father, and how does he respond? He complains. The message seems to be: "Dear Jewish Mothers, forget it, whatever you do by your sons will be wrong!" Listen instead to the social scientists cited. Whatever you did was right! In their view, at any rate.

Or, to put it another way:

"If third-generation Jewish male writers find you lacking because you have not read Freud, and denigrate you for virtues you ought to be proud of, remember that what's really bothering them is that you're not gentile."

The "unmelted" Jewish woman, the woman who has not become completely assimilated, threatens the security of the Jewish community's acceptability to other Americans (according to the stereotypers) by continually reminding the gentile world that Jews are, after all, different. Something's gone awry here, though, for according to the sociologist Marcus Hansen, most immigrant groups, by the third generation, feel secure enough within American society to begin to retrieve some of the ethnicity the second generation rejected, so that "what the son wished to forget, the grandson wishes to remember." Despite "Hansen's law," however, a good part of Alexander Portnoy's ravings on the couch consist of a rejection of all things Jewish, and an embracing of all things gentile. Portnoy is distressed because his parents—mostly, of course, his mother—appear embarrassingly un-American. He is still caught in the throes of an ethnic identity crisis, and many of the qualities he finds distasteful in his parents are precisely those that mark them out as Jews. Roth himself gives us clues to the roots of Portnoy's insecurity as Portnoy challenges his psychiatrist:

> So don't tell me we're American just like they are. No, no, these blond-haired Christians are the legitimate residents and owners of this place . . . O America! America! it may have been gold in the streets to my grandparents, it may have been a chicken in every pot to my father and mother, but to me, a child whose earliest movie memories are of Ann Rutherford and Alice Faye, America is a *shikse* nestling under your arm whispering love love love love love!

For Portnoy, the values and tastes of gentiles are safe and good, and they dwell in harmony and bliss behind their *goyishe* curtains, but Alex lives in guilt and anxiety "behind the aluminum 'Venetians' for which my mother has been saving out of her table money for years." Alex is anxious lest his outspoken mother be noticed since, unlike most American women, she doesn't seem to know her place.

> Only in America . . . do these peasants, our mothers, get their hair dyed platinum at the age of sixty, and walk up and down Collins Avenue in Florida in pedal pushers and mink stoles—and with opinions on every subject under the sun. It isn't their fault they were given a gift like speech—

look, if cows could talk, they would say things just as idiotic.

Why platinum? What color hair does Alice Faye have? If Jewish women dye their hair platinum in an attempt to give themselves what Jewish men are attracted to, why are they being scorned? Who else are they trying to please? Isn't that their final capitulation to the Jewish male? And his desires? As for their opinions being idiotic, knowing what we do about Portnoy, who could trust his evaluation of anything Jewish? Perhaps Alexander would have found them more palatable if mothers prefaced their remarks with the *shtetl* disclaimer, "I'm only a silly woman, but. . . ."

Jewish mothers become for some, like Alexander Portnoy, the objects of their children's anger and ridicule and are served up as scapegoats for their failures. The highly negative connotations of the Jewish Mother stereotype—and of the cultural attitudes of which it is but a symptom—make it difficult for Jewish women to affirm their identity with equanimity. They may find it necessary to stifle positive impulses of warmth and hospitality, of concern and nurturance. Their bowls of chicken soup have become philters of hemlock.

Mink Coats and Idealism

The Jewish American Princess and Jewish Mother stereotypes have certain features in common, just as young women of the third and fourth generations share certain characteristics and personality traits with their mothers. The Princess has inherited the Mother's *chutzpah*, her energy and lack of deference; but while the Mother focuses her attention on her children, the daughter is portrayed as concentrating on her future husband —someone whom she, too, can dominate and manipulate, and who will provide her access to the material possessions she is said to covet.

Characters like Marjorie Morningstar do not exemplify all of the qualities usually associated with the stereotypical Jewish

Princess, for second-generation authors like Wouk, in characterizing third-generation women, usually emphasize the conflicts young women felt between old and new values, particularly with regard to sexual morality. The sympathy of these authors is limited, however, by general notions of womanhood, so their fictions do not allow the potentially strong female characters they have created to express themselves fully, or to become wholly realized.

Herman Wouk endows Marjorie Morningstar with enough energy and determination to pursue a career even against the wishes of her family, and despite numerous setbacks. But Marjorie, a character talented enough to receive a certain amount of recognition, still cannot transcend what Wouk saw as the limitations of her sex.

The short-circuiting of Marjorie's acting career is inconsistent with her desire to be an actress. Possibly, in Wouk's view, Marjorie's ambition is an aberration, a failure to be adequately socialized toward the goal of finding the proper woman's place —in the home. Apropos, Marjorie, once dauntless and determined, experiences a failure of will, a loss of drive, and she takes up her wifely duties without regret. So Marjorie Morningstar becomes Mrs. Milton Schwartz of Westchester and, in fact, she seems to have been rewarded despite her sexual escapades with Noel Airman (who is also a pejorative figure—a male who derails women from their correct chaste journey to the marriage bed).

What is most interesting about *Marjorie Morningstar* for the purposes of this discussion is Wouk's ambivalent sympathy toward Marjorie as a character and toward her failed career and love affair with Airman. It appears that second-generation Jewish male authors writing about third-generation Jewish women have a more favorable, compassionate response to them than do third-generation Jewish male authors such as Philip Roth. While Marjorie Morningstar is regarded by many to be the first "real" Jewish American Princess, she is essentially presented as a positive character whose missteps along the proper female path symbolize Wouk's perception of modernizing American ways as an affront to sustaining traditional values.

Nineteen fifty-nine was the year that fully launched the new model Jewish Princess, Brenda Patimkin. In Philip Roth's *Goodbye, Columbus,* Brenda and her lover, Neil Klugman, are highly reminiscent of characters in some of the romantic novels of the thirties: Neil is poor and idealistic (he works in a library where he risks being fired by hiding art books for a kid who comes in every day) and Brenda is rich, arrogant, and self-centered. However, unlike the females of the thirties (one of whom might well have been Brenda's mother), Brenda is eager to sleep with Neil, although she still has ambivalent feelings about it. Neil persuades her to get a diaphragm, which she leaves in her bureau drawer, only to be discovered by her mother when Brenda is off at school. Her action, according to both Neil and Roth, is the result of not-so-veiled subconscious ties to her parents, whom she does not really want to deceive and disobey.

Neil sees Brenda as bound to her parents in other ways. He assumes that she shares their materialistic, *nouveau-riche* values, and that if he marries her he will have to abandon his own (albeit vaguely defined) ideals. Brenda's brother Ron, who is seen as absurd and destined only to go into his father's plumbing business so he can support a wife, serves as a foil for Neil, a terrifying vision of what might happen to him if he were to marry Brenda. Brenda, of course, is never allowed the opportunity to disabuse Neil of his assumptions.

Like her predecessors in the thirties, Brenda represents the trap of domesticity; her material demands are antagonistic to the idealistic ambitions of the man who has the misfortune to fall in love with her. This male-female dualism is by no means an unusual theme in Jewish culture. The woman has, traditionally, been said to be an earthbound creature who, because of her sensual, materialistic nature, threatens to distract the scholar from his holy tasks. Custom required the Jewish woman to be sexually modest and self-effacing in order to minimize the temptation she posed. Among American Jews, however, the dualism is not so clear-cut, for American Jewish men are not unequivocably committed to idealistic goals, but usually feel the tug of desire for temporal success. The Jewish American Princess stereotype operates to preserve the dualism by projecting all materialistic desires onto women, and by locating the roots of ambivalence in them, rather than in men themselves. When a young man meets a Jewish Princess, he thinks about "selling out" because *she* will insist on having a house, furniture, clothing, cars, and expensive vacations. This scheme does not allow for the fact that, as Veblen has pointed out, a man enhances his own status by providing for his wife, that she is but a "ceremonial consumer."

Julie Baumgold, with overzealous wit, put the finishing touches on the stereotypical Princess portrait in her article, "The Persistence of the Jewish American Princess," which appeared in *New York* magazine (1971). According to Baumgold and her reliable informants (including the aforementioned male authors plus two comedians—David Steinberg and Mel Brooks —David Susskind, and a pedigreed member of the species in question, identified only as "Ellen"), the Jewish Princess is recognizable by her outsized ego (inflated by eternally supportive parents), excessive concern for creature comforts and material goods, and, of course, her ability to "hold out" for marriage (old-style) or at least "a relationship" (updated version) before giving sexual favors. The outlines of the stereotype blur, however, enabling Baumgold to subsume under it nearly every well-known Jewish woman she can think of. But since Jacqueline Kennedy Onassis and other notable *shikses* are mentioned too, one might conclude that you don't have to be Jewish to be a Jewish Princess. Obviously a stereotyped projection of a certain kind of money-spoiled woman always existed in literature, but she was never labeled "Jewish" until Jewish writers made her part of the American comic pantheon—the way the movie version of *Gone with the Wind* made Butterfly McQueen a parody of the devoted, "dumb," Black servant.

Off Their Thrones

After enduring several decades of denigration and forced assimilation at the hands of the stereotypers, Jewish women—mothers and daughters alike—have begun to assert themselves, to find legitimate outlets for the energy that narrow female roles had not dissipated, but only mischanneled. Their protests are taking literary, intellectual, and political form.

In a number of recent novels, female Jewish authors have given an inside view of the so-called Jewish Princesses of the world. They have shown that social conditions that supposedly spoil these women actually constrict them, relentlessly shoving them toward the marriage canopy and symbols of status. Skills and talents are fostered only if they will enhance a young woman's marriageability.

Much of the criticism third-generation female authors have leveled at parents has been directed at mothers in particular too. In "Downers and Seances," a short story by Renata Adler, one of the characters remarks that Jane Austen would have had a great deal in common with a typical Jewish mother; both of them contend that finding and winning a suitable husband is the primary and proper goal of a young woman's existence. Some Jewish daughters could easily identify their own mothers in a character like Mrs. Bennet in *Pride and Prejudice*. But Mrs. Bennet is treated sympathetically as well as ironically.

Unlike Jane Austen's heroines, the protagonists of the novels we are discussing live uneasily between conflicting demands to become both a bride and an independent person. Some of them are female *shlemiels* like the main characters in *Sheila Levine Is Dead and Living in New York* by Gail Parent (1972), *The Launching of Barbara Fabrikant* by Louise Blecher Rose (1974), and *Fat Emily* by Susan Lukas (1974). These young women are too fat and unattractive to have the easy access to marriage that is supposed to be available to the Jewish Princess. At first, they try to avoid the marriage game because they are sure they will lose at it; later, Barbara and Emily decide that even though they might have some success, it isn't what they want anyway. But even Sasha, the pretty heroine of Alix Kates Shulman's *Memoirs of an Ex-Prom Queen* (1972), finds the Jewish Princess's throne a rickety scaffold indeed. Because she is attractive, she receives a good deal of attention from men— most of it in the form of harassment—and has no trouble finding husbands, but men are unwilling to treat her as a thinking, whole human being, either inside or outside marriage.

Sasha seems to have the legendary unshakable self-confidence of the Jewish Princess, but this quality is lacking in the female *shlemiels*. They have received their parents' attentions not as support but as reproach. None of them is encouraged to seek a career; education is offered, but only for matrimonial purposes, so their intelligence has outlets only in sarcasm and self-deprecating wit.

Gail Parent's novel, the funniest of the three, is also the most cynical. Sheila Levine, still unmarried at thirty, decides to commit suicide. Trained by her mother to clean up after herself, she goes about planning her own funeral, only to discover that, as difficult as it is for single women to *live*, it is even more difficult for them to *die*. Cemetery plots, for example, only come in pairs. Sheila finally manages to settle all the details, and attempts suicide. She fails, of course, but true to the comic spirit, Parent leaves Sheila recovering in the hospital, surrounded by scores of unmarried interns—infinite possibilities, for more of the same.

The other two novels, although less comic, offer more hope for the likelihood of transcendence. Although Emily and Barbara are younger than Sheila, only college freshmen, they not only resist their parents' expectations for them, but actively seek alternatives—not, of course, without enduring their share of humiliation by throwing their fates into the hands of unwilling, irresponsible young men. Barbara Fabrikant, a rabbi's daughter, has her epiphany when a Jewish professor whom she idolizes (and for whom she manages to lose twenty-five pounds) admits that he will be impotent and therefore unable to receive the gift of her virginity unless she wears a crucifix to bed. Barbara's refusal is an important moment of revelation and self-affirmation for her. Emily, too, achieves independence when she runs away from home and, denied refuge by her boyfriend, finds a job, and a house, and begins to lead her own life.

Barbara and Emily are never as funny as Sheila, for their disarming sarcasm is less consistent, revealing more of their underlying sadness, self-hatred, doubt, and failures of confidence. In Parent's comic scheme, Sheila can never resolve these feelings: after her suicide attempt, she merely totes them out again for another laugh. Authors Lukas and Rose, by imagining new possibilities for their characters—possibilities that do not exist within a scheme based on acceptance of traditional roles for women—undermine the comic convention.

In *Fear of Flying* (1974), Erica Jong abandons the convention altogether. Her heroine, Isadora Wing, takes herself quite seriously as she articulates her conflict between preserving her marriage as a form of sustenance and searching for some as yet undefined concept of female autonomy. A poet, Isadora must balance her need for men with her need for self-expression and the assertion of an independent identity. Although her creativity, experience, and self-knowledge put her far beyond Emily and Barbara, Isadora is still prone to some of the same insecurities they feel. Isadora traces her problems to her mother, but not because she is Jewish: "If only I had a *real* Jewish mother—easily pigeonholed and filed away—a real literary property. . . ."

Isadora's Jewish mother encourages her originality, not conformity—but what she really values is success. She does not urge her daughter simply to marry, but to take her craft seriously, telling her, "Above all, never be ordinary." Her teaching did not, however, give Isadora license, but rather acted as an implied expectation, placing on Isadora the onus of making a name for herself.

Nevertheless, Isadora goes ahead with her marriage to a psychiatrist, but, after several years, she begins to feel trapped. She leaves him for another psychiatrist, a British Laingian would-be existentialist anti-hero. But their brief affair in Europe ultimately falls short of her fantasies; it becomes banal and routine. At the end of it, Adrian returns to his mistress and children, leaving Isadora in a Paris hotel room, contemplating her fate. She reflects, "It sometimes seemed I would make any compromise, endure any ignominy, stay with any man just so as not to face being alone. But why?"

Isadora's ambivalence about husbands and children is an old theme in a new bottle. Fiction is expressing the dilemma of women who are unable to avoid social and psychological pressure on these issues; it is still the rare female character who can work through them without faltering. Feminist ideology notwithstanding, novelists have generally reflected society's expectations. If they no longer portray female characters as entirely content within the domestic realm, or joyfully giving up careers to marry and start families, they are mirroring new pressures on women both to recognize themselves as discontented and to confront their discontent.

Characters like Isadora Wing, who transcend the deterministic view of male authors in general and Jewish male authors in particular, open the way for the transition of the image of Jewish women in literature from stereotypic comic diminishment as Jewish Mothers and Jewish Princesses to real women living real lives. The heroines of Sue Kaufman's *Diary of a Mad Housewife* (1967), and Anne Roiphe's *Up the Sandbox* (1970), rebel against the domestic role of women. Their protest is, however, in an early stage in which oppression is recognized but neither confronted directly nor transcended. Kaufman's heroine takes refuge in adultery, while Roiphe's seeks escape in fantasy.

These characters, while the creations of Jewish authors, are not recognizably Jewish. Rhoda Lerman, in *Call Me Ishtar* (1973) turns to the rich body of Jewish and pre-Biblical mythology to reinvent and reinvigorate a *sui generis* female culture with a number of specifically Jewish characteristics. In quite another mode, but perhaps with similar intentions, the television program *Rhoda* shows that women can still be Jewish and funny without being the objects of ridicule. The program has taken Molly Goldberg out of the chicken-soup ethnic identification tag and given the modern Jewish woman a part that is acceptable—even admirable—one that incorporates and acknowledges her ethnic identity without depending on the stock ethnic joke. (Rhoda herself of course has evolved from a stock figure in another show, *Mary Tyler Moore,* a significant move in itself. But Rhoda's mother is still a Molly Goldberg type, although more up to date, and the younger sister has assumed the former Rhoda role of the failed Jewish American Princess.)

In 1974 sixteen-year-old Diana Bletter of Great Neck, Long Island, wrote a letter to *The New York Times* criticizing the image of young Jewish women usually transmitted by the

media. The letter focused her attack on the movie *The Heartbreak Kid,* seeing it as one in a long series of movies and books
filled with "anti-Jewish-women jokes." "They are making fun of
me, my mother, my sister, and all Jewish women," she wrote.
"The 'jokes' are brainwashing Jewish men to believe that Jewish
women are not good enough for them, and that the ideal wife
is a gentile one from North Dakota." Bletter points out that
nearly everyone involved in the production of *The Heartbreak
Kid,* including director Elaine May, and her daughter, actress
Jeannie Berlin, is Jewish. There is, then, a modicum of self-
hatred involved in the highly negative portrayal of Lila (played
by Berlin), a young Jewish bride who is deserted by her husband
Lenny on their Miami honeymoon for Kelly, "America's
numero uno." Bletter explains:

> She was what Lenny waited for all his life, sophisticated,
> wealthy, pretty and all WASP. Kelly is Marjorie Morning-
> star's non-Jewish counterpart. Although non-Jewish prin-
> cesses are made with the same ingredients as Jewish ones,
> they are never made fun of. Rather, they are idolized by
> Jewish men like Lenny Cantrow, who feel they would make
> perfect wives. By marrying Kelly, Lenny thinks that he can
> prove something to himself. . . . What is Lenny trying to
> prove? That a Jewish man can "catch" a Gentile woman?
> That Lenny deserves more than Lila, because of what she
> represented to him? Or, did he marry Kelly to become a
> part of the Gentile world, to forget about his own Jewish-
> ness?

Bletter also criticizes a 1973 David Susskind show on intermarriage, in which three of the four couples were Jewish men married to gentile women.

> It seemed these men somehow felt superior to Jewish wom-
> en. . . . All of them had gripes about their Jewish moth-
> ers and preferred not to identify with their Jewish cultures.
> . . . It seems absurd to think a non-Jewish producer would

ever host a talk show on intermarriage and in the course
of it dare put down gentile women and boast that Jewish
women make better wives.

Bletter concludes by calling upon all Jews to boycott movies in
which Jewish women are negatively portrayed, and she also
urges Jewish educators and rabbis to raise their voices against
pejorative female stereotypes.

Nor has protest of the stereotyping of Jewish women been
confined to the written word. The efforts of women within the
religious Jewish community, for example, give the lie to the
notion that their concern is only with the material. Observant
women have begun recently to ask for equality in both secular
and clerical institutions. Running through their demands is exu-
berance coupled with a sense of responsibility. They seek
changes in religious education and in ritual so that women will
be able to participate more fully and share with men the duties
of making decisions and carrying them out.

Although certain themes and images run continuously
through their history, American Jewish women are not, ultimately, reducible to any one set of characteristics or fully drawn
by any single description. Their varied class and national backgrounds produced different patterns of assimilation, and the
experience of each generation has, in certain ways, been unique.
Yet in their search to establish a valid identity, one that does not
diminish them either as women or as Jews, American Jewish
women of all ages and backgrounds have begun to move closer
together. They are questioning the roles that have been assigned
to them and the values on which those roles are based. They are
denying the stereotyped images by which they have been portrayed and replacing them with accurate representations of
themselves and expressions of their experience. Far from denying the tradition of Jewish womanhood, they are drawing upon
its strength to face modern challenges.

The experience of Jewish women in America has sometimes
been idiosyncratic and sometimes similar to that of other
women moving through social, political, and economic
change. Emigration and shifts of power often rupture cultural

value systems in such a way that women find their identities out of phase with received standards. Economic development also affects female roles and the images of women derived from their roles. American Jewish women have not been alone in their struggle with the problems arising from such changes, and their behavior has many parallels with that of women in like situations. In this sense, their story not only belongs to the chronicle of American Jewry, but also forms an important chapter in the history of women.

BIBLIOGRAPHY

Memoirs and Autobiographies

ANTIN, MARY. *The Promised Land,* Boston and New York: Houghton Mifflin, 1912, reprinted 1969.

BENJAMIN, I.J. *Three Years in America, 1859–1862,* 2 vols. Trans. by Charles Reznikoff. Philadelphia: Jewish Publication Society, 1956.

BENGIS, ESTHER. *I Am a Rabbi's Wife,* New York: Bloch Publishing, 1934.

BERG, GERTRUDE. "Let God Worry a Little Bit," in Jay David, ed., *Growing Up Jewish,* New York: William Morrow, 1969.

BYER, ETTA. *Transplanted People,* Chicago: The Author, 1955.

CAHAN, ABRAHAM. *The Education of Abraham Cahan.* Trans. by Leon Stein. Philadelphia: Jewish Publication Society, 1969.

CHAGALL, BELLA. *Burning Lights,* New York: Schocken Books, 1962.

COHEN, ROSE (RAHEL). *Out of the Shadow,* Garden City, N. Y.: Doubleday, Doran, 1918.

DAHLBERG, EDWARD. *Because I Was Flesh,* Norfolk, Conn.: New Directions, 1963.

DAVID, JAY, ed. *Growing Up Jewish,* New York: William Morrow, 1969.

Bibliography

DAWIDOWICZ, LUCY, ed. *The Golden Tradition: Jewish Life and Thought in Eastern Europe,* New York: Holt, Rinehart, 1967.

FERBER, EDNA. *A Peculiar Treasure,* Garden City, N. Y.: Doubleday, Doran, 1939.

FREEMAN-ISHILL, ROSE. *Tillie Freeman Goldstein: In Memoriam,* Berkeley Heights, N.J., 1948.

GOMPERS, SAMUEL. *Seventy Years of Life and Labor,* Vol. 1, New York: E. P. Dutton, 1925.

GOTTESFELD, CHUNE. *Tales of the Old World and the New.* Trans. by Jacob Richman. New York: Thomas Yoseloff, 1964.

HARKAVY, ALEKSANDER. *Bella and I,* New York: The Author, 1934.

HASANOVITZ, ELIZABETH. *One of Them,* New York: Houghton Mifflin, 1918.

HOWE, IRVING and GREENBERG, ELIEZER, eds. *Voices from the Yiddish,* Ann Arbor: University of Michigan Press, 1972.

KAZIN, ALFRED. *A Walker in the City,* New York: Harcourt, Brace, 1951.

KOBER, ARTHUR. *Bella, Bella, Kissed a Fella,* New York: Random House, 1951.

————. *My Dear Bella,* New York: Random House, 1941.

KOHUT, REBEKAH BETTELHEIM. *More Yesterdays,* New York: Bloch, 1950.

————. *My Portion,* New York: Boni & Liveright, 1925.

KUSSY, SARAH. "Jewish Life in Newark, N.J." *YIVO Annual* VI (1951).

LEVIN, SHMARYA. *Childhood in Exile,* Trans. by Maurice Samuel. New York: Harcourt, Brace, 1929.

————. *The Arena.* Trans. by Maurice Samuel. New York: Harcourt, Brace, 1932.

————. *Youth in Revolt.* Trans. by Maurice Samuel. New York: Harcourt, Brace, 1930.

LEVY, HARRIET LANE. *920 O'Farrell Street,* Garden City, N.Y.: Doubleday, 1947.

LEWISOHN, LUDWIG. *Up Stream: An American Chronicle,* New York: Boni & Liveright, 1922.

Bibliography

MARCUS, JACOB RADER. *Memoirs of American Jews, 1775–1865*, Philadelphia: Jewish Publication Society, 1955.

MENKEN, ALICE DAVIS. *On the Side of Mercy: Problems of Social Adjustment*, New York: Covici, Friede, 1933.

MEYER, ANNIE NATHAN. *It's Been Fun*, New York: Henry Shuman, 1951.

National Council of Jewish Women, Pittsburgh Section. *By Myself I'm a Book!*, Waltham, Mass.: American Jewish Historical Society, 1972.

ORNITZ, SAMUEL. *Bride of the Sabbath*, New York: Holt, Rinehart, 1951.

————. *Haunch, Paunch and Jowl*, New York: Boni & Liveright, 1923.

REZNIKOFF, CHARLES, NATHAN, and SARAH. *Family Chronicle*, New York: C. Reznikoff, 1929.

RIBALOW, HAROLD U. *Autobiographies of American Jews*, Philadelphia: Jewish Publication Society, 1965.

RUSKAY, SOPHIE. *Horsecars and Cobblestones*, New York: Beechhurst Press, 1949.

SANDBERG, SARA. *My Sister Goldie*, Garden City, N.Y.: Doubleday, 1968.

SCHNEIDERMAN, ROSE and GOLDTHWAITE, LUCY. *All for One*, New York: Paul S. Eriksson, 1967.

SHEKLOW, EDNA. *So Talently My Children*, Cleveland: World, 1966.

SINGER, ISAAC BASHEVIS. *A Day of Pleasure*, New York: Farrar, Straus, 1970.

————. *In My Father's Court*, New York: Farrar, Straus, 1966.

SINGER, ISRAEL JOSHUA. *Of a World that Is No More*. Trans. by Joseph Singer. New York: Vanguard Press, 1970.

SOLOMON, HANNA GREENEBAUM. *Fabric of My Life*, New York: Bloch, 1946.

STEFFENS, LINCOLN. *The Autobiography of Lincoln Steffens*, New York: Harcourt, Brace, 1931.

MORTON, LEAH (pseud. for Elizabeth G. Stern). *I Am a Woman—and a Jew*, New York: J. H. Sears, 1926.

STERN, ELIZABETH G. *My Mother and I*, New York: Macmillan, 1917.

Bibliography

TABAK, MARY. "My Grandmother Had Yichus." *Commentary,* April 1949, pp. 368–372.

WALD, LILLIAN. *The House on Henry Street,* New York: Henry Holt, 1915.

———. *Windows on Henry Street,* New York: Little, Brown, 1934.

WISE, ISAAC MAYER. *Reminiscences.* Trans. and ed. by D. Philipson, Cincinnati: L. Wise, 1901.

YEZIERSKA, ANZIA. *Red Ribbon on a White Horse,* New York: Charles Scribner, 1950.

ZUNSER, MIRIAM SHOMER. *Yesterday,* Harrisburg, Pa.: Stackpole Sons, 1939.

Printed Primary Sources

BINGHAM, THEODORE A. "Foreign Criminals in New York." *North American Review* CLXXXVII (September 1908).

Committee of Fifteen. *The Social Evil, with Special Reference to Conditions Existing in the City of New York,* New York, Committee of Fifteen, 1902.

———. *The Social Evil . . . ,* second edition, revised with new material edited by Edwin R. A. Seligman, New York: G. P. Putnam's Sons, 1912.

Committee of Fourteen in New York City. *Annual Reports,* New York 1913–1918.

EHRLICH, EMMA G. "Henrietta Szold & Louis Ginzberg." *American Jewish Historical Quarterly* LXI, 4 (June 1972), pp. 361–363.

LLOYD P. GARTNER. "The Jews of New York's East Side, 1890–93." *American Jewish Historical Quarterly* LIII (1964).

HAPGOOD, HUTCHINS. *The Spirit of the Ghetto,* New York: Funk & Wagnalls, 1902, reprinted 1965.

METZKER, ISAAC, ed. *A Bintel Brief,* Garden City, N.Y.: Doubleday, 1971.

MANNING, CAROLINE. *The Immigrant Woman and Her Job,* U.S. Dept. of Labor, Bulletin of the Women's Bureau, No. 74, Washington, D.C.: Government Printing Office, 1930.

MINER, MAUDE E. *Slavery of Prostitution: A Plea for Emancipation,* New York: Macmillan, 1916.

Bibliography

National Council of Jewish Women, *Proceedings,* 1897–1923.

New York State, Senate Document No. 29, *Report of the Commission of Immigration,* Washington, D.C.: Government Printing Office, April 5, 1909.

Papers of the Jewish Women's Congress, Philadelphia: Jewish Publication Society, 1894.

PHILIPSON, DAVID, ed. *Letters of Rebecca Gratz,* Philadelphia: Jewish Publication Society, 1929.

REMY, NAHIDA. *The Jewish Woman.* Trans. by Louise Mannheimer. New York: Bloch Publishing, 1895, reprinted 1916.

RUBINOW, I.M. "Economic Condition of the Jews in Russia." *Bulletin of the Bureau of Labor* XV, No. 72, Washington, D.C.: Government Printing Office, September, 1907.

RUSKAY, ESTHER. *Hearth and Home Essays,* Philadelphia: Jewish Publication Society, 1902.

SAPINSKY, RUTH. "The Jewish Girl at College." *The Menorah Journal* II (December 1916), pp. 294–300.

TURNER, GEORGE KIBBE. "The Daughters of the Poor." *McClure's Magazine* XXXIV (November 1909).

VAN KLEECK, MARY. *The Artificial Flower Makers,* New York: Russell Sage Foundation, 1913.

———. *Working Girls in Evening Schools: A Statistical Study,* New York: Russell Sage Foundation, 1914.

Newspapers and Magazines

The American Hebrew

The American Jewess

Hadassah Magazine

The Israelite

The Jewish Daily Forward

The Jewish Messenger

The Jewish Woman

New York Times

New York World

The Occident

Archival Sources

American Jewish Historical Society, Waltham, Mass.
  Material on National Council of Jewish Women, the Baron de Hirsch Fund, the Jewish Immigration Committee, the Industrial

Removal Office, and the National Association of Jewish Social Workers.

National Council of Jewish Women, New York Section

New York Public Library
Papers of Fannia Cohen

Tamiment Library
Papers of Rose Schneiderman

University of California, Regional Oral History Office
Interviews of Amy Braden, Alice Levison, Jennie Matyas, Rose Rinder.

YIVO Archives

Interviews

Dina Blond

Sylvia Brenner

Molly Chernikovsky

Pearl Halpern

Ida Moskowitz

Pauline Newman

Feigele Shapiro

Fiction, Drama, Poetry

AGNON, SAMUEL JOSEPH. "The Kerchief." In Saul Bellow, ed., *Great Jewish Short Stories.* New York: Dell, 1963.

ALEICHEM, SHOLEM. *Adventures of Mottel, the Cantor's Son.* Trans. by Tamara Kahana. New York: Henry Shuman, 1953.

———. "Hodel." In *Great Jewish Short Stories.*

ANGOFF, CHARLES. *Journey to the Dawn,* New York: Beechhurst Press, 1951.

ASCH, SHALOM. *America.* Trans. by James Fuchs. New York: Alpha, Omega, 1918.

———. *East River.* Trans. by A.H. Gross. New York: G.P. Putnam's Sons, 1946.

Bibliography

_____. *The Mother.* Trans. by Nathan Ausubel. New York: Liveright, 1930, reprinted 1970.

BAUM, CAMILLE. *A Member of the Tribe,* New York: Lyle Stuart, 1971.

BELLOW, SAUL. *Mosby's Memoirs and Other Stories,* New York: Viking Press, 1968.

_____, ed. *Great Jewish Short Stories,* New York: Dell, 1963.

BERCOVICI, KONRAD. *Dust of New York,* New York: Boni & Liveright, 1919.

BISNO, BEATRICE. *Tomorrow's Bread,* New York: Liveright, 1938.

BLECHMAN, BURT. *How Much?* London: Eyre & Spottiswood, 1963.

BLOCK, RUDOLPH EDGAR (pseud. Bruno Lessing). *Children of Men,* New York, 1903, reprinted Plainview, N.Y.: Books for Libraries, 1969.

BRINIG, MYRON. *Singermann,* New York: Farrar, Straus, 1929.

BRODY, ALTER, *Rapunzel,* in *Four Folk-Plays of the American Jew,* New York: Coward-McCann, 1928.

BSTSKY, SARAH ZWEIG, ed. *Onions and Cucumbers and Plums: 46 Yiddish Poems in English,* Plainview, N.Y.: Books for Libraries, 1969.

CAHAN, ABRAHAM. *The Imported Bridegroom and Other Tales of the New York Ghetto,* New York, 1898, reprinted, New York: MSS Information, 1972.

_____. *The Rise of David Levinsky,* New York, 1917, reprinted, Harper Torchbooks, 1960.

_____. *Yekl, A Tale of the New York Ghetto,* New York: D. Appleton, 1896.

CHAPMAN, ABRAHAM, ed. *Jewish-American Literature,* New York: New American Library, 1974.

COOPERMAN, JEHIEL B. and Sarah H., eds. and trans. *America in Yiddish Poetry,* Jericho, N.Y.: Exposition Press, 1967.

DAVIDMAN, JOY. *Anya,* New York: Macmillan, 1940.

DAVIDMAN, SHLOIMA. *A Jew's Head,* Brooklyn, N.Y.: The Author, 1943.

EISENBERG, AZRIEL L., ed. *The Golden Land: A Literary Portrait of American Jewry 1654 to the Present,* Cranbury, N.J.: Thomas Yoseloff, 1965.

EPSTEIN, SEYMOUR. *Leah,* Boston: Little, Brown, 1964.

Bibliography

FERBER, EDNA. *Fanny Herself,* Chicago: Grosset & Dunlap, 1919.

———. "The Fast," in Jerry D. Lewis, ed., *Tales of Our People,* New York: Bernard Geis, 1969.

FRIEDMAN, BRUCE JAY. *A Mother's Kisses,* New York: Simon and Schuster, 1964.

FUCHS, DANIEL. *Three Novels: Homage to Blenholt,* 1936; *Low Company,* 1937; *Summer in Williamsburg,* 1934; reprinted, New York: Basic Books, 1961.

GLASS, MONTAGUE. *Abe & Mawruss,* New York: Doubleday, Page, 1911.

———. *Potash & Perlmutter,* Chicago: Grosset & Dunlap, 1909, 2nd edition, 1924.

GOLD, HERBERT. *Fathers,* New York: Random House, 1967.

GOLD, MICHAEL. *Jews Without Money,* New York: International Publishers, 1930, reprinted, 1965.

GOLDBERG, ISAAC, ed. and trans. *Six Plays of the Yiddish Theater,* 1st series, Boston: John W. Luce, 1916; 2nd series, Boston, 1918.

GOULD, LOIS. *Necessary Objects,* New York: Random House, 1972.

GREENBERG, JOANNE. *Summering,* New York: Holt, Rinehart and Winston, 1966.

GREENBURG, DAN. *How To Be a Jewish Mother,* New York: Pocket Books, 1964.

———. *Scoring,* Garden City, N.Y.: Doubleday, 1972.

HALPER, ALBERT. *The Chute,* New York: Viking Press, 1937.

HECHT, BEN. *A Jew in Love,* New York: Covici, Friede, 1931.

KAUFMANN, MYRON S. *Remember Me to God,* Philadelphia: J.B. Lippincott, 1957; reprinted, New York: Dell, 1968.

———. *Thy Daughter's Nakedness,* Philadelphia: J.B. Lippincott, 1968.

KAUFMAN, SUE. *Diary of a Mad Housewife,* New York: Random House, 1967.

KELLY, MYRA. *Little Aliens,* New York: Scribner's, 1910.

———. *Little Citizens,* New York: McClure & Phillips, 1904.

———. *Wards of Liberty,* New York: McClure, 1907.

LAZARUS, EMMA. *Selections from her Poetry and Prose.* Ed. by Morris

U. Schappes. 3rd edition, New York: Emma Lazarus Federation of Jewish Women's Clubs, 1967.

LERMAN, RHODA. *Call Me Ishtar,* Garden City, N. Y.: Doubleday, 1973.

LEVIN, MEYER. *Frankie and Johnny,* New York: John Day, 1930.

———. *The Old Bunch,* New York: Viking Press, 1937.

LEWIS, JERRY D., ed. *Tales of Our People,* New York: Bernard Geis, 1969.

LIST, SHELLEY STEINMANN. *Did You Love Daddy When I Was Born?,* New York: Saturday Review Press, 1972.

LUKAS, SUSAN. *Fat Emily,* New York: Stein and Day, 1974.

MALIN, IRVING and STARK, IRWIN, eds. *Breakthrough,* New York: McGraw-Hill, 1964.

MIRSKY, MARK. *Blue Hill Avenue.* Indianapolis, Ind.: Bobbs-Merrill, 1972.

ODETS, CLIFFORD. *Awake and Sing,* New York: Random House, 1935.

OLSEN, TILLIE. *Tell Me a Riddle,* New York: Dell, 1971.

———. *Yonnondio,* New York: Delacorte, 1974.

PARENT, GAIL. *Sheila Levine Is Dead and Living in New York,* New York: G.P. Putnam's Sons, 1972.

PINSKI, DAVID. *Temptations.* Trans. by Isaac Goldberg. New York: Brentano's, 1919.

REZNIKOFF, CHARLES. *By the Waters of Manhattan,* New York: Boni & Liveright, 1930.

RIBALOW, HAROLD U., ed. *A Treasury of American Jewish Stories,* Cranbury, N.J.: Thomas Yoseloff, 1958.

RIIS, JACOB A. *Children of the Tenements,* New York: Macmillan, 1903; reprinted, Plainview, N.Y.: Books for Libraries, 1970.

———. *Out of Mulberry Street,* New York, 1893; reprinted, Upper Saddle River, N.J.: Gregg Press, 1970.

ROIPHE, ANN RICHARDSON. *Up the Sandbox,* New York: Simon and Schuster, 1971.

ROSE, LOUISE BLECHER. *The Launching of Barbara Fabrikant,* New York: David McKay, 1974.

ROSEN, NORMA. *Green,* New York: Harcourt, Brace and World, 1967.

ROSENFELD, ISAAC. *Passage from Home.* New York: Dial Press, 1946.

ROSENFELD, MAX, ed. and trans. *Pushcarts and Dreamers,* Cranbury, N.J.: Thomas Yoseloff, 1967.

ROSENFELD, MORRIS. *Songs from the Ghetto.* Trans. by Leo Wiener. Boston: Copeland and Day, 1898.

ROSS, LILLIAN. *Vertical and Horizontal,* New York: Simon and Schuster, 1963.

ROTH, HENRY. *Call It Sleep,* New York, 1935, reprinted New York: Avon Books, 1964.

ROTH, PHILIP. *Goodbye, Columbus,* Boston: Houghton Mifflin, 1959.

————. *Portnoy's Complaint,* New York, Random House, 1969.

RUBIN, RUTH. *Voices of a People,* 2nd edition, New York: McGraw-Hill, 1973.

SCHNEIDER, ISIDOR. *From the Kingdom of Necessity,* New York: G.P. Putnam's Sons, 1935.

SCHWARTZ, DELMORE. *The World Is a Wedding,* Norfolk, Conn.: New Directions, 1948.

SEIDE, MICHAEL. *The Common Thread,* New York: Harcourt, Brace, 1944.

SHABER, DAVID. "Escape from Mother." In Oscar Hardlin, ed., *Children of the Uprooted,* New York: Braziller, 1966.

SHULMAN, ALIX KATES. *Memoirs of an Ex-Prom Queen,* New York: Alfred A. Knopf, 1972.

SLESINGER, TESS. *Time: the Present,* New York: Simon and Schuster, 1935.

————. *The Unpossessed,* New York: Simon and Schuster, 1934, reprinted, New York: Avon Books, 1966.

TASHRAK (pseud. Israel Joseph Zevin). *Marriage Broker,* adapted by Irving Meites from *The Stories of Shulem the Shadchen,* New York: G.P. Putnam's Sons, 1960.

TODRIN, BORIS. *Out of These Roots,* Caldwell, Ohio: Caxton Printers, 1944.

WEIDMAN, JEROME. *Fourth Street East,* New York: Random House, 1970.

WEINGARTEN, VIOLET. *Mrs. Beneker,* New York: Simon and Schuster, 1968.

Bibliography

WELLMAN, RITA. *The Gentile Wife,* New York: Moffat, Yard, 1919.

WILSON, S.J. *Hurray for Me,* New York: Crown Publishers, 1964.

WINSLOW, THYRA SAMTER. "A Cycle of Manhattan," in Harold U. Ribalow, ed., *A Treasury of American Jewish Stories,* Cranbury, N.J.: Thomas Yoseloff, 1958.

WOLF, EMMA. *Other Things Being Equal,* Chicago: A.C. McClurg, 1892.

WOUK, HERMAN. *Marjorie Morningstar,* Garden City, N.Y.: Doubleday, 1955.

YEZIERSKA, ANZIA. *All I Could Never Be,* New York: Harcourt, Brace, 1932.

――――. *Arrogant Beggar,* Garden City, N.Y.: Doubleday, Doran, 1927.

――――. *Bread Givers,* Garden City, N.Y.: Doubleday, Doran, 1925; reprinted, New York: Braziller, 1975.

――――. *Children of Loneliness,* New York: Funk & Wagnalls, 1923.

――――. *Hungry Hearts,* Chicago: Grosset & Dunlap, 1920.

――――. *Salome of the Tenements,* New York: Boni & Liveright, 1923.

ZANGWILL, ISRAEL. *The Melting Pot,* New York, 1909, reprinted, New York: Macmillan, 1914.

Secondary Sources

AARON, DANIEL. *Writers on the Left,* New York: Harcourt, Brace & World, 1961.

ALTER, ROBERT. *After the Tradition: Essays on Modern Jewish Writing,* New York: E. P. Dutton, 1969.

ARENDT, HANNAH. *Rahel Varnhagen,* trans. by Richard & Clara Winston. New York: Harcourt, Brace, Jovanovich, 1974.

ARSENIAN, SETH. *Bilingualism and Mental Development,* New York: Columbia Teachers College, 1937.

ASKOWITH, DORA. *Three Outstanding Women,* New York: Bloch, 1941.

BALTZELL, E. DIGBY. *The Protestant Establishment: Aristocracy and Caste in America,* New York: Random House, 1964.

BANNER, LOIS C. *Women in Modern America,* New York: Harcourt, Brace, Jovanovitch, 1974.

BART, PAULINE. "Depression in Middle-Aged Women." In Vivian Gornick and Barbara Moran, eds., *Woman in Sexist Society,* New York: Basic Books, 1971.

BAUMGOLD, JULIE. "The Persistence of the Jewish American Princess." *New York,* 22 March 1971, pp. 25–31.

BEER, MAX. *Fifty Years of International Socialism,* London: Macmillan, 1935.

BELLMAN, SAMUEL I. "The 'Jewish Mother' Syndrome." *Congress Bi-Weekly,* 22 December 1965, pp. 3–5.

BERKSON, ISAAC B. *Theories of Americanization,* New York: Columbia Teachers College, 1920.

BERMAN, LOUIS. *Sex Role Patterns in the Jewish Family,* New York: Thomas Yoseloff, 1968.

BERMAN, MYRON. "The Attitude of American Jewry towards East European Jewish Immigration, 1881–1914." Dissertation, Columbia University, 1963.

BESDINE, MATTHEW. "Jewish Mothering." *Jewish Spectator,* February 1970.

BIRMINGHAM, STEPHEN. *Our Crowd,* New York: Harper & Row, 1967.

BISNO, ABRAHAM. *Abraham Bisno, Union Pioneer,* Madison: University of Wisconsin Press, 1967.

BLAU, ZENA SMITH. "In Defense of the Jewish Mother." *Midstream,* February 1967, pp. 42–49.

BLETTER, DIANA. "Hollywood's Heartbreaks." *Keeping Posted,* Bulletin of Temple Beth El, Great Neck, New York, February 1974, pp. 19–21.

BOSERUP, ESTER. *Woman's Role in Economic Development,* New York: St. Martin's Press, 1970.

BRANDSTADTER, EVAN. "The Emancipation of the American Jewess," paper presented to History Dept. of Brandeis University, 1971.

BRAV, STANLEY. "The Jewish Woman, 1861–1865." *American Jewish Archives* XVII (1965), pp. 34–75.

CHYET, STANLEY F. "Three Generations: An Account of American-

Bibliography

Jewish Fiction (1896–1969)." *Jewish Social Studies* XXXIV, 1 (January 1972), pp. 31–41.

COHEN, BERNARD, ed. *Sociocultural Changes in American Jewish Life as Reflected in Selected Jewish Literature,* Rutherford, N.J.: Fairleigh Dickinson University Press, 1972.

COHEN, ELLIOT E., ed. *Commentary on the American Scene: Portraits of Jewish Life in America,* New York: Alfred A Knopf, 1953.

COSER, ROSE. "Authority and Structural Ambivalence in the Middle-Class Family." In Rose Coser, ed., *The Family: Its Structure and Functions,* New York: St. Martin's Press, 1964.

CRAIN, JANE LARKIN. "Feminist Fiction." *Commentary,* December 1974, pp. 58–62.

DAVIS, MOSHE. *The Emergence of Conservative Judaism,* Philadelphia: Jewish Publication Society, 1963.

————. "Jewish Religious Life and Institutions in America." In Louis Finkelstein, ed., *The Jews,* New York: Schocken Books, 1971.

DUBNOW, S. M. *History of the Jews in Russia and Poland,* 3 vols., Philadelphia: Jewish Publication Society, 1916–1920.

EPSTEIN, MELECH. *Jewish Labor in the United States, 1882–1914,* 2 vols., New York: Trade Union Sponsoring Committee, 1950–1953.

FEINGOLD, HENRY. *Zion in America,* New York: Twayne, 1974.

FELDMAN, EGAL. "Prostitution, the Alien Woman, and the Progressive Imagination, 1910–1915." *American Quarterly* XI (Summer 1967).

FIEDLER, LESLIE. *Love and Death in the American Novel,* revised edition, New York: Stein and Day, 1966.

FINE, DAVID M. "Attitudes toward Acculturation in the English Fiction of the Jewish Immigrant, 1900–1917." *American Jewish Historical Quarterly* LXIII, 1 (September 1973), pp. 45–56.

FISCH, HAROLD. "Fathers, Mothers, Sons and Lovers: Jewish and Gentile Patterns in Literature." *Midstream* XVIII, 3 (March 1972), pp. 37–45.

FRIEDAN, BETTY. *The Feminine Mystique,* New York: W.W. Norton, 1963.

GANS, HERBERT. "Park Forest: Birth of a Jewish Community." In *Commentary on the American Scene.*

GLANZ, RUDOLF. *Jew and Irish: Historic Group Relations and Immigration,* New York: Alexander Kohut Memorial Foundation, 1966.

————. *Jew and Italian: Historic Group Relations and the New Immigration (1881–1924),* New York: Ktav Publishing House, 1971.

GLAZER, NATHAN. *American Judaism,* Chicago: University of Chicago Press, 1957.

GLAZER, RUTH. "West Bronx: Food, Shelter, Clothing." In *Commentary on the American Scene: Portrait of Jewish Life in America.*

GLICKSMAN, WILLIAM M. *In the Mirror of Literature,* New York: Living Books, 1966.

GOLDMAN, ALBERT, "Boy-man, schlemiel: the Jewish element in American humour." In Murray Mindlin, ed., *Explorations,* Chicago: Quadrangle Books, 1968.

GORDON, ALBERT I. *Jews in Transition,* Minneapolis: University of Minnesota Press, 1949.

GORDON, MICHAEL, ed. *The American Family in Social-Historical Perspective,* New York: St. Martin's Press, 1973.

GOREN, ARTHUR A. *New York Jews and the Quest for Community: The Kehillah Experiment, 1908–1922,* New York: Columbia University Press, 1970.

GREENBERG, LOUIS. *The Jews in Russia,* New Haven, Conn.: Yale University Press, 1966.

GRINSTEIN, ALEXANDER. "Profile of a Doll." In Norman Kiell, ed., *The Psychodynamics of American Jewish Life,* New York: Twayne, 1967.

GUTTMANN, ALLEN. *The Jewish Writer in America,* New York: Oxford University Press, 1971.

HANDLIN, OSCAR. *Adventures in Freedom,* New York: McGraw-Hill, 1954.

————. *The Uprooted,* Boston: Little, Brown, 1951.

HANSEN, MARCUS LEE. *The Problem of the Third Generation Immigrant,* Rock Island, Ill.: Augustana Historical Society, 1938.

Hebrew Union College-Jewish Institute of Religion, *Essays in American Jewish History,* Cincinnati: Hebrew Union College Press, 1959.

HELLER, JAMES GUTTHEIM. *Isaac Mayer Wise: His Life, Work, and Thought,* New York: Union of American Hebrew Congregations, 1965.

HERBERG, WILL. *Protestant, Catholic, Jew,* Garden City, N.Y.: Doubleday, 1955.

HERTZ, J.S. *Doios Bundistn* (Generations of Bundists), New York: Farlag Unser Tsait, 1956.

HIGHAM, JOHN. "Social Discrimination against Jews in America, 1830–1930." *Publications of the American Jewish Historical Society* XLVII (September 1957), pp. 1–33.

HINDUS, MILTON. "The School of Leitzim in American Jewish Writing." *Jewish Frontier* XXIX, 6 (August 1962), pp. 18–23.

HIRSHLER, ERIC E. *Jews from Germany in the United States,* New York: Farrar, Straus, 1955.

HOWE, IRVING. *The Critical Point: On Literature and Culture,* New York: Horizon Press, 1973.

The Jewish Labor Bund: A Pictorial History, 1897–1957, compiled by J. S. Hertz, New York: Farlag Unser Tsait, 1958.

JOSEPH, SAMUEL. *History of the Baron de Hirsch Fund,* New York: Baron de Hirsch Fund, 1935.

————. *Jewish Immigration to the United States from 1881 to 1910,* New York: Columbia University Press, 1914.

KATZ, JACOB. *Out of the Ghetto,* Cambridge, Mass.: Harvard University Press, 1973.

Keltun, Liz, ed., *The Jewish Woman: An Anthology. Response,* No. 18, Summer, 1973.

KENNEDY, RUBY JO REEVES. "Single or Triple Melting Pot? Intermarriage Trends in New Haven, 1870–1940." *American Journal of Sociology* XLIX, 4.

KNEELAND, GEORGE J. *Commercialized Prostitution in New York City,* New York, 1913; revised edition, Montclair, N.J.: Paterson Smith, 1969.

KRAMER, JUDITH R. and LEVENTMAN, SEYMOUR. *Children of the Gilded Ghetto,* New Haven, Conn.: Yale University Press, 1961.

LAVIN, DAVID E. *The Prediction of Academic Performance,* New York: Russell Sage Foundation, 1965.

LEBESON, ANITA LIBMAN. *Recall to Life: The Jewish Women in American History,* Cranbury, N.J.: Thomas Yoseloff, 1970.

LEVIN, ALEXANDRA. *The Szolds of Lombard Street: A Baltimore Family 1859–1909,* Philadelphia: Jewish Publication Society, 1960.

LEVINE, LOUIS. *The Women's Garment Workers: A History of the International Ladies' Garment Workers' Union,* New York: Viking Press, 1924.

LEVY, DAVID. *Maternal Overprotection,* New York: Columbia University Press, 1943.

LIPTZIN, SOLOMON. *Germany's Stepchildren,* Philadelphia: Jewish Publication Society, 1944.

————. *The Jew in American Literature,* New York: Bloch, 1966.

LOWENTHAL, LEO. *Literature, Popular Culture, and Society,* Palo Alto, Calif.: Pacific Books, 1968.

LOWENTHAL, MARVIN. *Henrietta Szold: Life and Letters,* New York: Viking Press, 1942.

MADISON, CHARLES. *Yiddish Literature: Its Scope and Major Writers,* New York: Frederick Ungar, 1968.

MALIN, IRVING. *Jews and Americans,* Carbondale: Southern Illinois University Press, 1966.

————, ed. *Contemporary American Jewish Literature,* Bloomington: Indiana University Press, 1973.

MANDEL, IRVING. "The Attitudes of the American Jewish Community toward Eastern European Immigration in the U.S." *American Jewish Archives,* June 1950.

MANNERS, ANDE. *Poor Cousins,* New York: Coward, McCann and Geoghegan, 1972.

MCLAUGHLIN, VIRGINIA YANS. "Patterns of Work and Family Organization: Buffalo's Italians." In Michael Gordon, ed., *The American Family in Social-Historical Perspective,* New York: St. Martin's Press, 1973.

MEYER, MICHAEL. *The Origins of the Modern Jew,* Detroit: Wayne State University Press, 1967.

MIELZINER, REV. DR. M. *The Jewish Law of Marriage and Divorce in Ancient and Modern Times,* Cincinnati: Bloch, 1884.

PANITZ, ESTHER. "In Defense of the Jewish Immigrant (1891–1924)." *American Jewish Historical Quarterly* LV, 1 (September 1965), pp. 57–97.

————. "The Polarity of American Jewish Attitudes towards Immigration (1870–1891)." *American Jewish Historical Quarterly* LIII, 2 (December 1963), pp. 99–130.

PHILIPSON, DAVID. *The Reform Movement in Judaism,* New York: Macmillan, 1931.

PLAUT, W. GUNTHER. *The Growth of Reform Judaism,* New York: World Union for Progressive Judaism, 1966.

————. *The Rise of Reform Judaism,* 2 vols., New York: World Union for Progressive Judaism, 1963.

POLL, SOLOMON. *The Hasidic Community of Williamsburg: A Study in the Sociology of Religion,* New York: Schocken Books, 1969.

PORTER, JACK NUSAN and DREIER, PETER. *Jewish Radicalism: A Selected Anthology,* New York: Grove Press, 1973.

REISS, LIONEL S. and HINDUS, MILTON. *A World at Twilight,* New York: Macmillan, 1971.

RIBALOW, HAROLD U., ed. *Mid-Century,* New York: Beechhurst Press, 1955.

RISCHIN, MOSES. *The Promised City: New York's Jews,* Cambridge, 1962, reprinted, New York: Harper & Row, 1970.

ROSE, PETER I. *The Ghetto and Beyond,* New York: Random House, 1969.

SANDERS, RONALD. *The Downtown Jews,* New York: Harper & Row, 1969.

SCHAPPES, MORRIS U. *The Jews in the United States: A Pictorial History 1659 to the Present,* New York: Citadel Press, 1958.

SHERMAN, C. BEZALEL. *The Jew within American Society: A Study in Ethnic Individuality,* Detroit: Wayne State University Press, 1961.

SHOHET, AZRIEL. *Im Hilufei Tekufot* [Hebrew], Jerusalem, 1960.

SIDORSKY, DAVID, ed. *The Future of the Jewish Community in America,* New York: Basic Books, 1974.

SINCLAIR, ANDREW. *The Better Half: The Emancipation of the American Woman,* New York: Harper & Row, 1965.

Sisters of Exile: Sources on the Jewish Woman, New York: Ichud Habonim Labor Zionist Youth, 1974.

SKLARE, MARSHALL. *America's Jews,* New York: Random House, 1971.

————. *Conservative Judaism: An American Religious Movement,*

New York: Schocken Books, 1955; 2nd edition, 1972.

————, ed. *The Jews: Social Patterns of an American Group,* Glencoe, Ill.: Free Press, 1958.

SLATER, PHILIP E. "Social Change and the Democratic Family." In Philip E. Slater and Warren G. Bennis, eds., *The Temporary Society,* New York: Harper & Row, 1968.

SOLOMON, BARBARA MILLER. *Ancestors and Immigrants: A Changing New England Tradition,* Cambridge, Mass.: Harvard University Press, 1956.

SROLE, LEO, et al. *Mental Health in the Metropolis,* Vol. 1, New York: McGraw-Hill, 1962.

STEIN, LEON. *The Triangle Fire,* Philadelphia: J.B. Lippincott, 1962.

STRODTBECK, FRED L. "Family Interaction, Values and Achievement." In David McClelland et al., eds., *Talent and Society,* Princeton: D. Van Nostrand, 1958.

SUHL, YURI. *Ernestine L. Rose and the Battle for Human Rights,* New York: Reynal, 1959.

SZAJKOWSKI, ZOSA. "The Attitude of American Jews to East European Jewish Immigration, 1881–1893." *Publications of the American Jewish Historical Society* XL (1950–1951), pp. 221–280.

TCHERIKOWER, ELIAS. *The Early Jewish Labor Movement in the U.S.* Trans. by A. Antonovsky. New York: Yivo Institute for Jewish Research, 1961.

TELLER, J.L. *Strangers and Natives: The Evolution of the American Jew from 1921 to the Present,* New York: Dial Press, 1968.

TOBIAS, HENRY J. *The Jewish Bund in Russia: From Its Origins to 1905,* Stanford, Calif.: Stanford University Press, 1972.

VISHNIAC, ROMAN. *Polish Jews: A Pictorial Record,* New York: Schocken Books, 1947.

WELTER, BARBARA. "The Cult of True Womanhood: 1820–1860." In *The American Family in Social-Historical Perspective.*

WIENER, LEO. *The History of Yiddish Literature in the Nineteenth Century,* New York: 1899; 2nd edition, New York: Hermon Press, 1972.

WILLETT, MABEL HURD. *The Employment of Women in the Cloth-*

ing Trade. Dissertation, Columbia University, 1902.

WILLIAMS, BERYL. *Lillian Wald: Angel of Henry Street,* New York: Julian Messner, 1948.

WISCHNITZER, MARK. *To Dwell in Safety,* Philadelphia: Jewish Publication Society, 1948.

WOLFENSTEIN, MARTHA. "Two Types of Jewish Mothers." In Margaret Mead and Martha Wolfenstein, eds., *Childhood in Contemporary Cultures,* Chicago: University of Chicago Press, 1955.

WYDEN, BARBARA and SCHWARTZ, GWEN GIBSON. *The Jewish Wife,* New York: P.H. Wyden, 1969.

ZBOROWSKI, MARK and HERZOG, ELIZABETH. *Life Is with People,* New York, 1952, reprinted, Schocken Books, 1962.

ZEITLIN, ROSE. *Henrietta Szold: Record of a Life,* New York: Dial Press, 1952.

ZIMMERN, O. "Seven Months in America." *Sociological Review* V (1912), pp. 202–214.

INDEX

Index

Bolsheviks, 81

Brandeis, Louis, 178–179

Braut, Bessie, 155–156

Bread Givers (Yezierska), 103–104, 198–199, 219–220

Breckenridge, Desha, 51

Brenner, Rose, 213

Bressler, David, 177, 178

Bride of the Sabbath (Ornitz), 112, 118, 150, 205–206, 224, 225

Brith ceremony, 11

Brody, Alter, 108, 197–198

Brooks, Mel, 254

Burroughs, John, 38

Byer, Etta, 108–109

Cahan, Abraham, 59, 63, 73, 108, 135, 191, 193–196, 201, 204, 222, 225, 229

Call It Sleep (H. Roth), 246

Call Me Ishtar (Lerman), 258

Celibacy, 8

Chagall, Bella, 57, 60

Cheder, 60, 61, 62

Chernikovsky, Molly, 92–98, 132

Chernikovsky, Morris, 95, 97

Child labor laws, 122

Children of the Tenements (Riis), 106

Chute, The (Halper), 233

Circumcision, 11

Civil War, 30, 32

Clara de Hirsch Home for Girls, 169, 181

Cloak Manufacturers' Association, 146

Clothing, 67, 102

Clothing industry. *See* Garment industry

"Colossus, The" (Lazarus), 38

Congregation Beth Elohim, Charleston, S.C., 24

Congregation B'nai Jeshurun, New York City, 28

Conservative Judaism, 5, 11, 52

Courtship, 62

"Cycle of Manhattan, A" (Winslow), 203, 207–208, 209–210, 224, 227–228

Dahlberg, Edward, 225

"Dance to Death, The" (Lazarus), 38

"Daughters of the Poor, The" (Turner), 171

Deborah, 12, 13

Diary of a Mad Housewife (Kaufman), 258

Divorce, 6–7, 27, 63

"Downers and Seances" (Adler), 255

Dowries, 23, 63, 222

Dress and Waist Manufacturers' Association, 146

Dubnow, S. M., 55, 73

Dzalodski, Maria, 86–87

East European Jewish women, 38, 39, 55–89; anti-Czarist groups, 76; appearance and manners, changes in, 190, 204–210, 222–227; beggars, 114; boarders, 103–109; compared with Italian women, 137–139; cultural conflict, 179–185; economic arrangements, 67–70, 121–125, 189, 191–199; education, 60–62, 72–74, 121–129, 227–228; family disruption, 116–119; food, 65–67, 102; *Haskalah* movement, 64, 71–72; immigration, 55–56, 94–95, 164–170; leisure, 199–203, 211–214; marriage, 62–64, 72; personality traits, 56, 189–190; prostitution issue, 115–116, 170–175; pushcart trade, 100–102; religious tradition, 57–60; retail shop system, 96–99; unassimilated, 214–218; Zionist movement, 75–76. *See also* Garment industry; Labor movement

East River (Asch), 182, 191, 225

Economic responsibilities, 15, 67–70, 121–125, 189, 191–199

Edelstadt, Dovid, 83–84

Education: American, 121–129; East European, 60–62, 72–74, 121–129, 227–228; marriage and, 127–129; Sunday Schools,

284

Index

Index

Index

Index

Index